WHAT YOUR COLLEAGU

*AI has transformed education, but since everytl
are still looking for the best ways to benefit from it. The authors have broken down a
complex, rapidly evolving subject and generated a framework for teaching AI literacy
to K–12 students. This book provides a foundation for distinguishing science from
fiction and for avoiding the pitfalls that come with the recent breakthroughs in AI.*

—Philippos Mordohai
Professor of Computer Science, Stevens Institute of Technology
Hoboken, NJ

*An accessible entry point into the complex world of AI education, this foundational
resource establishes and explains core concepts while inspiring educators to delve
deeper into AI literacy across disciplines. It is a valuable launching pad for the further
development of AI fluency.*

—Sonja Strydom
Deputy Director, Centre for Learning Technologies,
Stellenbosch University
Stellenbosch, South Africa

*This handbook is a valuable resource for educators and educational researchers. It
offers practical ways and resources for integrating AI literacy into various subjects,
addressing the interdisciplinary nature of AI. This book will show us how to apply
AI to transform K–12 learning. It is a must-read for everyone who wants to prepare
the future generation for the AI era.*

—Thomas Chiu
Assistant Professor, The Chinese University of Hong Kong
Program Coordinator, BSc Learning Design and Technology
Ma Liu Shui, Hong Kong

*This is a great addition to your resource library. The authors do a tremendous job
of laying the foundation for why addressing AI literacy is so vital. They follow
it up with some helpful examples of how to do this within existing content that
is taught.*

—Kevin Dykema
District Math Specialist, Mattawan Consolidated Schools
Mattawan, MI

The rapid development of Generative AI has brought us to an inflection in both society and education. This excellent book by Lyublinskaya and Du is a timely, balanced, and incisive resource. It offers highly practical guidance for educators aiming to effectively serve their students and society as we navigate these transformative times.

—Rian Roux
Lecturer (Pathways), University of Southern Queensland
Toowoomba, Queensland, Australia

At a time when artificial intelligence is reshaping every aspect of our lives, this book provides a timely guide for educators. Bridging theory and practice, the authors explain basic AI concepts and offer a framework, practical tools and lesson examples that can be used by educators to develop students' critical AI literacy skills.

—Manolis Mavrikis
Professor of Artificial Intelligence in Education,
University College London
London, UK

Teaching AI Literacy Across the Curriculum: A K–12 Handbook is a must-read for educators seeking to integrate AI literacy into their teaching. This comprehensive guide offers a pedagogical framework, practical tools, and over 20 lesson ideas, making AI accessible without needing advanced technical skills. Emphasizing ethical and responsible AI use, it equips teachers to foster 21st-century digital literacy across all subjects and grade levels. It is highly recommended for K–12 educators.

—Zsolt Lavicza
Professor, Johannes Kepler UniversityLinz,
Upper Austria, Austria

Teaching AI Literacy Across the Curriculum

Teaching AI Literacy Across the Curriculum

A K–12 Handbook

Irina Lyublinskaya

Xiaoxue Du

CORWIN

CORWIN

FOR INFORMATION:

Corwin

A SAGE Company

2455 Teller Road

Thousand Oaks, California 91320

(800) 233-9936

www.corwin.com

SAGE Publications Ltd.

1 Oliver's Yard

55 City Road

London EC1Y 1SP

United Kingdom

SAGE Publications India Pvt. Ltd.

Unit No 323-333, Third Floor, F-Block

International Trade Tower Nehru Place

New Delhi 110 019

India

SAGE Publications Asia-Pacific Pte. Ltd.

18 Cross Street #10-10/11/12

China Square Central

Singapore 048423

Vice President and Editorial
  Director: Monica Eckman

Senior Acquisitions Editor: Debbie Hardin

Senior Editorial Assistant: Nyle De Leon

Project Editor: Amy Schroller

Copy Editor: Denise McIntyre

Typesetter: C&M Digitals (P) Ltd.

Proofreader: Jeff Bryant

Cover Designer: Rose Storey

Marketing Manager: Margaret O'Connor

This book is printed on acid-free paper.

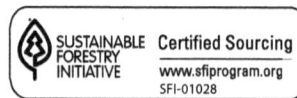

SUSTAINABLE FORESTRY INITIATIVE   Certified Sourcing
www.sfiprogram.org
SFI-01028

25 26 27 28 29 10 9 8 7 6 5 4 3 2 1

Contents

Table of Subject-Specific Standards   xi

Table of Examples, Lessons, and Units   xvii

Preface   xxi
     BOOK OVERVIEW   xxii
     HOW TO USE THIS BOOK   xxiv

Acknowledgments   xxv

About the Authors   xxvii

PART I   THEORETICAL FOUNDATIONS   1

1   ETHICS AND GLOBAL PERSPECTIVES ON AI LITERACY EDUCATION   3
     ETHICS AND EDUCATION   3
     GLOBAL PERSPECTIVES ON AI LITERACY EDUCATION   11

2   PEDAGOGICAL FRAMEWORK FOR AI LITERACY   19
     CURRENT RESEARCH   20
     THEORETICAL FOUNDATIONS FOR INTEGRATING AI LITERACY INTO THE CURRICULUM   22
     OUR PEDAGOGICAL FRAMEWORK FOR AI LITERACY   33

3   APPLYING OUR PEDAGOGICAL FRAMEWORK FOR AI LITERACY   39

4   PREPARING TO INTEGRATE AI LITERACY INTO EXISTING CURRICULUM   59
     RESEARCH OVERVIEW   59
     SUMMARY OF THE PROFESSIONAL LEARNING RECOMMENDATIONS FOR CLASSROOM TEACHERS   61

RECOMMENDATION 1: UTILIZE PRINCIPLES OF
BACKWARD DESIGN   64

RECOMMENDATION 2: DEVELOP CULTURAL AND
INCLUSIVENESS COMPETENCY   66

RECOMMENDATION 3: DEEPEN UNDERSTANDING
OF AI TECHNOLOGY   68

RECOMMENDATION 4: INCORPORATE AI TECHNOLOGY
INTO STUDENT TASKS   68

RECOMMENDATION 5: BECOME A FACILITATOR OF
STUDENT LEARNING   70

RECOMMENDATION 6: ENGAGE IN COLLABORATIVE
REFLECTION   71

RECOMMENDATION 7: EVALUATE THE IMPACT OF
AI ON STUDENT LEARNING   72

PART II   PRACTICAL APPLICATIONS   79

5 AI LITERACY IN SCIENCE EDUCATION   81

SCIENCE STANDARDS AND FIVE BIG IDEAS IN AI   82

LESSON SUGGESTIONS   86

INTEGRATING AI CONCEPTS INTO MIDDLE SCHOOL
UNIT ON ECOSYSTEMS   99

6 AI LITERACY IN MATHEMATICS EDUCATION   111

MATHEMATICS STANDARDS AND FIVE BIG IDEAS IN AI   112

LESSON SUGGESTIONS   116

INTEGRATING AI CONCEPTS INTO HIGH SCHOOL
ALGEBRA UNIT ON STRUCTURE OF ALGEBRAIC
EXPRESSIONS   134

7 AI LITERACY IN LANGUAGE ARTS EDUCATION   147

ENGLISH LANGUAGE ARTS STANDARDS AND FIVE
BIG IDEAS IN AI   148

LESSON SUGGESTIONS   152

INTEGRATING AI CONCEPTS INTO MIDDLE SCHOOL
ELA UNIT "MAN VS. MACHINE: EXAMINING THE
POWER DYNAMICS OF CREATING IN LITERATURE"   168

8 AI LITERACY IN SOCIAL STUDIES
EDUCATION   179

SOCIAL STUDIES STANDARDS AND FIVE BIG IDEAS IN AI   180

LESSON SUGGESTIONS   184

INTEGRATING AI CONCEPTS INTO ELEMENTARY SCHOOL
UNIT "JOURNEYS OF HOPE: USING AI TO UNDERSTAND
IMMIGRATION STORIES"   197

PART III   FRAMEWORK REVISITED   **211**

9 ASSESSMENT OF AI LITERACY
FRAMEWORK   213

CURRENT RESEARCH OVERVIEW   213

ASSESSMENT OF AI LITERACY FRAMEWORK   215

ASSESSMENT OF AI LITERACY RESOURCES   220

OVERVIEW OF ASSESSMENT OF AI LITERACY RESOURCES   221

Epilogue: How Will AI Transform K–12 Learning?   225

Glossary   227

References   229

Index   235

online
resources

Visit the companion website for downloadable resources.
https://companion.corwin.com/courses/TeachingAILiteracy

Table of Subject-Specific Standards

STANDARD	ABBREVIATION	EXPLAINED	SUBJECT	PAGE REFERENCE
CCSS.ELA-Literacy	RF.2.3	Know and apply grade-level phonics and word-analysis skills in decoding words.	ELA	156
CCSS.ELA-Literacy	L.4.4	Determine or clarify the meaning of unknown and multiple-meaning words and phrases based on Grade 4 reading and content, choosing flexibly from a range of strategies.	ELA	161
CCSS.ELA-Literacy	RL.6.3	Describe how a particular story's or drama's plot unfolds in a series of episodes as well as how the characters respond or change as the plot moves toward a resolution.	ELA	152
CCSS.ELA-Literacy	RI.7.2	Determine two or more central ideas in a text and analyze their development over the course of the text; provide an objective summary of the text.	ELA	166
CCSS.ELA-Literacy	W.8.1	Write arguments to support claims with clear reasons and relevant evidence.	ELA	168
CCSS.ELA-Literacy	W.9-10.1	Write arguments to support claims in an analysis of substantive topics or texts, using valid reasoning and relevant and sufficient evidence.	ELA	159

(Continued)

(Continued)

STANDARD	ABBREVIATION	EXPLAINED	SUBJECT	PAGE REFERENCE
CCSS.ELA-Literacy	SL.11-12.1	Initiate and participate effectively in a range of collaborative discussions (one-on-one, in groups, and teacher-led) with diverse partners on Grades 11–12 topics, texts, and issues, building on others' ideas and expressing their own clearly and persuasively.	ELA	163
CCSS.Math. Content	3.OA.B.5	Apply properties of operations as strategies to multiply and divide.	Mathematics	127
CCSS.Math. Content	3.OA.D.9	Identify arithmetic patterns (including patterns in the addition table or multiplication table), and explain them using properties of operations.	Mathematics	120
CCSS.Math. Content	6.SP.B.5	Summarize numerical data sets in relation to their context.	Mathematics	116
CCSS.Math. Content	7.RP.A	Analyze proportional relationships and use them to solve real-world and mathematical problems.	Mathematics	131
CCSS.Math. Content	8.G.A.2	Understand that a two-dimensional figure is congruent to another if the second can be obtained from the first by a sequence of rotations, reflections, and translations; given two congruent figures, describe a sequence that exhibits the congruence between them.	Mathematics	124
CCSS.Math. Content	HSA-APR.A.1	Understand that polynomials form a system analogous to the integers, namely, they are closed under the operations of addition, subtraction, and multiplication; add, subtract, and multiply polynomials.	Algebra	134

STANDARD	ABBREVIATION	EXPLAINED	SUBJECT	PAGE REFERENCE
CCSS.Math. Content	HSA-SSE.A.2	Use the structure of an expression to identify ways to rewrite it.	Algebra	134
CCSS.Math. Content	HSS-ID.B.6	Represent data on two quantitative variables on a scatter plot, and describe how the variables are related.	Statistics and Probability	122
CCSS.Math. Content	HSF-LEA.1	Distinguish between situations that can be modeled with linear functions and with exponential functions	Statistics and Probability	129
CCSS.Math. Content	HSS-CP.A.2	Understand that two events A and B are independent if the probability of A and B occurring together is the product of their probabilities, and use this characterization to determine if they are independent.	Statistics and Probability	118
ISTE	1.1	Empowered Learner: Students leverage technology to take an active role in choosing, achieving, and demonstrating competency in their learning goals, informed by the learning sciences.	Computer Science	39, 41, 44, 46, 49, 52, 70
ISTE	1.3	Knowledge Constructor: Students critically curate a variety of resources using digital tools to construct knowledge, produce creative artifacts, and make meaningful learning experiences for themselves and others.	Computer Science	70
ISTE	1.4	Innovative Designer: Students use a variety of technologies within a design process to identify and solve problems by creating new, useful, or imaginative solutions.	Computer Science	39, 41, 44, 46, 49, 52

(Continued)

STANDARD	ABBREVIATION	EXPLAINED	SUBJECT	PAGE REFERENCE
ISTE	1.5	Computational Thinker: Students develop and employ strategies for understanding and solving problems in ways that leverage the power of technological methods to develop and test solutions.	Computer Science	39, 41, 44, 46, 49, 52
NCSS.D2	Civ.7.K-2	Apply civic virtues when participating in school settings.	Social Studies	191
NCSS.D2	Geo.7.3-5	Explain how cultural and environmental characteristics affect the distribution and movement of people, goods, and ideas.	Social Studies	197
NCSS.D2	Geo.7.6-8	Explain how changes in transportation and communication technology influence the spatial connections among human settlements and affect the diffusion of ideas and cultural practices.	Social Studies	188
NCSS.D2	His.12.6-8	Use questions generated about multiple historical sources to identify further areas of inquiry and additional sources.	Social Studies	185
NCSS.D2	His.13.6-8	Evaluate the relevancy and utility of a historical source based on information such as maker, date, place of origin, intended audience, and purpose.	Social Studies	185
NCSS.D2	Civ.4.9-12	Explain how the U.S. Constitution establishes a system of government that has powers, responsibilities, and limits that have changed over time and that are still contested.	Civics	193

STANDARD	ABBREVIATION	EXPLAINED	SUBJECT	PAGE REFERENCE
NCSS.D2	Eco.2.9-12	Use marginal benefits and marginal costs to construct an argument for or against an approach or solution to an economic issue.	Economics	195
NCSS.D2	His.5.9-12	Analyze how historical contexts shaped and continue to shape people's perspectives.	History	66
NCSS.D2	His.6.9-12	Analyze the ways in which the perspectives of those writing history shaped the history that they produced.	History	66
NGSS	4-ESS2-2	Analyze and interpret data from maps to describe patterns of Earth's features.	Science	95
NGSS	4-PS3-2	Make observations to provide evidence that energy can be transferred by sound, light, heat, and electric currents.	Science	86
NGSS	MS-LS2-1	Analyze and interpret data to provide evidence for the effects of resource availability on organisms and populations of organisms in an ecosystem.	Life Science	99
NGSS	MS-LS2-2	Construct an explanation that predicts patterns of interactions among organisms across multiple ecosystems.	Life Science	99
NGSS	MS-LS2-4	Construct an argument supported by empirical evidence that changes to physical or biological components of an ecosystem affect populations	Life Science	99
NGSS	MS-LS4-4	Construct an explanation based on evidence that describes how genetic variations of traits in a population increase some individuals' probability of surviving and reproducing in a specific environment.	Life Science	89

(Continued)

(Continued)

STANDARD	ABBREVIATION	EXPLAINED	SUBJECT	PAGE REFERENCE
NGSS	MS-PS1-1	Develop models to describe the atomic composition of simple molecules and extended structures.	Physical Science	91
NGSS	HS-ESS1-5	Evaluate evidence of the movements of continental and oceanic crust to explain ages of crustal rocks.	Earth Science	96
NGSS	HS-LS1-3	Plan and conduct an investigation to provide evidence that feedback mechanisms maintain homeostasis.	Biology	88
NGSS	HS-PS2-1	Analyze data to support the claim that Newton's second law of motion describes the mathematical relationship among the net force on a macroscopic object, its mass, and its acceleration.	Physics	64
NGSS	HS-PS2-2	Use mathematical representations to support the claim that the total momentum of a system of objects is conserved when no net force acts on the system.	Physics	93

Table of Examples, Lessons, and Units

NUMBER	TOPIC	GRADE BAND	PAGE #
Example 1.1	Use of AI in Surgery	na	12
Example 1.2	Developing Programming Skills in Elementary Education	na	12
Example 1.3	Access to Virtual Learning	na	14
Example 2.1	Thermal Sensors	na	24
Example 2.2	AI-Based Games	na	25
Example 2.3	Recommender Systems	na	26
Example 2.4	Voice Assistants	na	27
Example 2.5	Face Recognition and Bias	na	27
Example 2.6	Bridge-Building Challenge	na	30
Lesson 3.1	Foundations of AI	Middle School	41
Lesson 3.2	Data Representation and Decision Making	Middle School	44
Lesson 3.3	Machine Learning	Middle School	46
Lesson 3.4	Natural Interaction and Creativity	Middle School	49
Lesson 3.5	Society Impact	Middle School	52
Lesson 4.1	Exploring Motion and Predictive Algorithms	High School	64
Lesson 4.2	Reexamining the U.S. Civil War	High School	66
Example 4.1	ISTE Artificial Intelligence in Education	na	68
Example 4.2	Interactive Classroom Experiences With WolframAlpha	na	68
Lesson 4.3	Speech Recognition	Middle School	70
Example 4.3	Connect: ISTE + ASCD's Free Online Community	na	71
Example 4.4	Evaluating STEM Practices in AI-Related Tasks	na	72

(Continued)

(Continued)

NUMBER	TOPIC	GRADE BAND	PAGE #
Lesson 5.1	Renewable Energy	Elementary School	86
Lesson 5.2	Homeostasis and Body Control	High School	88
Lesson 5.3	Natural Selection and Evolution	Middle School	89
Lesson 5.4	Atomic Structure of Matter	Middle School	91
Lesson 5.5	Conservation of Momentum	High School	93
Lesson 5.6	Earth's Features	Elementary School	95
Lesson 5.7	How Old Is Earth?	High School	96
Lesson 5.8	Genetic Engineering and Natural Genetic Variations	High School	97
Science Unit	Ecosystems	Middle School	99
Lesson 6.1	Statistics in Digital Photography	Middle School	116
Lesson 6.2	Probability Trees and Weather Prediction	High School	118
Lesson 6.3	Number Patterns	Elementary School	120
Lesson 6.4	Line of Best Fit	High School	122
Lesson 6.5	Geometric Transformations and Tessellations	Middle School	124
Lesson 6.6	Properties of Operations	Elementary School	127
Lesson 6.7	Comparing Linear, Quadratic, and Exponential Models With Technology	High School	129
Lesson 6.8	AI for Social Good	Middle School	131
Mathematics Unit	Structure of Algebraic Expressions	High School	134
Lesson 7.1	Analyzing Character Development	Middle School	152
Lesson 7.2	Phonics in Action	Elementary School	156
Lesson 7.3	Mastering Evidence-Based Writing	High School	159
Lesson 7.4	Identifying Words With Multiple Meanings	Elementary School	161
Lesson 7.5	Debating the Future of AI	High School	163
Lesson 7.6	Analyzing the Social Impact of Scientific Innovations	Middle School	166
ELA Unit	Man vs. Machine: Examining the Power of Dynamics of Creation in Literature	Middle School	168
Lesson 8.1	World War I	Middle School	185
Lesson 8.2	Along the Silk Road	Middle School	188

NUMBER	TOPIC	GRADE BAND	PAGE #
Lesson 8.3	Celebrating Together	Elementary School	191
Lesson 8.4	Understanding Political Parties and Voter Registration	High School	193
Lesson 8.5	Bridging the Gap	High School	195
Social Studies Unit	Journey of Hope: Using AI to Understand Immigration Stories	Elementary School	197

Preface

We live in an age where artificial intelligence (AI) is rapidly changing everything. Think about it: AI is already shaping how we shop, how we get our news, and even how doctors diagnose diseases. It's no exaggeration to say that AI is transforming every aspect of our lives, including education. For our students to thrive in this world, they need more than just the ability to use technology; they need to understand how it works, its potential, and its limitations. They need AI literacy. And the good news is, educators around the globe are recognizing this urgency. We're seeing a surge of initiatives aimed at integrating AI concepts into K–12 classrooms (UNESCO, 2022).

AI isn't just about technology; it's a fascinating blend of many different fields. Think philosophy, psychology, neuroscience, math—they all play a role in shaping how we build intelligent systems. And it's not a new idea either! Pioneers like Alan Turing (who gave us the famous Turing test to see if a machine could think like a human) and Frank Rosenblatt (who developed early neural networks, the foundation of today's machine learning) were already exploring these ideas back in the mid-20th century (Taylor & Dorin, 2020). Their work paved the way for large language models (LLMs) like GPT-4, a powerful model that can understand and generate human-like text. LLMs are already shaking up fields like education, offering incredible potential for personalized learning and creative applications. But with this potential come important questions. How will LLMs affect jobs? What are the ethical considerations we need to address? As AI keeps advancing, it's crucial that we learn to use it wisely and responsibly, ensuring it benefits humanity and creates a more equitable society. And that starts with bringing AI literacy into education.

So how do we actually bring AI literacy into our classrooms? That's where things get really interesting! This book dives deeply into the latest research and best practices for designing engaging lessons that integrate AI literacy into K–12 education. We'll explore everything from the Big Five Ideas in AI (Touretzky, Gardner-McCune, & Seehorn, 2023) to practical strategies for teaching AI core concepts across different subjects. You'll discover how to empower your students to not only understand AI but also to develop the critical thinking skills to evaluate its impact and use it ethically and responsibly. Imagine students designing their own AI projects, collaborating with their peers, and reflecting on the societal implications of AI! AI literacy has the potential to spark curiosity, boost critical thinking, and foster a love of lifelong learning, but it all comes down to how we, as educators, choose to integrate it. This book will help you navigate those choices and ensure your approach is thoughtful, intentional, and truly beneficial for your students.

Although this book doesn't delve into the technical intricacies of AI or its underlying mechanisms, we believe that by engaging with the book activities and adapting them to your own needs, you will begin your own AI literacy journey, gaining a deeper understanding of AI capabilities, limitations, and implications.

In writing this book, we have utilized Generative AI to support our creative writing process, ensuring our content is insightful and accessible. Generative AI has helped brainstorm ideas, refine our thoughts, and make sure our message is clear and engaging. This experience reinforced our belief in the power of AI tools to enhance creativity and learning. But more importantly, it reflects our commitment to walking the walk when it comes to AI integration. We hope this book serves as a valuable resource for teachers, teacher educators, curriculum developers, and researchers, offering practical strategies and insights to bring AI literacy into K–12 classrooms and empower a new generation of tech-savvy learners.

BOOK OVERVIEW

This book is divided into three parts, each designed to guide you as you explore how to integrate AI literacy into your teaching. Throughout the book you will also find different types of practical tools to support you in bringing AI literacy to your classroom, including:

- Examples that illustrate specific AI features and capabilities, provide resources for teaching and professional development

- Scenarios to engage in discussions around ethical considerations and potential biases in AI

- Lessons and instructional units aligned with discipline-specific educational standards that demonstrate ways to integrate AI concepts across various subjects

- Web resources that include templates, graphic organizers, and other teaching materials https://companion.corwin.com/courses/TeachingAILiteracy

Part I provides educators with the theoretical foundations for integrating AI literacy into existing curricula, so that busy teachers don't feel like they have yet another subject to teach. We begin in Chapter 1 by exploring ethics and social justice issues related to AI literacy in education. We go on to discuss the current research about AI in K–12 education and introduce a new pedagogical framework for AI literacy that we developed (Chapter 2). This framework provides a structured approach for teachers to foster AI literacy in their students, guiding them to build foundational knowledge, apply AI concepts to real-world problems, and cultivate ethical awareness in the responsible use of AI. In Chapter 3, we delve deeper into how this framework can be put into practice, providing concrete examples and illustrating how it supports the development of students' cognitive, social-emotional, and technological skills. Finally, in Chapter 4 we offer practical recommendations for educators to prepare for integrating AI literacy into their curricula.

Part II shifts from theory to practice, providing concrete examples and strategies for integrating AI literacy into your existing curriculum. In Chapters 5 through 8 we delve into specific core disciplines—Science, Mathematics, English Language Arts, and Social Studies—offering guidance and examples for different grade bands. When appropriate advocate for using AI tools that allow students to actively explore the Five Big Ideas in AI: perception, representation and reasoning, learning, natural interaction, and societal impact (Touretzky et al., 2023). To deepen understanding, we draw parallels between how AI systems function and the process of human learning, demonstrating how concepts like data processing, decision making, and feedback loops can be mirrored in engaging classroom activities. Throughout these chapters, we emphasize a thoughtful and purposeful approach to AI integration. This means carefully considering learning outcomes, within the specific discipline and in terms of AI literacy, and designing student experiences that foster meaningful connections. We also provide guidance on navigating potential challenges and ensuring that technology is used effectively to enhance learning.

Finally in **Part III**, in Chapter 9 we provide a brief overview of the current research on assessment in AI literacy, introducing an Assessment of AI Literacy Framework for evaluating students' understanding and offering examples of assessment tools that can be adapted for K–12 classrooms. We conclude the book with discussion of possible ways AI can transform teaching and learning in the future.

HOW TO USE THIS BOOK

- *Understand the landscape*: Begin with Chapter 1 to gain a broad understanding of global perspectives in AI literacy education, including important considerations like ethical issues, equity and access, cultural and social impacts, and curriculum design.

- *Adopt the pedagogical framework for AI literacy*: Embrace the design–create–reflect (DCR) process introduced in Chapter 2 as a foundational approach to integrating AI literacy. This framework promotes active learning, critical thinking, and creative application.

- *Examine effective practices*: Study the examples presented in Chapter 3 to understand how the pedagogical framework can be applied in real-world classrooms aiding students in developing cognitive, social-emotional, and technological skills related to AI.

- *Prepare for integration of AI literacy*: Use Chapter 4 to identify strategies for equipping yourself to integrate AI literacy into curricula, including professional development opportunities and resources.

- *Explore diverse examples*: Dive into Chapters 5 through 8 to discover practical strategies for integrating AI literacy across various grade bands and subjects, with examples illustrating how AI concepts connect to specific disciplinary standards and learning objectives.

- *Assess AI literacy*: Explore and adapt the assessment resources suggested in Chapter 9 to evaluate student progress in AI literacy. These resources can help you measure students' understanding of AI concepts and their ability to apply them creatively.

- *Adapt to your context*: Tailor the strategies and examples in this book to fit your school's or district's specific needs and resources, creating a customized approach to AI literacy education.

By embracing the integration of AI literacy in your teaching, you are not only equipping students with essential skills for the future but also empowering them to become informed and ethical users of this transformative technology. Ultimately, you are the key to fostering AI literacy in your students.

Acknowledgments

We extend our sincere gratitude to Debbie Hardin, Senior Acquisitions Editor, STEM, at Corwin Press, for her invaluable contributions to this book. Her meticulous attention to detail, insightful suggestions, and unwavering support have been instrumental in shaping this book into its final form.

Corwin Press would like to thank the following:

Whitney Aragaki, Teacher, Hawai'i Department of Education, Hilo, HI

Jennifer R. Meadows, Associate Professor, Tennessee Tech University

Kevin Dykema, District Math Specialist, Mattawan Consolidated Schools, Mattawan, MI

Perry Shank, Sr. Director of Research and Development, Harrisonburg, VA

About the Authors

Dr. Irina Lyublinskaya is a Professor of Mathematics and Education at Teachers College, Columbia University, New York. She holds PhD in Theoretical and Mathematical Physics from the Leningrad State University, Russia. She taught high school and university mathematics and science for more than 35 years. She is a recipient of various awards, including Radioshack/Tandy Prize for Teaching Excellence in Mathematics, Science, and Computer Science; NSTA Distinguished Science Teaching Award and citation;

Education's Unsung Heroes Award for innovation in the classroom; and NSTA Vernier Technology Award. Her research interests are in the areas of STEM education, teacher education, curriculum development, and international comparative education. She authored/co-authored 22 books, 15 book chapters, and more than 100 peer-reviewed papers and proceedings in these fields.

Dr. Xiaoxue Du is the Senior Director of AI Strategy and Operations at the University of Chicago, with a track record of leading digital transformations and driving strategic initiatives across industries. With a deep commitment to advancing AI literacy, she has developed curricula and resources to help K–12 educators integrate AI concepts into classrooms in engaging and responsible ways. Her work spans AI-enriched learning experiences, game-based AI education, and ethical AI adoption in schools. Previously, she collaborated with the MIT Media Lab on research and teaching in AI literacy and human–AI interaction and worked with a top consulting firm, where she specialized in AI strategy, digital transformation, and operational excellence. Dr. Du actively writes and teaches about human–AI interaction, focusing on preparing the next generation of learners and educators to navigate an AI-driven world. She holds a doctorate from Teachers College, Columbia University, where she conducted mixed-methods research to study complex sociotechnical systems.

PART I

Theoretical Foundations

Chapter 1: Ethics and Global Perspectives on AI Literacy Education

Chapter 2: Pedagogical Framework for AI Literacy

Chapter 3: Apply Our Pedagogical Framework for AI Literacy

Chapter 4: Preparing to Integrate AI Literacy into Existing Curriculum

CHAPTER 1

Ethics and Global Perspectives on AI Literacy Education

The rapid integration of artificial intelligence (AI) in education has raised important ethical concerns, emphasizing the need for AI literacy to ensure that these technologies are used responsibly and equitably. As AI becomes more prevalent in classrooms, it has the potential to enhance learning experiences and exacerbate existing inequalities if not carefully implemented. Teachers and students alike must be equipped with the skills to critically engage with AI, ensuring that it supports fair and transparent learning environments for all. Globally, AI literacy education takes on various forms, shaped by regional priorities, resources, and cultural contexts. However, several common themes emerge across different regions: the importance of addressing bias and discrimination in AI, the need for privacy and data security, ensuring transparency in AI decision making, closing the Digital Divide, and preparing teachers and students for the AI-driven future (Casal-Otero et al., 2023). This chapter explores ethical issues and examines how AI literacy education is being approached across the globe, with a focus on K–12 education (Sperling et al., 2024).

ETHICS AND EDUCATION

AI literacy education is essential in addressing the ethical issues that arise from the increasing integration of AI in education. The increasing presence of AI in classrooms comes with critical concerns, such as algorithmic bias, privacy violations, and accountability in decision making. These concerns have real-world implications for educational practices and student outcomes. Teachers must understand how AI operates, not just from a technical standpoint but also in terms of its societal and ethical consequences. AI literacy can empower teachers and students to critically engage with technology, giving everyone the tools to evaluate the benefits and risks of AI. In doing so, students and teachers alike develop the ability to critically evaluate AI applications, discern potential biases, and understand the broader societal implications of their use. With these abilities they are empowered to make informed decisions that prioritize ethical considerations alongside technological advancements. As the global landscape evolves toward an AI-driven future, equipping students and teachers with these essential skills ensures they can navigate not only the technical complexities but also the ethical challenges inherent in this new reality. Let's examine these ethical issues in more depth.

BIAS AND DISCRIMINATION

As you might already know, AI algorithms are often trained on historical data, which can carry biases that reflect societal inequalities. As a result, AI algorithms can perpetuate existing biases in data, leading to discriminatory outcomes in areas like admissions, grading, and personalized learning. An AI-driven grading tool, for example, could unfairly favor students from backgrounds that are overrepresented in its training data, while disadvantaging those who don't fit these patterns. Similarly, in admissions processes, AI systems designed to predict student success might disproportionately favor applicants from schools or regions that historically perform well, which could be influenced by access to better resources, socioeconomic status, or geographic location. This bias could lead to the system undervaluing students who are equally capable and from underrepresented backgrounds or schools with fewer resources. These subtle (and sometimes not so subtle!) forms of bias in AI-driven educational tools can perpetuate inequalities, reinforcing stereotypes, and creating barriers to success for those already marginalized in the system.

Scenario 1.1

Imagine you're a teacher grading two essays on the same topic.

- Essay A: Written by a student who consistently participates in class, asks thoughtful questions, and turns in assignments on time. The essay is well written but has a few minor grammatical errors.

- Essay B: Written by a student who is often quiet in class, rarely participates, and has missed a few deadlines. The essay is also well written, with similar content quality to Essay A, but has a few more grammatical errors.

Questions:

- How would you grade these two essays?

- Would you give them the same grade or different grades?

- If different, which one would receive the higher grade?

Just as teachers can unconsciously favor students based on pre-existing impressions, AI systems can exhibit bias due to skewed training data or flawed algorithms. In both cases, seemingly objective evaluations can be influenced by factors unrelated to actual performance. The **halo effect** in grading parallels AI's tendency to generalize based on limited data, whereas **confirmation bias** reflects AI's potential to reinforce existing patterns. Recognizing and addressing these biases is crucial for ensuring human and machine assessments are fair, accurate, and equitable.

PRIVACY AND DATA SECURITY

The collection and use of student data raise concerns about privacy breaches and misuse of sensitive information. As AI systems in education increasingly rely on collecting data—from demographic information to behavioral patterns and even health-related metrics—protecting student privacy becomes a crucial ethical issue. Without appropriate safeguards, this data could be exposed to misuse, breaches, or exploitation, putting the security and dignity of students at risk. A relevant example can be seen in the use of AI-powered health-monitoring tools in schools. Some schools have adopted wearable devices that track students' physical activity, sleep patterns, and heart rates to promote health and well-being.

Although these tools can provide valuable insights into student wellness and support health interventions, they also collect highly sensitive biometric data. If this data is not adequately protected, it could fall into the wrong hands or be used for purposes beyond the original intent, such as insurance companies accessing student health records or unauthorized third parties using it for commercial purposes.

• The **halo effect** is a type of cognitive bias where our overall impression of a person influences how we feel and think about their specific traits.

• **Confirmation bias** is the tendency to search for, interpret, favor, and recall information in a way that confirms or strengthens our preexisting beliefs or values.

Scenario 1.2

Your school decided to use an AI-powered learning platform that tracks student progress and behavior. It collects data like how long students spend on each task, which questions they struggle with, and even their emotional state based on facial expressions during online lessons.

> ## REFLECTION QUESTIONS
>
> - What potential benefits and challenges do you see in using such an AI-powered learning platform in your classroom?
>
> - How comfortable would you feel with this level of student data collection? What concerns do you have about student privacy and data security in this scenario?
>
> - Do you think there are any ethical implications of using AI to track student emotions during online lessons? How might this impact the student–teacher relationship or the overall learning environment?

Although this data can help teachers personalize instruction and identify students who need extra support, it's highly sensitive. If this data were accidentally shared publicly or accessed by unauthorized individuals, it could reveal private details about students' learning difficulties, emotional struggles, or even their home environment (based on background noise during online classes). This not only violates student privacy but could also lead to stigma, bullying, or discrimination.

Even with the best intentions, using AI tools in the classroom requires careful consideration of data privacy. Teachers need to be aware of what data is being collected, how it's being used and stored, and who has access to it. Open communication with students and parents about data practices is essential to build trust and ensure ethical use of AI in education.

ACCOUNTABILITY AND TRANSPARENCY

A major challenge in AI use in education is the lack of transparency in how AI systems make decisions. AI algorithms often operate as "black boxes," where the internal processes that lead to specific outcomes are difficult to understand. This lack of transparency makes it hard to identify potential biases or errors, particularly in education, where fairness and equity are paramount. When decisions affecting students' futures—such as admissions, grading, or placement in advanced courses—are influenced by AI, the absence of clear decision-making processes can erode trust and accountability. For example, in many schools, AI-powered systems are being used to recommend students for so-called gifted programs or advanced placement courses. These systems often rely on a mix of student performance data, standardized test scores, and behavioral metrics.

Scenario 1.3

Your school is facing increasing pressure to more effectively identify and support students who are high achievers. The current identification process, relying heavily on teacher recommendations and standardized tests, has been criticized for its subjectivity and potential biases. The school district is considering adopting an AI-powered placement system to streamline the process and ensure a fairer, more data-driven approach.

A committee of teachers, administrators, and parents has been formed to evaluate several vendor proposals. As a member of this committee, you are tasked with scrutinizing the AI systems and asking probing questions to ensure the chosen system aligns with the district's values and priorities. You understand the potential benefits of AI but also recognize the need for careful consideration and ethical implementation. What questions will you ask the vendors to address concerning transparency, fairness, data privacy, and the impact on students and teachers?

If teachers, students, and parents don't fully understand how student metrics are weighted and combined, students from underrepresented groups or those who don't perform well on standardized tests may be overlooked, even if they possess the potential to excel in advanced courses. Without transparency, it's nearly impossible to ensure that the AI system is not reinforcing existing biases, such as favoring students from more privileged backgrounds who have better access to test preparation resources. A transparent AI system would allow educators to review and adjust the criteria to ensure fair and inclusive decision making for all students.

REFLECTION QUESTIONS

- How does your AI system make decisions about student placement? Can you provide clear explanations for the factors considered and how they are weighted in the decision-making process?

- What specific student data is collected and how is it used? What safeguards are in place to protect student data privacy and security?

- How does your system incorporate teacher input and observations, and how does it empower students in the placement process? What evidence do you have that your system is effective in identifying students who are high achievers and improving their educational outcomes?

DIGITAL DIVIDE: ACCESSIBILITY ACROSS DISCIPLINES

The Digital Divide goes far beyond simply providing access to technology (Chang et al., 2014); it's about ensuring every student can engage meaningfully with technology. Achieving equity in AI literacy education requires a multifaceted approach—from motivating students to offering accessible materials across disciplines (Roshanaei et al., 2023). As educators, we have a crucial role in advocating for and implementing solutions that address these challenges, ensuring that all students have the tools, skills, and encouragement they need to thrive in an AI-driven world (Kong et al., 2024). To prepare students for the challenges of the future, AI literacy should be integrated across curriculum to broaden access, not just within science, technology, engineering, and mathematics (STEM) disciplines (Cantú-Ortiz et al., 2020).

In this book we provide multiple examples of how AI literacy can be integrated with various school disciplines such as social studies, English Language Arts (ELA), science, and mathematics. For instance, a middle school science unit on ecosystems (Chapter 5) allows students to explore different types of datasets, learning how choices in data labeling and dataset construction influence how computers learn. In an ELA example (Chapter 7), students examine themes of power, creation, and creators in literary texts, drawing connections between these literary concepts and the use of AI for social good. This approach makes AI concepts more tangible for students and teachers and illustrates the pervasive influence of technology, fostering a comprehensive understanding of AI's broader implications.

STUDENT AUTONOMY AND AGENCY

AI systems that track and monitor students' activities excessively can significantly limit their autonomy and sense of control over their learning. Although these technologies are often designed to personalize learning experiences and provide targeted support, there is a risk that they can undermine students' ability to make independent decisions about their education. When AI platforms constantly track student progress, suggest learning paths, or even intervene in task selection, students may feel like they are merely following instructions rather than actively participating in their learning journey. As an example, AI systems that monitor students' engagement in online classrooms often track metrics like time spent on tasks, frequency of clicks, or even facial expressions during virtual lessons. These systems may flag students who are perceived as "disengaged" or "distracted" based on these data points, prompting teachers to intervene.

Scenario 1.4

You're a high school teacher using an AI-powered online learning platform that monitors student engagement during virtual lessons. One day, the system repeatedly flags a particular student, Sarah, for appearing disengaged. However, you know Sarah to be a bright and capable student who actively participates in class discussions and consistently submits high-quality work. You're faced with a dilemma:

- Trust the AI: The AI system is flagging Sarah as disengaged, suggesting she might need additional support

or intervention. Perhaps there's something going on that you're not aware of, and the AI is picking up on subtle cues.

- Trust your own judgment: You know Sarah to be a good student, and you haven't observed any signs of disengagement during class. You're concerned that the AI might be misinterpreting her facial expressions or that there might be other factors influencing her behavior that the AI isn't considering.

REFLECTION QUESTIONS

- How do you balance the AI's data-driven insights with your own observations and knowledge of the student?

- Should you intervene with Sarah based solely on the AI's flags, or should you gather more information first?

- How can you ensure that the use of AI in the classroom doesn't create a climate of surveillance and anxiety for students?

- What are the potential consequences of overrelying on AI to monitor student engagement, and how can these be mitigated?

Although such systems aim to enhance learning outcomes by identifying students who might need additional support, they can also contribute to feelings of surveillance, reducing students' sense of privacy and autonomy. When students feel that every movement or moment of inattention is being tracked and judged, they may become more focused on meeting the system's engagement criteria rather than genuinely engaging with the content.

CULTURAL SENSITIVITY AND DIVERSITY

AI systems can struggle to understand and respond to diverse cultural contexts, potentially reinforcing stereotypes or marginalizing certain groups (Southworth et al., 2023). Careful design and inclusive datasets are crucial to mitigate this risk. This is particularly concerning in environments like classrooms, where students come from a wide range of cultural backgrounds, and it is critical that all students feel seen, heard, and valued.

Scenario 1.5

You're a middle school English teacher using an AI-powered chatbot to help students practice their conversational skills and vocabulary. You notice that when some of your students, who are English Language Learners, interact with the chatbot, it frequently misunderstands their phrasing or cultural references. This leads to frustrating conversations where the chatbot gives irrelevant or even insensitive responses, making these students feel excluded and discouraged from participating.

REFLECTION QUESTIONS

- How can you address the cultural insensitivity of the AI chatbot and create a more inclusive learning environment for all your students?

- Should you continue using the chatbot despite its limitations, or should you explore alternative tools that are more culturally sensitive?

- How can you leverage this experience to teach your students about the potential biases in AI and the importance of creating technology that is inclusive and respectful of diverse cultures?

- What steps can you take to advocate for more culturally responsive AI tools in education and ensure that all students have equal access to the benefits of technology.

Writing styles, argument structures, and even the use of metaphors or examples can vary greatly across cultures. An AI system that is not designed with this diversity in mind might penalize students for using unfamiliar rhetorical strategies, even if their reasoning and creativity are strong. This reinforces a narrow view of what constitutes "good" academic performance, which may privilege some students over others.

These interconnected challenges demand a multifaceted approach to ensure that AI technology serves as a force for good in education, fostering equitable access, promoting ethical practices, and empowering all learners to thrive. Having examined a range of critical ethical considerations in education, we are now ready to reflect on the broader implications of these issues.

GLOBAL PERSPECTIVES ON AI LITERACY EDUCATION

Global perspectives on AI literacy education emphasize a shared understanding that AI is fundamentally shaping the future, making it essential for students worldwide to grasp its implications. Therefore, it is our responsibility as educators to equip students with the knowledge and skills necessary to navigate an increasingly AI-driven world. By fostering critical thinking, ethical awareness, and responsible AI use, AI literacy empowers students to engage thoughtfully with these technologies, preparing them to make informed decisions and contribute to a more equitable and just society in the face of rapid technological advancements.

As the world embraces the integration of AI, four key perspectives emerge, each shaping the trajectory of AI literacy education: the recognition of AI's growing impact, the emphasis on foundational skills, the importance of teacher training, and the pursuit of equity and inclusion. Let's consider each of these perspectives in more detail.

THE RECOGNITION OF AI'S GROWING IMPACT

The transformative nature of AI is universally acknowledged, and countries across the world are incorporating AI literacy into their educational frameworks to prepare students for an AI-driven future. Students must not only understand AI technologies but also recognize their societal and ethical implications.

The goal of education is to foster a generation that can think critically about AI's role in decision making, innovation, and governance.

EXAMPLE 1.1

Use of AI in Surgery

AI is increasingly being used to make decisions in health care, finance, and law. In surgery, AI is being used in a variety of ways to enhance precision, efficiency, and patient outcomes.

FIGURE 1.1 ● Robotic surgery room

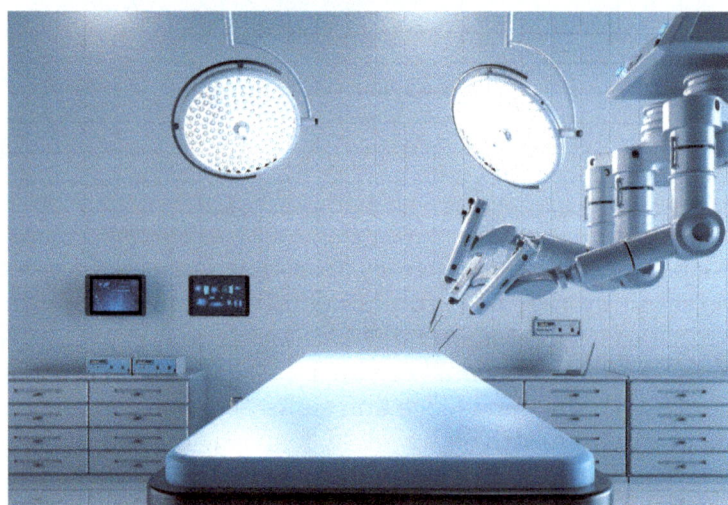

Source: istock.com/PhonlamaiPhoto

Students who understand the underlying mechanisms of AI and its potential biases are better equipped to challenge unjust outcomes and offer innovative solutions. AI literacy education helps students recognize that AI technologies can empower and limit decision-making processes, depending on how they are designed and deployed. As such, a critical understanding of AI's impact is essential for students to navigate and influence the future of AI development and its societal integration.

THE EMPHASIS ON FOUNDATIONAL SKILLS IN AI LITERACY

At the core of AI literacy education is the development of foundational skills, particularly in STEM. These skills enable students to not only use AI technologies but also to understand how they function, how to design them, and how to critically evaluate their applications. Foundational skills in programming, data analysis, and problem solving are crucial for students to move beyond being passive users of AI and instead become active creators and thinkers who can improve and innovate within the field.

EXAMPLE 1.2

Developing Programming Skills in Elementary Education

Students can develop computational thinking through robotics, coding, and basic programming as early as primary school.

FIGURE 1.2 ● Coding robots in elementary school

Source: Source: istock.com/insta_photos

Computational thinking teaches students to break down complex problems into smaller, manageable parts, which is a core concept in developing AI algorithms. Moreover, these foundational skills help students engage with AI technologies from a multidisciplinary perspective, connecting the technical aspects of AI with real-world applications across various fields such as environmental science, social justice, or economics.

THE IMPORTANCE OF TEACHER TRAINING TO ACHIEVE SUCCESS IN AI LITERACY

Teachers are central to the success of AI literacy education. We are the ones who introduce students to AI concepts, guide ethical discussions, and help students apply AI to real-world problems. However, teaching AI literacy requires a specific set of skills and knowledge that many of us as educators may not yet possess. This creates a global need for professional development and training that equips teachers with the technical expertise and the pedagogical strategies to integrate AI literacy into their classrooms. Teacher training in AI literacy must go beyond the basics of how AI technologies work. It should also cover the ethical implications of AI, so that teachers can facilitate meaningful discussions with students about these issues. As teachers we need to understand not only the mechanics of AI but also how to frame AI as a tool that can either support or undermine equity and justice, depending on how it is used. Additionally, teachers must be prepared to guide students in applying AI concepts to solve real-world problems, making the learning experience practical and impactful. In Chapter 4 we include research-based recommendations and resources to help you prepare for integration of AI literacy into your curriculum.

THE PURSUIT OF EQUITY AND INCLUSION IN AI LITERACY

A central challenge in AI literacy education is ensuring that it is accessible and inclusive for all students, regardless of their socioeconomic background or geographic location. AI has the potential to exacerbate existing inequities if equity is not addressed properly. Therefore, a global focus on equity in AI literacy education aims to bridge the Digital Divide and ensure that AI literacy does not become a privilege reserved for a few. Efforts to promote equity and inclusion in AI literacy education involve providing students with access to the necessary tools and resources, ensuring diverse representation in AI datasets, and encouraging the development of culturally responsive AI systems.

EXAMPLE 1.3

Access to Virtual Learning

In situations where financial constraints or geographic barriers prevent students from learning specific courses, AI-powered educational platforms can step in to bridge the gap. These platforms, equipped with vast libraries of knowledge and interactive learning tools, essentially act as virtual teachers, offering students the opportunity to explore subjects and gain valuable skills, regardless of their circumstances. AI-powered educational platforms can provide students with step-by-step tutorials and interactive simulations, guiding their explorations of topics that are not accessible to them in schools. These platforms could also connect students with online communities where they can ask questions, share their projects, and learn from others with similar interests.

FIGURE 1.3 ● A middle school student learning electronics virtually

Source: istock.com/ KarlosVBrito7

By fostering an inclusive approach to AI literacy, educators can ensure that all students, especially those from communities that are historically and currently underserved, are empowered to engage with AI technologies in ways that benefit their personal and professional development. Equity in AI literacy also involves preparing students to critically assess how AI systems affect different communities. This includes teaching students to question who designs AI systems, whose voices are included in decision-making processes, and who is affected by the outcomes. An inclusive AI literacy curriculum encourages students to think about how AI can be used to promote social good and ensure that technological advancements benefit everyone, not just the privileged few.

Chapter Summary

The importance of AI literacy extends far beyond mastering technical skills; it provides a crucial foundation for addressing the ethical challenges posed by AI integration into society. As AI systems increasingly influence decisions in areas such as healthcare, criminal justice, and employment, it becomes vital to teach students how to critically assess the ethical implications of these technologies. Making AI literacy accessible and inclusive ensures that all students understand the societal impacts of AI, particularly how biases can be embedded and perpetuated if systems are not designed and implemented responsibly. This chapter underscores that confronting these ethical challenges requires a global educational approach that adapts to regional contexts and perspectives.

AI's rapid transformation of the educational landscape makes the urgency to integrate AI literacy into curricula and pedagogy more pressing than ever (Lee et al., 2021). However, despite its evolving presence, there is still a notable gap in research and resources for AI literacy education (Micheuz, 2020; Yue et al., 2021). This poses a significant challenge for educators, who need to acquire the necessary knowledge and skills to effectively introduce AI concepts into their classrooms (Touretzky et al., 2019). Some countries, recognizing this need, have already made efforts in promoting AI literacy in K–12 education, creating comprehensive AI curricula that address technical proficiency and ethical considerations. However, to truly meet the global challenge, more efforts are needed to ensure development of educational frameworks that are adaptable to diverse cultural and regional needs.

Although the foundations of AI literacy may be universal, its application is not one size fits all. Regional variations in priorities, resources, and cultural contexts require tailored approaches to ensure that AI literacy education is relevant and effective across different settings. Teachers play a pivotal role in this process, guiding students through not only the technical aspects of AI but also its ethical and societal implications. As we move forward, the responsibility lies with educators to ensure that students are equipped with the critical thinking skills and ethical awareness necessary to navigate an AI-driven world responsibly and inclusively.

Wrap-Up Questions

- As AI becomes increasingly integrated into education, what are some key ethical considerations we must address to ensure responsible and equitable use of these technologies, for example,
  - How can we protect student data and privacy in an AI-powered learning environment?
  - How can we ensure that AI algorithms used in education are transparent, fair, and free from bias?
- How can we foster cross-cultural understanding and collaboration in an AI-powered world, ensuring that diverse perspectives are valued and respected?
- How can we leverage AI to address global educational challenges, such as access to quality education in underserved communities?
- How can we prepare students to be responsible global citizens who can navigate the ethical complexities of AI in a rapidly changing world?

The questions that we asked throughout this chapter, though challenging, are crucial stepping stones on the path to responsible and informed AI literacy education. We don't expect you to provide immediate answers; rather, we hope this initial exploration has sparked curiosity and a desire for deeper understanding. As we progress through the book, we delve into these ethical dilemmas, global perspectives, and their implications for teaching and learning about AI. Together, let's navigate the complexities and opportunities that lie ahead.

CHAPTER 2

Pedagogical Framework for AI Literacy

In this chapter we'll

- Briefly review current research about AI in K–12 education
- Learn about theoretical foundations for integrating AI literacy into curriculum
- Introduce a new Pedagogical Framework for AI Literacy

Did you know that the term **artificial intelligence (AI)** was first introduced in 1955 as a counterpoint to human intelligence? The term simply referred to computer programs that make decisions that typically would be required of humans (Griffey, 2019). In education AI was first used in 1965 at Stanford University, with a computer program developed to teach students basic math and science concepts (Brezina, 2020). In the 1970s intelligent tutoring systems were introduced in K–12 education, and since then AI has been used in various educational settings, from K–12 schools to universities (Kahn & Winters, 2021).

• Artificial intelligence (AI) is technology that enables computers and machines to simulate human learning, comprehension, problem solving, decision making, creativity, and autonomy.

We have been using AI in teaching and learning for more than four decades, but in the past decade AI technology experienced very rapid development. In particular, the arrival of Generative AI (GenAI) was a huge advance because it is a tool that is so different from any digital tools that we have experienced in the past. It immediately raised student excitement and teacher concerns about using AI in schools.

Before we introduce our Pedagogical Framework for AI Literacy, let's briefly review current research about use of AI in education and existing theoretical frameworks that we used to develop our pedagogical framework.

CURRENT RESEARCH

Our students are quickly finding new and innovative ways to incorporate AI into their studies, from using intelligent algorithms to assist assignment completion to utilizing chatbots to improve their argumentation skills. Can teachers leverage the power of AI tools to create engaging and stimulating learning environments that foster curiosity and excitement for their students? We think so: We strongly believe that as AI technology continues to evolve, it has the potential to offer our students more opportunities to learn. Recent advancement in learning technology and learning sciences helped to expand the range of concepts students can explore with different robotic systems and machine learning platforms (Castro-Alonso et al., 2021). Research also shows that GenAI could serve as peers, partners, mentees, or tutors to improve associated cognitive and affective learning outcomes (Mogavi et al., 2024). In particular, through analysis of major social media platforms Mogavi et al. (2024) found that ChatGPT has:

- been instrumental in helping students improve their reading, writing, grammar, sentence-building, and conversational language skills;

- been used to create tailored learning experiences for individual students;

- proven to be a valuable asset for supporting home learning by providing assistance with assignments and helping parents teach complex concepts;

- the potential to empower students with disabilities and special needs by providing them with accessible learning resources.

• Digital literacy describes skills and ways of thinking related to the use of technology, including the technical competence to communicate, evaluate and interpret digital information, navigate websites, and understand why all these skills are important.

In the past, students learned about AI in school from their computer science teachers. Thus, the majority of early AI resources and curricula were developed for teachers who had prior training in computational thinking and experience in programming. However, as AI-powered experiences and applications become an increasingly important part of everyday personal and professional life, being AI literate becomes an increasingly important component of K–12 **digital literacy** and **digital citizenship**.

• Digital citizenship is the responsible and respectful use of technology to engage online, find reliable sources, and protect and promote human rights.

As a result, more recent AI literacy curricula have begun to expand beyond computer science to include interdisciplinary approaches and perspectives (Su et al., 2022). Here is one such example:

In the slums of Dharavi in Mumbai (one of the largest slums in Asia, and the iconic location of the film *Slumdog Millionaire*), a group of young women (eight to sixteen years of age) recognized women's safety was a critical problem in their community. Despite having no prior programming experience, they were driven by the feeling they could affect real change in the lives of those close to them. Through guidance from a local mentor, some online videos, and MIT's App Inventor, they were able to build the Women Fight Back app, which focuses on women's safety and has features like SMS alerts, location mapping, distress alarm, and emergency calls to contacts (Tissenbaum et al., 2019, p. 35).

These new AI literacy curricula not only provide students with a comprehensive understanding of AI, but also include discussions of its impact on society, covering a broad range of topics, from the use of AI in civic engagement and scientific inquiry to the exploration of AI applications and their ethical implications (UNESCO, 2022).

International AI literacy initiatives have underscored the importance of developing teaching capacities in local regions across the globe (Pedro et al., 2019). Research studies across the world emphasize the need to prepare teachers to integrate AI literacy into their classroom settings, as this can help cultivate students' critical awareness of AI's societal impact and promote responsible use of the technology in different scenarios. For example:

> The Weizmann Institute of Science in Israel conducted a professional development program for in-service high school biology teachers to develop understanding of AI-Grader, a natural language processing (NLP) and AI-powered assessment technology that analyzes constructed responses and open-ended questions in biology and generates an automated score based on an analytic grading rubric. The professional development program included three group sessions and teachers' independent, hands-on assignments. The AI-Grader's results for the teachers' own class were presented, explained, and discussed during interviews. Teachers proposed related follow-up activities that they later conducted with their classes (Nazaretsky et al., 2022).

> In Harvard University and MIT, in the USA, K–12 teachers were engaged in a two-day codesign workshop to identify opportunities to integrate AI education into core curriculum to leverage learners' interests. During the codesign workshops, teachers and researchers cocreated lesson plans where AI concepts were embedded into various core subjects (Lin & Van Brummele, 2021).

There is still much work to be done for widespread adoption of AI literacy in classrooms across the world. This includes the development and evaluation of teacher professional-development materials that prepare educators with essential knowledge and pedagogical practices necessary to adapt and integrate AI literacy into their teaching (Darling-Hammond et al., 2022; Pedro et al., 2019). Teachers need more resources and support to effectively use AI to create student-centered learning environments. The availability of resources, curricular materials, and ongoing professional-development opportunities are all core factors that contribute to teachers' self-perceived readiness to teach AI curriculum (Milliken et al., 2019).

We strongly believe that AI technologies can act as a catalyst for preparing teachers to innovate pedagogy and design practices that are inclusive, collaborative, and culturally relevant. In this chapter we provide a conceptual framework for teachers to use to integrate AI literacy into their existing curriculums while also promoting the responsible use of AI in teaching and learning.

THEORETICAL FOUNDATIONS FOR INTEGRATING AI LITERACY INTO THE CURRICULUM

Our goal is to support teachers in integrating AI into their disciplines to prepare diverse K–12 students to succeed, act responsibly, and engage in an increasingly AI-powered society. Let's be honest: this is a complex process. So to make it more comprehensible, we're introducing a Pedagogical Framework for AI Literacy that we developed based on three theoretical frameworks:

- Five Big Ideas in AI that define AI concepts, essential knowledge, and skills
- Human-centered design (HCD) process that provides a structure for the approach to teaching with AI
- Science of learning and development (SoLD) that supports inclusiveness of the curriculum.

Let's look at each of these foundational frameworks.

FIVE BIG IDEAS IN AI

The Five Big Ideas in AI were developed by The Artificial Intelligence (AI) for K–12 Initiative (https://ai4k12.org/) to provide national guidelines and resources for AI education for K–12 audiences. The five ideas are (Figure 2.1)

1. perception,
2. representation and reasoning,
3. learning,
4. natural interaction, and
5. social impact,

all of which are essential for understanding how AI operates and its impact on society (Touretzky et al., 2023).

FIGURE 2.1 ● Five Big Ideas in AI Wheel

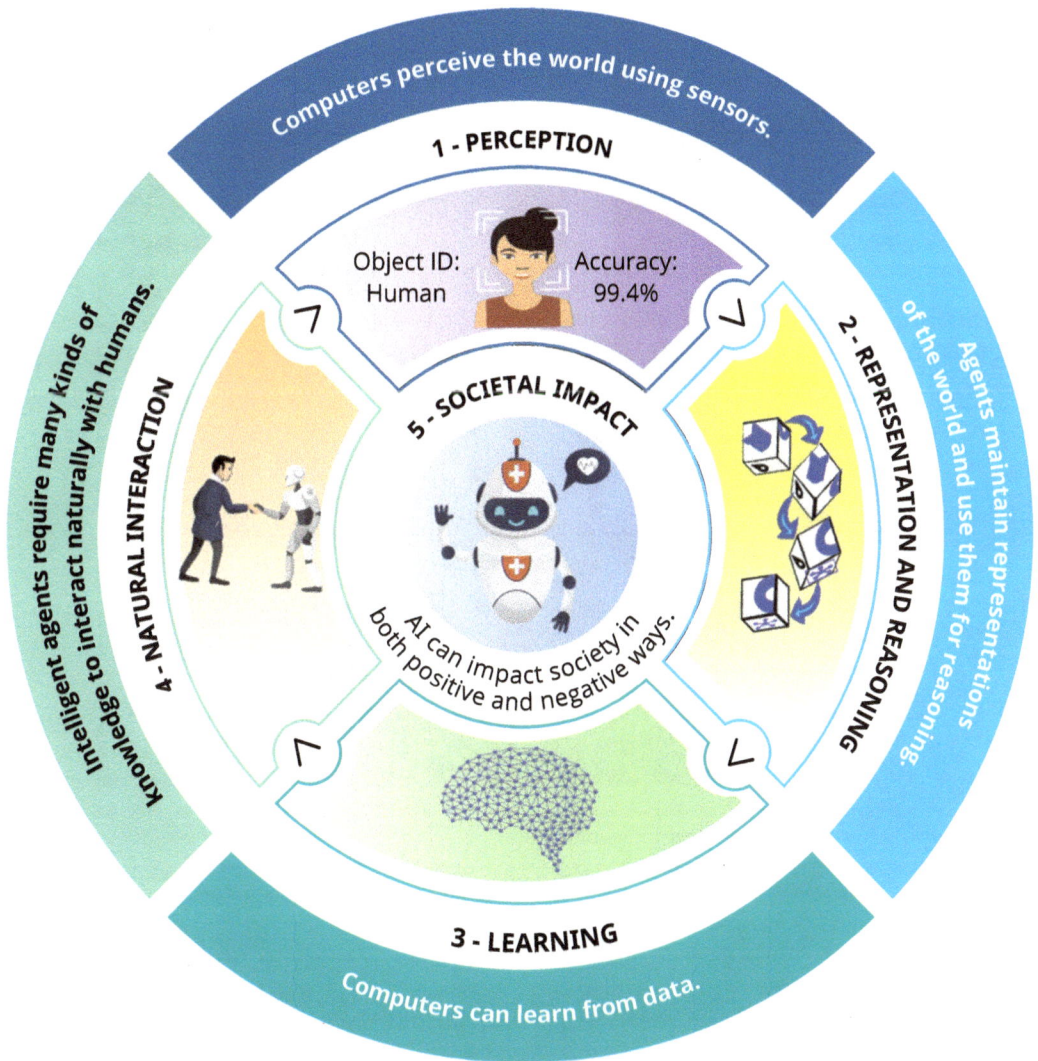

Source: AI4K12.org

Perception refers to how computers perceive the world by gathering data from various sensors. Sensors are devices that detect and measure physical phenomena such as light, sound, temperature, pressure, motion, and so on. These sensors convert physical signals into electrical signals that can be understood by the computer.

EXAMPLE 2.1

Thermal Sensors

Thermal imaging (also called thermography) is used to monitor changes in athletes as injury prevention methods. Thermography can detect thermal asymmetry that could lead to injury, with its consequent impact on performance and health of athletes.

FIGURE 2.2 ● Thermography of upper torso

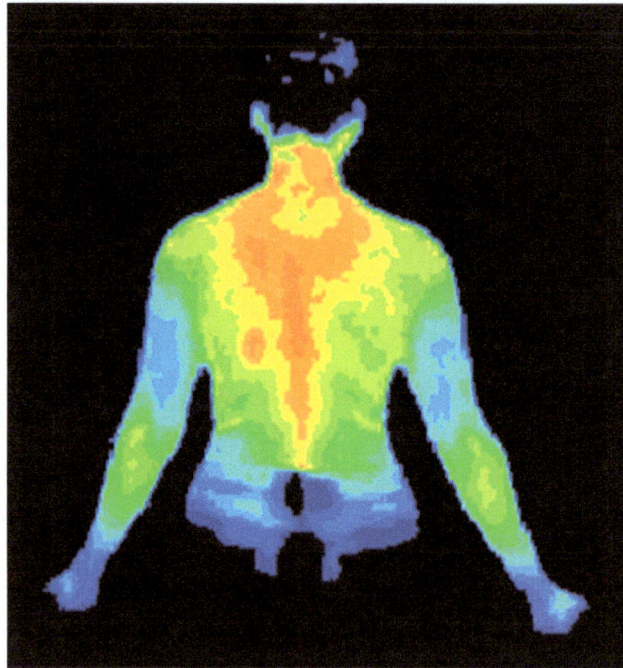

Source: istock.com: AnitaVBD

"Representation" and "reasoning" refer to how agents maintain representations of the world and use them for reasoning. Computers construct representations using data structures, and these representations support reasoning algorithms that derive new information from what is already known. This allows machines to process data and make decisions based on it.

EXAMPLE 2.2

AI-Based Games

Play Magnus game available on board of all United Airlines inflight entertainment systems features an AI-based chess engine that mimics World Chess Champion Magnus Carlsen's style of play from ages five and older.

FIGURE 2.3 ● United Airlines entertainment—Play Magnus chess game

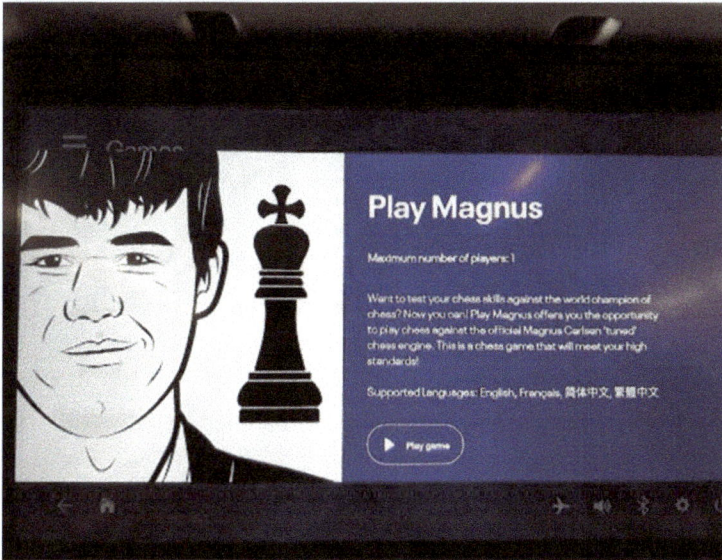

Credit: Play Magnus. Used with permission.

"Learning"—in other words, machine learning—refers to a way for computers to find patterns in data. Thus, learning is another key idea in AI that explains how computers can learn from data and make predictions. Computers need lots of data, which usually comes from people or sometimes the computer can acquire data on its own. AI sources data by accessing online databases, using **Application Programming Interfaces (APIs)** to connect to data feeds, scraping web content, and processing user inputs or interactions to gather targeted information for analysis. Additionally, AI systems can use sensors and other devices to gather real-time data from the environment, such as images, audio, and other sensory inputs. This ability to autonomously acquire and analyze data allows AI to continuously learn and improve its performance, making it highly effective for a wide range of applications.

• **Application Programming Interface (API)** is a connection between computers or programs.

EXAMPLE 2.3

Recommender Systems

When you shop online on platforms like Amazon, eBay, or Walmart, the recommender systems use machine learning to analyze your browsing history, purchase history, items you've added to your cart, as well as other users' behavior. They use this data to suggest products that you might be interested in purchasing.

FIGURE 2.4 ● Shopping recommendation system

Dog toys based on your purchases

Source: istock.com/ AlinaMD

"Natural interaction" refers to communication or interaction between humans and machines that feels intuitive, effortless, and similar to how people interact with each other. In natural interaction, technology adapts to human behavior and preferences, making the interaction process smoother and more intuitive for users.

"Societal impact" of course refers to how AI affects daily life. AI can affect society in positive and negative ways. It is changing the way we work, travel, and communicate with each other. It is crucial to discuss how AI is affecting society and establish guidelines for ethically designing and deploying AI-based systems.

EXAMPLE 2.4

Voice Assistants

Amazon Alexa is a voice assistant that can perform a variety of tasks, including answering questions, playing music, and controlling smart home devices.

FIGURE 2.5 ● Voice assistant

Source: Istock.com/ jittawit.21

EXAMPLE 2.5

Face Recognition and Bias

Face recognition technology involves the automated identification or verification of individuals based on their facial features. Face recognition algorithms are trained on datasets. If the training data is skewed toward certain demographics (e.g., race, gender, age), the algorithm may perform better for those groups and worse for others.

(Continued)

(Continued)

FIGURE 2.6 ● Security with face recognition technology

Source: istock.com/EvgeniyShkolenko

REFLECTION QUESTIONS

- Which of the Five Big Ideas in AI do you find most intriguing or relevant to your teaching context? Why?

- How might you incorporate these big ideas into your curriculum to enhance students' understanding of AI concepts?

HUMAN-CENTERED DESIGN PROCESS

HCD is a creative approach to problem solving. This approach begins by understanding the people you're designing for and concludes with tailored solutions crafted to meet their needs, achieved through empathy, idea generation, prototyping, collaboration, and implementation (IDEO, 2015).

Design thinking is a nonlinear, iterative human-centered process of problem solving and innovation. This process helps achieve the balance between different elements of HCD (IDEO, 2015). In this book we focus on the five-steps design-thinking process (Figure 2.7) proposed by the Hasso Plattner Institute of Design at Stanford (https://dschool.stanford.edu/).

FIGURE 2.7 ● Design-thinking process (retrieved from https://www.interaction-design.org/)

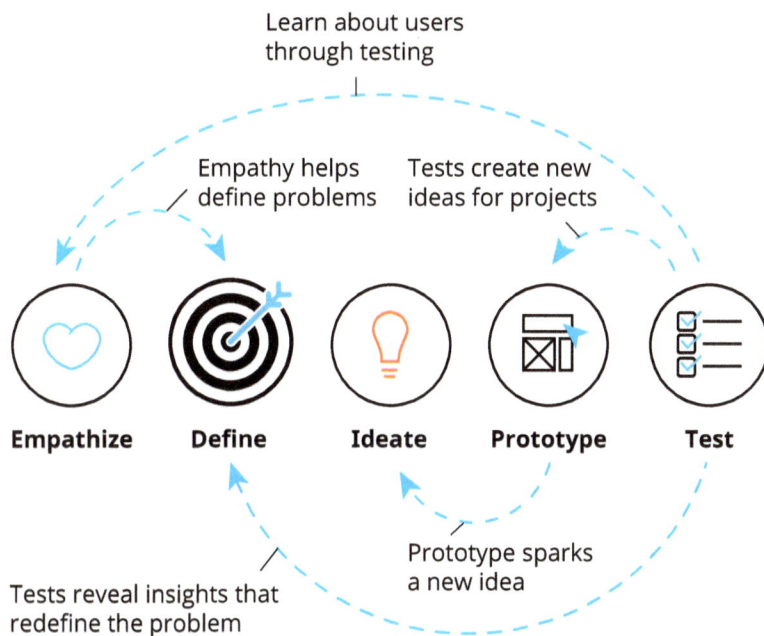

Learn about users through testing

Empathy helps define problems

Tests create new ideas for projects

Empathize   **Define**   **Ideate**   **Prototype**   **Test**

Prototype sparks a new idea

Tests reveal insights that redefine the problem

Source: Interaction Design Foundation

The five steps are

- empathize,
- define,
- ideate,
- prototype, and
- test.

These steps are not always sequential and can be completed in parallel, out of order, and repeated as needed. Let's dig into these ideas more deeply by applying them to a hypothetical bridge-building challenge. In this challenge, students are grouped into teams and given a brief on materials, budget constraints, and the required load the bridge must hold. The challenge is to build a model that maximizes strength and minimizes cost.

EXAMPLE 2.6

Bridge-Building Challenge

- *Empathize*: Students may conduct research to understand the needs and preferences of potential users of the bridge, such as the volume of traffic, environmental conditions, and aesthetic preferences. Students could also interview stakeholders, such as engineers and city planners, to gain insights into the requirements and constraints of the project.

- *Define*: Based on the insights gathered during the *empathize* stage, students define the problem they need to solve. This involves identifying the key requirements and constraints of the bridge challenge, for example, to construct a model bridge using limited materials that can support a predetermined weight, cost less than a set budget, and have a minimal environmental impact. They might also aim for an aesthetically pleasing design that could be implemented in a real-world situation.

- *Ideate*: With a clear understanding of the problem, students brainstorm ideas for designing the bridge (Figure 2.8) and explore various design concepts and creative solutions that could maximize strength and minimize costs. Ideas might include using recycled materials, innovative geometric structures for added strength, or modular designs for easy assembly. The goal is to generate a wide range of ideas that meet the defined criteria.

FIGURE 2.8 ● Sample bridge sketches

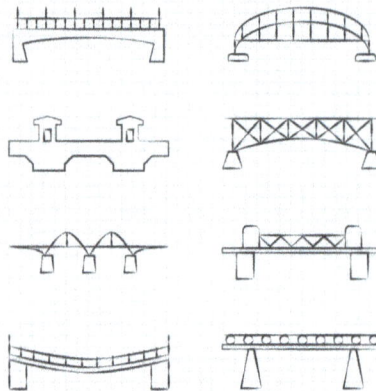

Source: istock.com/MicrovOne

- *Prototype*: Selecting one or two of their best ideas, students build prototypes of their bridge designs to test and iterate on their ideas. Prototypes could range from simple paper models to more sophisticated 3D models constructed from materials provided in the challenge brief. Students may use iterative prototyping, building and refining multiple versions of their designs to optimize strength and cost effectiveness.

- *Test*: Students test their prototypes to evaluate how well they meet the requirements and constraints of the challenge. They assess the strength of their bridges by loading them with weights or applying simulated forces. Students also consider factors such as stability, durability, and cost effectiveness in their evaluations. Based on the test results, students refine their designs, iterating on the prototype to improve its performance and meet the project objectives. The final bridges could be tested in a class competition. Students gather data on which designs held the most weight and why, relating these findings back to their initial research and design choices.

The design-thinking process provides a structured framework for teachers to explore and experiment with instructional strategies, which can lead to effective teaching practices and improved student-learning outcomes (Xiao & Chan, 2022). We also learned from various studies that the design-thinking process can be effectively applied to AI literacy education to engage students in development of authentic projects that explore and apply AI concepts and skills in real-world situations (Chiu et al., 2024).

REFLECTION QUESTIONS

- How can the five steps of the design-thinking process be applied in your classroom or subject area?

- How might you guide students through the process of solving a real-world problem using the design-thinking process?

SCIENCE OF LEARNING AND DEVELOPMENT (SOLD)

Education goes beyond academics; it encompasses nurturing the holistic development of a whole child. The "whole child model" is an educational approach that recognizes the importance of supporting children's physical, emotional, social, and cognitive growth. The SoLD framework consolidates evidence from the learning sciences and various educational research fields on proven strategies that foster the necessary relationships and learning experiences to enhance children's health, development, and transferable skills (Darling-Hammond et al., 2020). Drawing on insights from the SoLD framework, the SoLD Alliance outlined five fundamental principles for creating optimal learning environments in schools and other settings (https://soldalliance.org/):

1. positive developmental relationships;
2. environments filled with safety and belonging;
3. rich learning experiences and knowledge development;
4. development of skills, habits, and mindsets; and
5. integrated support systems.

These principles can be used to guide the design of learning settings that are equitable, relationship rich, holistic, rigorous, positive, and engaging of students' interests and abilities. Let's dig into these ideas more deeply using our bridge-building challenge from earlier:

- Positive developmental relationships: Students collaborate in teams to conduct research on potential users and environmental conditions for the bridge, thereby strengthening their relationships within the team.

- Environments filled with safety and belonging: Students develop their understanding of the bridge's requirements and constraints in a classroom environment that encourages open discussion and risk taking.

- Rich learning experiences and knowledge development: Students apply their prior knowledge to solving the real-world tasks, exploring innovative solutions such as using recycled materials or designing unique structures.

- Development of skills, habits, and mindsets: Students engage in iterative processes constructing initial models, testing them, and making necessary adjustments, which develop resilience and critical thinking through hands-on experience.

- Integrated support systems: With access to a variety of resources—including materials, tools, and expert advice—students effectively test and refine their designs based on empirical data, learn from their successes and failures.

REFLECTION QUESTIONS

- In what ways can the SoLD framework be integrated into your teaching practices to promote responsible use of AI technologies?

- How might you guide students in using AI technologies to build a positive and safe environment within their community?

By now you might have realized that designing and implementing an effective AI literacy program is a multifaceted process that requires careful consideration of the technical, social, and ethical implications of AI. To support teachers in integrating AI literacy into the K–12 classrooms, we build upon these theoretical frameworks to propose the Pedagogical Framework for AI Literacy.

OUR PEDAGOGICAL FRAMEWORK FOR AI LITERACY

Our Pedagogical Framework for AI Literacy comprises three fundamental components: design, create, and reflect (Figure 2.9). It is aimed at assisting teachers in building students' knowledge of AI literacy, developing their ability to apply AI concepts to resolve real-world problems, and reflecting the values in responsible use of AI. In this chapter we explained our Pedagogical Framework for AI Literacy. In Chapter 3 we'll illustrate how this framework can be used to design learning experiences for students.

FIGURE 2.9 ● Pedagogical Framework for AI Literacy

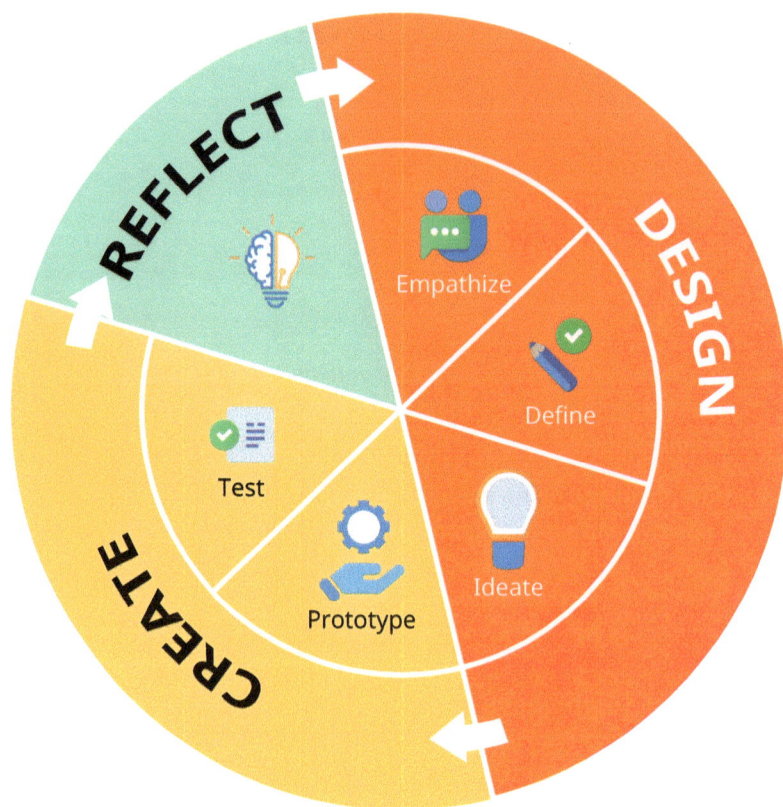

Icon Sources: istock.com/bakhtiar_zein; istock.com/PeterSnow

DESIGN

The core of the HCD is involving users directly in the design process. The HCD approach encourages students to tackle real-world problems creatively and innovatively. As we learned earlier, this involves a cyclical design process, thereby fostering creative problem solving and continuous innovation. As part of the design process students are also expected to assess AI applications for their practicality, accuracy, ethical considerations, and impact, fostering a critical understanding of technology use.

So, we decided to include two competencies within the Design component; one that expects students to apply the design-thinking process to develop AI-driven solutions (D1) and the other focusing on students' ability to critically evaluate AI systems based on their understanding of the Five Big Ideas in AI (D2) (see Table 2.1). Therefore, the Design component includes three steps of the design-thinking process: *empathize*, *define*, and *ideate*.

TABLE 2.1 ● Summary of Competencies, Learning Outcomes, and Theoretical Basis for Our Pedagogical Framework for AI Literacy

COMPETENCIES	LEARNING OUTCOMES	THEORETICAL BASIS
Design: positions students as designers and encourages student-led initiatives in student-centered, authentic learning experience.		
D1. Applying design-thinking process	Students demonstrate proficiency in a deliberate design process, including generating and refining ideas, testing theories, and creating innovative artifacts or solutions to authentic problems.	HCD, Five Big Ideas in AI
D2. Evaluating AI applications	Students critically evaluate and apply AI technologies, including assessing their effectiveness, accuracy, perspective, and credibility in various applications and contexts.	Five Big Ideas in AI
Create: creates learning experience for students to become active problem solvers and apply the knowledge to solving real-world problems.		
C1. Applying AI to solve real-world problems	Students identify problems that can be effectively addressed with AI technologies, such as data analysis, abstract models, and algorithmic thinking, and develop solutions using a contextualized approach.	HCD, Five Big Ideas in AI
C2. Decomposing complex problems into manageable parts	Students break down complex problems into manageable parts, extract essential information, and develop descriptive models to understand complex systems and facilitate problem solving.	HCD, Five Big Ideas in AI
Reflect: develop critical awareness of AI with its societal innovation, while encouraging students to foster digital citizenship and actively use AI to solve real-world problems.		
R1. Developing ethical awareness in AI	Students think critically about the ethical implications of AI technologies and evaluate their impact on society, including issues such as bias, discrimination, and privacy.	Five Big Ideas in AI
R2. Responsible use of AI technologies with real-world application for the community through collaboration	Students use AI technologies in a responsive and intentional manner, including strategies for managing personal data, maintaining digital privacy and security, and sustaining a culture of innovation and change.	SoLD

At the *empathize* step, the design competencies expect students to understand the users' needs, thoughts, and emotions to gain insights into their experiences. This informs the next, *define*, step, where students synthesize and interpret insights gathered during the *empathize* step to articulate the problem and develop a focused problem statement that guides the rest of the design of an AI-driven solution. They also evaluate AI applications that could be leveraged for this task. In the *ideate* step students brainstorm potential solutions, generating a wide range of ideas that address the defined problem and leverage AI capabilities. The evaluation of AI applications is interwoven within the design-thinking steps. This competency also expects that students consider the ethical implications of AI, including privacy and bias.

The Design component is critical in shaping personalized learning experiences in classrooms. It fosters a supportive and inclusive atmosphere, encouraging strong relationships and a community-oriented classroom culture. Students are positioned as active "knowledge builders" within an inquiry-based learning environment, enhancing engagement and participation.

CREATE

The Five Big Ideas in AI call for students to be able to identify issues and employ technology-assisted strategies like data analysis, abstract modeling, and algorithmic thinking. This process requires students to be competent in decomposing complex problems into manageable parts, thus enhancing their problem-solving capabilities and deepening their understanding of complex systems. So, we identified two critical competencies in the Create competencies: one that expects students to apply AI to solve real-world problems (C1); the other that requires students to use representation and reasoning to break down problems and develop descriptive models that simplify understanding complex systems (C2) (see Table 2.1). Therefore, the Create component includes two steps of the design-thinking process: prototype and test.

In the *prototype* step, students transform selected ideas into tangible prototypes or representations decomposing complex problems. They build, iterate, and refine their prototypes, leveraging AI capabilities to address the user's needs. They simulate and test the prototype in various scenarios to evaluate its performance, accuracy, and robustness. The AI-driven solutions could include, but are not limited to, data preparation and model training, algorithm development, and so on. Then, during the *test* step of the design-thinking process, students rigorously evaluate and validate their prototypes with the users. They use feedback to inform further iterations and refinements of the prototype. Last, considering the societal impact, students assess the ethical implications of their AI-driven solutions, ensuring they contribute positively to society and address concerns like privacy and bias.

The Create component is essential in developing personalized learning experiences in classrooms. It empowers students to be active "creators" of knowledge, fostering a sense of ownership and agency in their problem-solving process.

REFLECT

Drawing directly from the "societal impact" idea of the Five Big Ideas in AI, the Reflect component of the framework requires students to assess the positive and negative impacts of AI within societal contexts. We also used guiding principles of SoLD to highlight the value of positive developmental relationships through collaborative and responsible use of AI in safe learning environments. So, the Reflect component includes two competencies: critical awareness of societal impact of AI (R1) and the responsible use of AI (R2) (see Table 2.1).

In developing their critical awareness of the societal impact of AI, students are tasked with analyzing how AI systems can affect society, with a particular focus on issues such as bias, discrimination, and privacy. Thus, students explore real-world applications of AI that fosters a culture of change and innovation. By understanding the societal implications of AI, students are better equipped to develop and advocate for technologies that promote equity, protect privacy, and contribute to positive societal change. This holistic approach ensures that future AI developments are more inclusive and ethically sound, driving progress and innovation in the field.

In the competency about responsible use of AI, students are expected to integrate resources for ethical guidance and data security, which helps students become thoughtful, ethical individuals ready to use technology in their communities. This competency requires environments filled with safety and belonging, encouraging open discussions about AI impacts such as privacy and bias.

Chapter Summary

In this chapter you learned about theories that are foundations for our Pedagogical Framework for AI Literacy. First and foremost, the Five Big Ideas in AI framework serves as a foundation in introducing AI concepts of perception, representation and reasoning, learning, natural interaction, and societal impact. Second, the design-thinking process, a creative and iterative approach, guides students through steps of empathizing, defining, ideating, prototyping, and testing their AI-related projects. Third, the SoLD framework focuses on responsible AI use by emphasizing social good, ethical considerations, and the creation of positive and safe learning environments. Building upon these frameworks, we propose a three-component Pedagogical Framework for AI Literacy. The Design component positions students as active designers, fostering student-led initiatives within a student-centered and authentic learning experience. The Create component empowers students to become active problem solvers by applying their AI knowledge to real-world challenges. Finally, the Reflect component cultivates critical awareness of AI's societal impact, encourages responsible digital citizenship, and inspires students to actively utilize AI to address real-world issues.

Wrap-Up Questions

- How might you implement the three components of our Pedagogical Framework for AI Literacy (design, create, reflect) in your classroom activities?

- Can you think of an example of a student-led initiative or project that aligns with the components of the framework?

- Why is reflection important in fostering students' critical awareness of AI and its societal impact?

- How can you encourage students to reflect on their use of AI technologies and the ethical considerations involved?

CHAPTER 3

Applying Our Pedagogical Framework for AI Literacy

In this chapter we'll

- Examine how our Pedagogical Framework for AI Literacy supports effective practices for teaching AI literacy

- Review specific tasks illustrating application of the pedagogical framework for developing AI literacy into K–12 education

- Explore how integrating AI literacy strengthens cognitive, social-emotional, and technological skills

Now that we have a Pedagogical Framework for AI Literacy (see Chapter 2) you may ask: How do I use it in practice? How does it help me to select effective pedagogical practices for teaching AI literacy? How do I help students develop AI competencies identified by the pedagogical framework?

In this chapter we aim to illustrate how our Pedagogical Framework for AI Literacy can be used to design learning experiences for students that will help them develop AI literacy and strengthen their cognitive, social-emotional, and technological skills. We walk you through applying the *design–create–reflect* (DCR) process defined by the Pedagogical Framework for AI Literacy by using tasks for middle school students that explore different Big Ideas in AI (Table 3.1). Each task uses a real-world context that engages students in active learning of related AI concepts (AAAI & CSTA, n.d.) and support development of following core information and communication technology (ICT) competencies (International Society for Technology in Education [ISTE], 2024):

- 1.1 Empowered Learner: Students leverage technology to take an active role in choosing, achieving, and demonstrating competency in their learning goals, informed by the learning sciences.

- 1.4 Innovative Designer: Students use a variety of technologies within a design process to identify and solve problems by creating new, useful, or imaginative solutions.

- 1.5 Computational Thinker: Students develop and employ strategies for understanding and solving problems in ways that leverage the power of technological methods to develop and test solutions.

TABLE 3.1

LESSON	FIVE BIG IDEAS IN AI	AI LITERACY CONCEPTS
3.1 Design a Netflix Recommender (p. 41)	1–5 Overview	Foundations
3.2 Design an Accessibility Sensor for Students with Hearing Disabilities (p. 44)	1 and 2	Sensing, Processing, Representation, Reasoning
3.3 Global Climate Change Challenge (p. 46)	3	Nature of Learning, Neural Networks, Datasets
3.4 Fashion Design with Generative AI (p. 49)	4	Natural Language Processing
3.5 Creating a Search-and-Rescue Autonomous Agent (p. 52)	5	AI for Social Good

The ICT competencies are outlined in the student standards developed by the International Society of Technology in Education (ISTE, 2024). These standards are developed based on learning sciences research and the real-world experiences of teachers like you. They show us how to use technology in a way that makes a difference for every student and to help us create high-impact, sustainable, scalable, and equitable learning experiences for all learners.

Lesson: Foundations of AI

3.1

Design a Netflix Recommender

In this lesson we are going to ask students to design the algorithm for the Netflix streaming services recommender system. This task emphasizes the key AI concepts, algorithms, and data-handling practices necessary to develop basic AI literacy. Students are also exposed in this task to the ethical dilemmas and challenges of AI. The teacher can support students by scaffolding their work through the steps of the DCR process.

For Middle School

DESIGN

The Netflix recommender system is designed to suggest new movies, shows, books, or games tailored to the preferences of its users. This task encourages students to integrate the Netflix recommender system into a chatbot specifically designed for a community of their choice, for example, a book club, a sport team, student family, and so on.

Let's look at an example of how a teacher can facilitate the *define* step of this process. Teachers can introduce students to the way Netflix can recommend a user who watched *Spiderman* to watch *Iron Man*.

As noted, there are two types of the recommender systems used by Netflix: collaborative-based and content-based (see Figure 3.1).

Collaborative-based systems recommend new items based on past interactions between users and items, essentially trying to find other users similar to oneself. Let's walk through an example of how it works:

- The user watches *Spiderman*.
- The collaborative-based algorithm looks for users with similar preferences in movies, for example, Tim watched *Spiderman* and *Iron Man*.
- Based on analysis of multiple users like Tim, the algorithm suggests the user to watch *Iron Man* next.

Content-based systems do not consider other users and instead require additional information about users and items to make recommendations:

- The user watches *Spiderman*.
- The content-based algorithm analyzes the features of *Spiderman*, such as genre, actors, and so on, and the movie-watching history of the user.
- Based on this analysis, the algorithm suggests the user to watch *Iron Man*.

TIPS

Scaffolding student learning through the *design* component of the DCR process:

- Empathize: Identify different stakeholders involved with Netflix (e.g., users, content creators, Netflix as a company) in your community and discuss their potential needs and preferences.

- Define: Identify and justify the objectives for the recommender system, and based on that select the type of the recommender system, collaborative-based or content-based.

- Ideate: Brainstorm ideas for an algorithm for the Netflix recommender system that addresses user individual needs and minimizes biases.

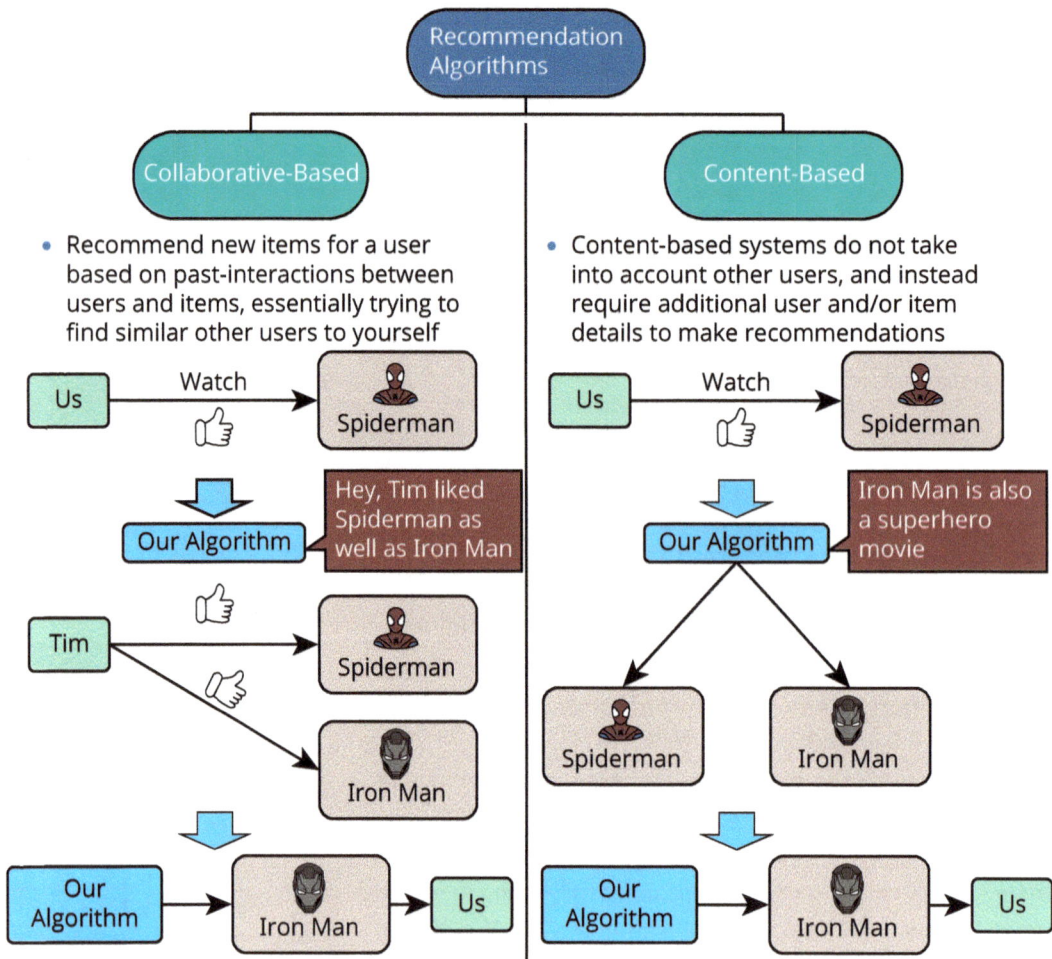

FIGURE 3.1 ● Collaborative-Based vs. Content-Based Recommendation Algorithms (Liu et al., 2023)

Source: Copyright by AACE. Reprinted from with permission of AACE.

In this example the two types of recommender system suggested the same movie; however, that is not always the case. This would be a good place to talk about bias in AI algorithms and to discuss with the students why the two recommendation algorithms could lead to different suggestions.

CREATE

After the *ideate* step, students will prototype and test their Netflix recommender algorithm. The teacher's scaffolding should focus on organizing student collaboration and peer feedback necessary for iterative design and evaluation of the algorithm.

REFLECT

After students have designed the new Netflix recommender system, students should reflect on the positive and negative implications of employed algorithms on user decision making. Reflection should engage students in discussing the influence of recommender systems on user choices and behaviors. Students can be asked to critically analyze the ethical dimensions involved in crafting algorithms that interact with humans, touching on privacy concerns, consent, and the risk of perpetuating biases.

Here are some questions you can ask to guide student discussion:

- How do recommender systems learn from user data?

- How can bias manifest in recommender systems, and what are its implications?

- How do recommender systems affect consumer behavior and decision making?

- In what ways might recommender systems reinforce or challenge societal norms and values?

- What future developments can we expect in the field of AI-driven recommendations?

Central to this reflective exercise is the developer's ethical responsibilities, the importance of transparency, fairness, and the overarching impact of AI technologies on the fabric of society.

SUMMARY FOR LESSON 3.1

In Lesson 3.1, students gain an essential understanding of how recommender systems function and the complexity of human–AI interaction. Students also delve into the responsibilities of users in engaging with AI recommendations conscientiously, fostering an awareness of algorithmic biases, and the significance of seeking out diverse viewpoints.

TIPS

Scaffolding student learning through the *create* component of the DCR process:

- Prototype: Collaboratively design the algorithm of the Netflix recommender system, incorporating peer feedback to refine functionality and design.

- Test: Evaluate the Netflix recommender system in terms of accuracy, sensitivity to individual needs of the users, learning ability of the algorithm, and plan for future improvements.

REFLECTION QUESTIONS

- How can we ensure that students not only understand the technical aspects of recommender systems but also appreciate the societal implications and ethical considerations involved?

- Why is it important for students to seek out diverse viewpoints, especially in the context of AI recommendations? How can we emphasize this significance in our teaching?

- What strategies or activities can be employed to raise students' awareness of algorithmic biases in recommender systems?

Lesson: Data Representation and Decision Making

3.2

Design an Accessibility Sensor for Students with Hearing Disabilities

In this lesson students develop competencies related to perception (Big Idea in AI #1) and representation and reasoning (Big Idea in AI #2) and apply their understanding of *sensing* to design sensors that enhance accessibility and inclusivity in educational environments. Sensors mirror human senses and detect imperceptible data to enrich data collection capacity. Specifically, they are devices that facilitate data collection through actions such as swiping a smartphone or passing through automatic doors. These sensors might include devices such as microphones that capture sound data, which can then be converted into visual or tactile feedback, or motion sensors that detect gestures to control devices or navigate interfaces. The teacher can support students in designing an accessibility sensor by scaffolding their work through the steps of the design-thinking process.

DESIGN

In this task students apply knowledge of data sensing and processing to design accessibility sensors to aid access to educational resources for individuals with hearing disabilities or loss.

To facilitate the *empathize* step of this process, the teacher can provide students with a template to organize their research and plan their work (see Table 3.2). This graphic organizer can help students to identify educational tasks individuals with hearing disabilities and hearing loss might face in various learning spaces and the type of data that will need to be processed by AI sensors to create an assistive device. You'll find a blank template posted to our companion website at https://companion.corwin.com/courses/TeachingAILiteracy

CREATE

After students develop initial ideas for their accessibility sensors, they shift toward building and testing their sensors.

REFLECT

In this task the aim of the reflection is to deepen students' understanding and critical thinking regarding how AI systems simulate aspects of human perception and cognition. In the reflection process, you might want to begin the conversation with an overview of how AI technologies, such as sensors, are designed to process information, make decisions, and learn from experiences like human

TIPS

Scaffolding student learning through the *design* component of the DCR process:

- Empathize: Research the challenges that individuals with hearing disabilities and hearing loss face in various educational spaces, such as classroom, library, or online.

- Define: Identify and select the type of sensor to make a particular learning space accessible for individuals with hearing disabilities and hearing loss.

- Ideate: Brainstorm sensor systems that could support students with individuals with hearing disabilities and hearing loss in different learning spaces.

TABLE 3.2 ● *Empathize* Step: Working Plan Template with Sample Answers

TARGET ACTION	CHALLENGES/ NEEDS	TYPE OF DATA FOR AI TO SENSE	TYPE OF SENSOR(S) TO COLLECT DATA	AI NEEDS FOR DATA PERCEPTION TO COMPLETE THE TARGET ACTION
Understanding spoken content in classrooms	Difficulty in hearing and understanding the teachers	Audio recordings of classroom teaching; real-time spoken words	Microphones with noise-cancellation features; speech-to-text converters	Noise filtering algorithm; transcribe spoken words accurately
Receiving classroom notification	Ensuring timely important announcements	Priority levels of different notification	Mobile phone notification; classroom announcement systems	Personalization based on students' schedule and preference
Staying aware of classroom activities and transitions	Keep track of class schedules and changes	Classroom timetable and schedule data; real-time activity tracking	Motion sensors, visual sensors	Activity recognition algorithm Time management and scheduling AI
Other Tasks:				

beings learn (Mitchell, 2020). This comparison provides a foundation for examining the capabilities and limitations of AI in replicating human-like perception and cognition.

Students then delve into the ethical implications of these technologies. This includes discussions on privacy concerns, as AI systems often require vast amounts of data, including sensitive personal information, to function effectively. Here are sample questions that can be used to guide this discussion.

- How do machines use data to make decisions?
- What are sensors and what role do they play in helping computers collect data?
- Why is it important to understand the distinctions between sensing and perceiving when it comes to computers?
- How do humans process information differently from computers?

SUMMARY FOR LESSON 3.2

In this task students learn the fundamental concepts of data and data analysis. They learn how data comprises information, facts, and figures that can be collected, organized, and analyzed for various purposes. By designing algorithms within a project-based environment, students see the practical side of AI in solving specific real-life problems. Doing that they also explore how AI processes data and makes decisions.

TIPS

Scaffolding student learning through the *create* component of the DCR process

- Prototype: Select one or two of the best ideas; build collaboratively the accessibility sensor, incorporating peer-review feedback to refine functionality and design.

- Test: Conduct usability testing assessing the ease of use and user satisfaction. Based on the test results, refine the design to improve it.

3.3

Lesson: Machine Learning

Global Climate Change Challenge

For Middle School

This task emphasizes AI's role as a practical tool for addressing real-world problems. Building upon the Big Idea in AI #3 (Learning), students learn about how datasets can affect algorithm performance and examine the role of neural networks in visual classifications where a human-labeled dataset trains an AI model to find patterns and associations and to link specific inputs with desired outputs. This process is crucial, as it involves direct human input to ensure data is well structured and categorized, guiding the AI through its learning phase. Let's now consider scaffolding of this task through the DCR process.

DESIGN

• **Supervised machine learning** is an AI technique that uses labeled data to train algorithms to recognize patterns and predict outcomes.

In this task students are positioned as environmental scientists to design a **supervised machine learning (ML)** model to tackle an environmental issue caused by climate change.

To complete the *define* step, students can use an Identity Wheel graphic organizer to reflect on how their personal identities influence their choice of the environmental issue to be addressed in this task (see Figure 3.2). You'll find this template posted to our companion website at https://companion.corwin.com/courses/TeachingAILiteracy.

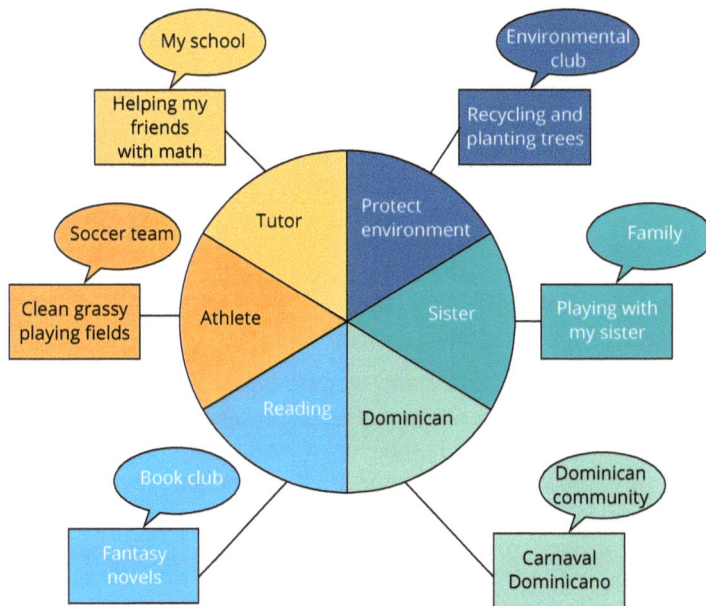

Student instructions for completing the Identity Wheel

- Select the six most important identities that you use to describe yourself—for example, home country, gender, language, personal values, and principles, etc.
- Fill in each "slice" of the wheel with information about your own identities.
- For each identity, write a statement of what you value most as part of that identity in the rectangles that radiate from the wheel.
- For each identity you selected, describe what community you belong to in the speech bubbles.
- Select the environmental issue and community where you believe you have the most concerns and can have the most impact

Based on this activity, students next develop a problem statement that defines the environmental issue they want to address. For example,

- I will develop an AI model specifically trained for waste classification and recognition to improve recycling in my community.
- I will create an AI model that analyzes satellite images and drone footage to detect changes in land use and habitat degradation.

TIPS

Scaffolding student learning through the *design* component of the DCR process:

- Empathize: Research the impacts of climate change on communities, ecosystems, and the economy.

- Define: Identify personal and community concerns about climate change, focusing on one environmental issue to develop a machine learning (ML) solution. Focus on how ML tools and techniques can be applied to find solutions.

- Ideate: Brainstorm a wide range of ideas and solutions that address the defined problem. Explore multiple applications of ML in tackling a selected environmental issue.

Next, students create and test a supervised ML model aimed to address the environmental issue of their choice.

REFLECT

After students create the ML model, they evaluate ethical aspects of their model using the Machine Learning Ethical Matrix (see Table 3.3). Students can analyze potential biases and evaluate the balance of benefits and risks. Teachers need to guide students on how to ethically and effectively gather or access relevant data. You'll find a customizable ethical matrix template posted to our companion website at https://companion.corwin.com/courses/TeachingAILiteracy

This matrix can serve as a structured framework for assessing the ethical implications of ML models. Specifically, students can use this matrix after developing their algorithms to determine whether and how models need to be refined to ensure that they not only are effective in addressing environmental issues but also uphold high ethical standards. The ethical issues can also be discussed as a whole class.

TIPS

Scaffolding student learning through the *create* component of the DCR process:

- Prototype: Select one or two of the best ideas, build the supervised ML model (Gerrish, 2019) aimed to address an environmental issue of your choice to ensure it meets the needs of its intended users.

- Test: Assess the precision, sensibility, and accuracy of the ML model. Based on the test results, refine the design to improve the model.

TABLE 3.3 ● Machine Learning Ethical Matrix

STAKEHOLDERS	VALUES				
	PERSONALIZATION	ACCURACY	TRUSTWORTHINESS	DIVERSITY	FAIRNESS
Computer scientists	NA	Responsible for designing accurate model	Responsible for designing trustworthy model	Responsible for designing ML model with diversity perspectives	Responsible for designing ML model with fairness
Users	Experience personalized recommendations	Receive accurate recommendations	Receive clear explanations or justifications	Exposed to a broader range of options	Mitigate biases in recommendations
Content providers	Customize and personalized recommendations	Ensure accurate content and representation from information sources	Ensure trustworthy content and representation from information sources	Value diversity aim to provide users with a wide range of content options	Emphasize fairness, ensure that recommendations are not biased or favor certain content providers over others

Here are some questions you can ask to guide student discussion:

- In what ways can continuous learning from AI systems lead to unforeseen consequences?

- What are the implications of bias in data used for training AI systems, and how can these biases be addressed?

- How does AI's need for large datasets affect privacy and data security?

SUMMARY FOR LESSON 3.3

The climate change challenge provides students with opportunities to examine how algorithms learn from data to create classification models and understand the profound effect data quality has on ML outcomes.

REFLECTION QUESTIONS

- What are different ways educators can frame the climate change challenge to engage students in exploring how algorithms learn from data to create ML models?

- What activities can be used in the classroom to help students grasp the impact of data quality on ML outcomes?

- How might educators facilitate discussions around the ethical considerations involved in using ML algorithms to address environmental challenges caused by climate change?

Lesson: Natural Interaction and Creativity

3.4

Fashion Design with Generative AI

This task emphasizes the role Generative AI (GenAI) can play in developing student creativity through natural interaction (Big Idea in AI #4). Let's now consider how the teacher can support students in this task through the DCR process.

For Middle School

DESIGN

In this task students act as fashion designers developing a collection of garments for an upcoming Spring/Summer fashion show while employing GenAI

Scaffolding student learning through the *design* component of the DCR process:

- Empathize: Explore specific GenAI tools that are relevant to fashion design, such as AI-driven design software like Adobe's generative design features, Clo3D, or AI pattern-making tools. Research how artists, designers, and critics use GenAI in real-world tasks.

- Define: Identify key challenges and opportunities in the integration of GenAI into fashion design.

- Ideate: Select one or more ideas to develop initial design concepts and parameters for your fashion collection.

as creative assistant to ensure their designs keep up with the latest trends in the fashion industry. Students explore a wide array of silhouettes, lengths, and embellishments to uncover designs that are trendsetting and cohesive with the overall theme of their collection.

CREATE

Students can train AI models to recognize and synthesize elements from various artistic styles or genres, turning vast datasets into a creative palette for innovation. By feeding these models with carefully selected images of textures, patterns, and existing fashion pieces, students train the AI to understand what makes a design appealing and to generate new patterns that reflect these learned preferences. GenAI can then generate diverse variations, offering a rich palette of options that might not have been considered otherwise.

In the *prototype* step, students can leverage their understanding of GenAI, particularly **Generative Adversarial Networks (GANs)** and deepfake technologies, to craft innovative fashion design patterns. These AI technologies excel in analyzing and processing diverse inputs—ranging from images and sounds to textual descriptions—and generating outputs that closely resemble authentic artistic creations. This capability is rooted in AI's perception skills, enabling machines to "see" and "interpret" the nuances of artistic elements accurately. Figure 3.3 shows an example of the fashion design prototypes created using ChatGPT 4.0.

The first design shown on the left of Figure 3.3 is a modern reinterpretation of the classic Renaissance dress, skillfully blending historical inspiration with cutting-edge technology. This dress is meant

FIGURE 3.3 ● Sample Fashion Collection

Source: Created with ChatGPT 4.0

to be crafted from smart fabric that alters its pattern in response to environmental changes, symbolizing the adaptability and ongoing evolution of fashion. The design second from left transforms the traditional doublet into a futuristic blazer, utilizing transparent, breathable materials. The piece on the right is enhanced with integrated wearable technology, adding a modern twist that reflects the intersection of historical influences and futuristic visions within urban culture. Finally, on the far right you'll see high-tech sneakers that combine historical aesthetic cues with contemporary functionality. These sneakers feature adaptive cushioning and interactive, color-changing surfaces, epitomizing the seamless fusion of past and present, and showcasing the innovative direction of future footwear.

REFLECT

After creating and then sharing their fashion collections, students can discuss how biases might influence the outcome of their fashion designs. For example, students might discuss how the cultural background of the training data set affects the design outcomes, or whether any trends or styles were overrepresented or underrepresented in the design.

They also explore how parameters such as style, culture, and material could introduce biases into the style transfer process. Students should examine societal and cultural biases that may manifest in aesthetic preferences. Such discussion is aimed at fostering a deep understanding of how GenAI can be used to enhance creative decision making and innovation in fashion design while also pointing out unconscious biases to students that could have influenced their decisions.

Here are some questions you can ask to guide student discussion:

- Can you identify any potential biases in the dataset of style images provided for the activity? How might these biases affect the resulting artworks?

- How do you think the parameters such as style, culture, and material affect the final appearance of the fashion collection? Are there any biases inherent in these parameter settings?

- How might societal or cultural biases be reflected in the aesthetic preferences for style transfer artworks?

- How can we ensure diversity and inclusivity in the creation and appreciation of such artworks?

- How can we cultivate awareness and sensitivity to biases in our artistic practice?

SUMMARY FOR LESSON 3.4

The application of GenAI technologies in art design allows students to examine the complexities of this technology in creative fields. It encourages students to explore AI technologies through a lens of discovery and innovation, focusing on understanding and empathy as they tackle real-world problems with AI solutions.

TIPS

Scaffolding student learning through the *create* component of the DCR process:

- Prototype: Use GenAI to create a fashion design in an upcoming campus fashion show. Focus on the specific applications and implications of AI in fashion and pay attention to the ethical, aesthetic, and practical considerations.

- Test: Evaluate the level of personalization, uniqueness, trend forecasting accuracy, and theme consistency, and plan for future improvement.

3.5

Lesson: Societal Impact

Creating a Search-and-Rescue Autonomous Agent

For Middle School

• An autonomous agent
is a system or entity that can act independently and make decisions without direct human intervention.

• A block-based program
is a type of programming environment where users can create computer programs by assembling visual blocks that represent different commands or functions.

The widespread adoption of **autonomous agents** raises ethical and social questions regarding issues such as job displacement, algorithmic bias, privacy concerns, and accountability. Grounded in Big Idea in AI #5 (Societal impact) this task engages students in designing autonomous agents that *benefit* society while minimizing potential risks and drawbacks. Let's walk through the DCR process for this task.

DESIGN

This task places a student in an active role of innovator, who creates a **block-based program** that responds to sensory inputs or user interactions, simulating a search-and-rescue mission by an autonomous agent.

CREATE

Students experiment with basic block-based programming to initiate a response from an autonomous agent in completing a search-and-rescue mission. They develop, test, and iterate the algorithm to ensure their agents can effectively complete search-and-rescue missions.

During the *prototype* step of the process, the teacher can provide students with a **starter template** for a block-based program that students have to develop.

Here is an example of instructions that teachers can provide to the students to create a basic starter template in Scratch for a search-and-rescue autonomous agent (Scratch is a project of the Scratch Foundation, in collaboration with the Lifelong Kindergarten Group at the MIT Media Lab. It is available for free at https://scratch.mit.edu):

1. Initial setup:
   - Create a new Scratch project.
   - Delete the cat **sprite** if it's present.
   - Create a backdrop representing the environment where the search-and-rescue mission will take place.

2. Create sprites:
   - Create a sprite to represent the autonomous agent (e.g., a robot).
   - Optionally, create additional sprites to represent obstacles, rescue targets, or other elements in the environment.

Source: Scratch Foundation. Scratch is a project of the Scratch Foundation, in collaboration with the Lifelong Kindergarten Group at the MIT Media Lab. It is available for free at https://scratch.mit.edu.

3. Movement controls:
   - Implement movement controls for the agent sprite using the arrow keys or other controls.
   - Drag out "when green flag clicked" block from the Events category and "forever" block from the Control category.

• **A starter template** in AI-based code refers to a predesigned structure or framework that provides a foundation for building AI applications or systems. These templates typically include basic functionalities and serve as a starting point for developers and researchers, allowing them to focus on customizing the code for their specific needs rather than starting from scratch.

In Scratch, a **sprite** refers to a graphical character or object that can move, interact, and perform actions within a project.

Scaffolding student learning through the *design* component of the DCR process:

- Empathize: Understand the challenges faced by rescue teams and the importance of efficiency and accuracy in locating individuals in distress. This step encourages students to consider the perspectives and needs of rescuers and those being rescued.

- Define: Identify key challenges such as obstacle navigation, optimization of search paths, and timely completion of rescue missions.

- Ideate: Brainstorm various strategies autonomous agents could use to address the defined challenges. This might include different algorithms for pathfinding, strategies for obstacle avoidance, and methods for quickly locating the target.

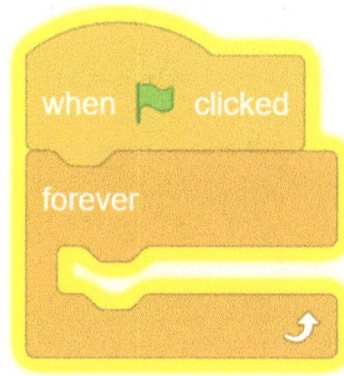

Source: Scratch Foundation. Scratch is a project of the Scratch Foundation, in collaboration with the Lifelong Kindergarten Group at the MIT Media Lab. It is available for free at https://scratch.mit.edu.

Source: Scratch programming

- Use "if then" statements from the Control category to move the robot sprite when arrow keys are pressed using "move" and "turn" blocks from the Motion category.

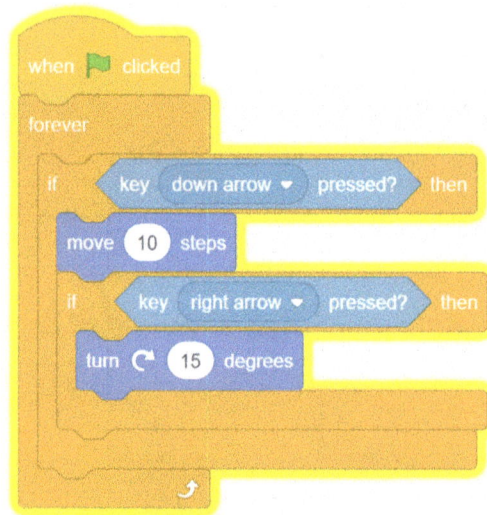

Source: Scratch is a project of the Scratch Foundation, in collaboration with the Lifelong Kindergarten Group at the MIT Media Lab. It is available for free at https://scratch.mit.edu.

4. Collision detection:

- Implement collision detection to prevent the agent sprite from moving through obstacles.

- Use "if then" block from the Control category and the "touching [ ]?" block from the Sensing category to detect collisions with other sprites.

- If the agent sprite is touching an obstacle, make it stop moving or change direction.

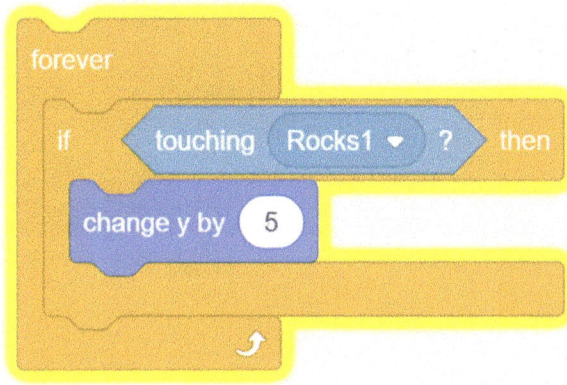

Source: Scratch Foundation. Scratch is a project of the Scratch Foundation, in collaboration with the Lifelong Kindergarten Group at the MIT Media Lab. It is available for free at https://scratch.mit.edu.

5. Search-and-rescue logic:

   • Implement logic for the agent to search the environment for rescue targets and perform rescue actions.

   • Use loops, conditionals, and sensing blocks to scan the environment and detect rescue targets.

   • When a rescue target is detected, trigger rescue actions such as moving the rescue sprite to safety.

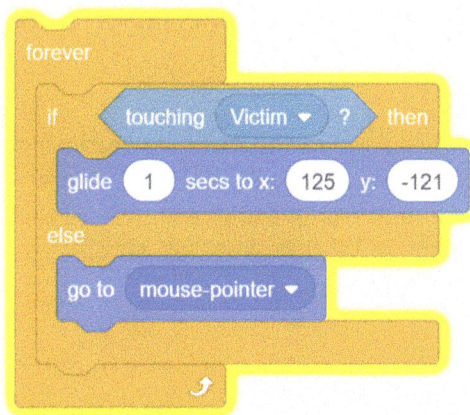

TIPS

Scaffolding student learning through the *create* component of the DCR process:

   • Prototype: Develop a block-based program, ensuring that autonomous agents can effectively complete search-and-rescue missions.

   • Test: Observe the autonomous agent's performance, identifying its strengths and needs for improvement. Testing provides critical feedback that can be used to improve the algorithm design.

Source: Scratch Foundation. is a project of the Scratch Foundation, in collaboration with the Lifelong Kindergarten Group at the MIT Media Lab. It is available for free at https://scratch.mit.edu.

6. Interaction with rescue targets:

   • Implement interaction logic to rescue targets once they're located.

   • For the agent sprite: You can use broadcasting or messaging to signal the rescue sprite to follow the autonomous agent sprite once it's reached.

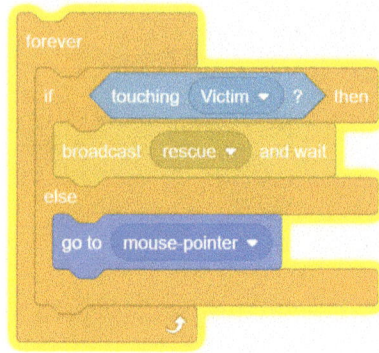

Source: Scratch is a project of the Scratch Foundation, in collaboration with the Lifelong Kindergarten Group at the MIT Media Lab. It is available for free at https://scratch.mit.edu.

- For the rescue sprite: You can use motion blocks to make the rescue sprite follow the agent sprite after message is received.

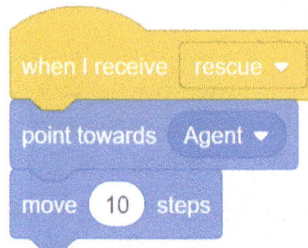

Source: Scratch Foundation. Scratch is a project of the Scratch Foundation, in collaboration with the Lifelong Kindergarten Group at the MIT Media Lab. It is available for free at https://scratch.mit.edu

Source: Scratch programming

By following these instructions, students can create a basic starter template for a search-and-rescue autonomous agent in Scratch, complete with movement controls, collision detection, and search-and-rescue logic, and use this template to customize and test their autonomous agents.

REFLECT

Teachers can engage students in a debate about using autonomous agents in solving societal challenges focusing on potential bias used in training autonomous agents. You can assign teams of students to be proponents or critics of autonomous agents, and allow them to defend their arguments (see Table 3.4).

Following the debate, students can engage in the discussions about the societal impact of AI on various communities.

Here are some suggested questions for this discussion:

- What are the potential societal benefits of widespread AI adoption, and how can these be maximized?
- What role do governments, corporations, and individuals play in ensuring that AI is developed and used ethically?

TABLE 3.4 ● Potential Arguments of Proponents and Critics of Autonomous Agents for Student Debate

POSITION 1: PROPONENTS OF AUTONOMOUS AGENTS	POSITION 2: CRITICS OF AUTONOMOUS AGENTS
• Autonomous agents offer a promising solution to many societal challenges by leveraging advanced technologies such as AI and ML.	• Although autonomous agents hold promise in addressing societal challenges, there are significant concerns regarding their potential for bias and discrimination.
• These agents can process vast amounts of data and make decisions more efficiently and objectively than humans, potentially leading to better outcomes in areas like healthcare, transportation, and public safety.	• Many autonomous systems are trained on biased datasets, which can perpetuate and even exacerbate existing societal inequalities.
• Autonomous agents are not susceptible to human biases or prejudices, which can often influence decision making in traditional systems.	• For example, if an autonomous agent is trained on historical data that reflects systemic biases, it may inadvertently reproduce those biases in its decision-making processes.
• By relying on algorithms and data-driven approaches, autonomous agents can mitigate bias and discrimination, leading to fairer and more equitable outcomes for all members of society.	• Furthermore, the lack of transparency and accountability in autonomous systems can make it challenging to identify and rectify biased outcomes.
	• As a result, there is a risk that autonomous agents may unintentionally discriminate against certain groups or individuals, leading to unfair and unjust outcomes in areas such as employment, criminal justice, and healthcare.

SUMMARY FOR LESSON 3.5

This task enables students to explore the societal impact of AI through the lens of a search-and-rescue mission conducted by an autonomous agent. By engaging in coding and problem-solving activities, students gain insight into how AI technologies can be used to address societal challenges, such as emergency response and public safety.

REFLECTION QUESTIONS

- How effectively did the project-based approach of designing autonomous agents for search and rescue engage students in exploring the societal impact of AI?

- In what ways did the debate about the pros and cons of using autonomous agents deepen students' understanding of AI's societal impact? How did it encourage critical thinking and reflection?

- How might the task be refined or expanded to further develop students' understanding of the societal impact of AI and their ability to critically evaluate the ethical implications of AI technologies in various contexts?

Chapter Summary

The development of AI literacy competencies identified in the peda-gogical framework can be achieved through tasks similar to the tasks provided in this chapter. Through such immersive tasks, students gain insights into designing AI solutions that cater to users' needs, fostering a human-centered approach within the DCR process. The student tasks lead to development of critical thinking and ethical reasoning skills nec-essary to navigate and shape the future of AI in an informed and respon-sible manner. Moreover, by exploring AI applications, students gain a holistic understanding of its role in modern society.

For teachers, the DCR process naturally leads to effective pedagogical practices such as project-based, inquiry-based, and collaborative learn-ing, discussions and debates, and so, on engaging students in real-world practices, brainstorming diverse solutions, and being prompted to think outside the box.

Wrap-Up Questions

- How might the student tasks outlined in the chapter be adapted or customized to suit the specific needs and interests of diverse student populations in K–12 education?

- Reflecting on the tasks provided, how do you envision integrating the Five Big Ideas in AI into your own teaching practices to foster critical thinking and ethical reasoning among your students?

- Consider the potential challenges or barriers you might encounter when implementing the Pedagogical Framework for AI Literacy in your classroom. How can these challenges be addressed or overcome?

- As educators, how can we ensure that students not only gain technical knowledge about AI but also develop a nuanced understanding of its societal implications and ethical considerations? What strategies or resources could support this holistic approach to AI literacy education?

CHAPTER 4

Preparing to Integrate AI Literacy Into Existing Curriculum

In this chapter we'll:

- Briefly review what research says about preparing to integrate AI literacy into curriculum

- Share recommendations for preparing to integrate AI literacy into curriculum

- Review examples illustrating effective professional learning practices

Now that you have become more familiar with the Pedagogical Framework for AI Literacy and explored different ways this framework can be used to engage students in inquiry-based learning, you may feel a little overwhelmed. You might be asking yourself, How do I prepare to teach AI literacy? Where do I start? Are there specific recommendations you have for me? We answer these questions and more in this chapter.

RESEARCH OVERVIEW

We need teachers who are AI literate who can help all students to prepare for the complex world they are entering and meet the societal demands for problem solvers who can use AI responsibly, ultimately widening AI access for everyone. That means educators need to be familiar with AI technologies and be able to integrate AI into classroom teaching. Moreover, we need teachers who can overcome cultural and financial barriers and limited resources to support the implementation process, especially for students with limited financial resources and access.

AI technologies are gradually shaping personal and professional lives all around the world. AI has a unique potential to level the playing field by providing all students with access to high-quality educational materials. The use of AI technology offers schools the chance to reinvigorate their curriculum and support all students in their pursuit of lifelong learning (National Academies of Sciences, Engineering, and Medicine, 2018). Meaningful inclusive AI literacy education requires teachers to shift away from the traditional sage-on-the-stage lecturing model and develop broader pedagogical practices to relearn, rethink, and reframe learning and teaching to take advantage of collaboration, problem solving, and community building in the AI-infused curriculum with real-world contexts (Laupichler et al., 2022).

Recent studies explored the strategies, challenges, and outcomes associated with preparing teachers for integrating AI technologies into their teaching practices (Casal-Otero et al., 2023). Specifically, research emphasizes the importance of hands-on, experiential learning, allowing educators to interact directly with AI tools and applications. This approach not only enhances technical skills but also fosters teachers' deeper understanding of the pedagogical implications of AI in the classroom. Research has highlighted the need to develop teachers' technological pedagogical content knowledge (TPACK) to support professional growth in AI literacy (Gutiérrez-Fallas & Henriques, 2020; Wei et al., 2020).

Furthermore, collaborative learning communities and mentorship programs have been identified as effective means of facilitating knowledge exchange and skill development among educators. Fullan (2015) emphasized the need to create shared meaning among teachers in aligning diverse perspectives and experiences toward a common vision for professional growth and learning. This collaborative and inclusive process not only enhances the effectiveness of professional development but also contributes to a culture of continuous learning and improvement within the educational community. It recognizes that meaningful and sustainable professional development requires a shared commitment to growth, collaboration, and a shared vision for advancing educational practices (Fullan, 2015).

Studies have also highlighted the significance of a multidisciplinary approach to AI literacy professional development. By incorporating perspectives from computer science, education, and ethics, teachers are better prepared to navigate the complexities of AI integration in diverse educational settings (Chiu & Chai, 2020; Wu et al., 2020).

REFLECTION QUESTIONS

- What are the key challenges you might face when integrating AI technologies into your classroom, and how can effective professional development address these challenges?

- How can professional development programs be tailored to meet the diverse needs and skill levels of teachers when it comes to AI integration?

- What additional resources or support systems might be necessary to complement professional development efforts and ensure successful AI integration in educational settings?

SUMMARY OF THE PROFESSIONAL LEARNING RECOMMENDATIONS FOR CLASSROOM TEACHERS

In Chapter 2 we introduced the Pedagogical Framework for AI Literacy, and in Chapter 3 we explored how this framework can support effective practices for teaching AI literacy. In this chapter we apply the same framework to define the professional learning goals for teachers to develop their own AI literacy and to prepare for integrating AI literacy into their curriculum. Recall the three fundamental components of the Pedagogical Framework for AI Literacy: design, create, and reflect. The DCR process is the foundational pillar that positions teachers as designers of student-centered AI-infused learning experiences. Let's explore how we can build professional learning activities within this process.

DESIGN

The *design* component calls for analyzing content-specific curriculum goals and carefully considering student needs and interests. Embracing a backward design methodology (Wiggins & McTighe, 1998), teachers define discipline-specific and AI literacy learning objectives and outcomes. Teachers then brainstorm ideas for student-centered tasks that integrate AI concepts. Thus, during the *design* component of professional learning the primary focus for teachers is on developing proficiency in backward design, developing competencies in culturally responsive and inclusive pedagogy, and deepening understanding of AI concepts.

RECOMMENDATIONS

1. Develop proficiency in utilizing backward design methodology to align curriculum goals with AI literacy learning objectives and outcomes, ensuring coherence and relevance in instructional planning.

2. Cultivate cultural competency and inclusiveness, deepening understanding of diverse cultural perspectives and their intersection with AI literacy.

3. Continuously deepen understanding of AI concepts and their implications for education, staying updated on advancements in AI technology and its applications across disciplines.

CREATE

Building on the *design* component, the *create* component encourages teachers to develop and implement student tasks that integrate digital tools and AI concepts. The *create* component emphasizes the dynamic nature of learning, where teachers act as facilitators, guiding students through interactive, collaborative, and authentic AI literacy experiences. Thus, professional learning focuses on instructional design and effective classroom practices.

RECOMMENDATIONS

4. Actively incorporate digital tools and AI concepts into student tasks and activities, leveraging technology to enhance learning experiences and develop students' AI literacy skills.

5. Transition from a traditional teacher-centered approach to a facilitator role in the classroom, guiding students through interactive, collaborative, and authentic AI literacy experiences that reflect real-world applications of AI concepts.

REFLECT

Finally, the *reflect* component encourages teachers to critically examine the successes and challenges encountered during the implementation of AI-infused tasks. Thus, professional learning focuses on collaborative reflective practices to analyze student engagement, learning outcomes, and the effectiveness of AI literacy integration. This introspective process not only enhances individual teaching practices but also contributes to the collective knowledge of the professional learning community, fostering a culture of shared insights and continuous growth.

RECOMMENDATIONS

6. Take advantage of opportunities for collaborative reflection with other teachers to critically examine the successes and challenges encountered during the AI literacy integration.

7. Evaluate the effectiveness of AI literacy integration in achieving desired learning outcomes, collecting evidence of student learning to inform future instructional decisions and improvements.

REFLECTION QUESTIONS

- What ideas do you have about aligning content-specific curriculum goals with AI literacy learning objectives?

- What authentic learning experiences in your classroom can be supported by integration of AI concepts?

- How might you navigate the complexities of engaging in critical analysis of your integration of AI in classroom practices with other teachers?

These seven recommendations for professional learning can be used independently or in combination to help teachers engage in effective pedagogical practices that support development of student AI literacy across different disciplines. Now let's look at some specific examples and additional resources to help you use these recommendations to prepare for integrating AI literacy into your classroom.

RECOMMENDATION 1: UTILIZE PRINCIPLES OF BACKWARD DESIGN

Develop proficiency in utilizing backward design methodology to align curriculum goals with AI literacy learning objectives and outcomes, ensuring coherence and relevance in instructional planning.

TIPS

Using backward design methodology to plan AI literacy integration

- Familiarize yourself with the three stages of backward design (https://jaymctighe.com/resources), which involves identifying desired learning outcomes (stage 1) and then planning assessments (stage 2) and instructional activities (stage 3) to achieve those outcomes.

- Consider the essential knowledge, skills, and dispositions that students need to develop to be AI literate, such as understanding the ethical implications of AI, analyzing data, and designing AI systems.

- Use our Planning AI Literacy Integration Template modified from the Understanding by Design (UbD) template (Wiggins & McTighe, 1998) to align discipline-specific learning outcomes with the identified AI literacy learning objectives and outcomes. The template is available on our companion website at https://companion.corwin.com/courses/TeachingAILiteracy .We also included a tutorial on prompt engineering for instructional design that can be used as a supplement to the template.

4.1 Lesson: Exploring Motion and Predictive Algorithms

For High School

In this physics lesson students learn the basic principles of motion and explore how predictive algorithms similar to those used in AI can be applied to analyze and predict motion. The Planning AI Literacy Integration template provides you with a guided process to align subject-specific and AI literacy outcomes. Table 4.1 shows a possible way this template can be completed for this lesson.

STAGE 1 DESIRED RESULTS		
INSTRUCTIONAL GOALS	**SUBJECT-SPECIFIC**	**AI LITERACY**
What subject-specific content standards will this unit address? *NGSS Performance expectations:* *HS-PS2-1: Analyze data to support the claim that Newton's second law of motion describes the mathematical relationship among the net force on a macroscopic object, its mass, and its acceleration.*	***Transfer*** What kinds of long-term independent accomplishments are desired?	
	Students will be able to independently use their learning to analyze and predict the motion of objects in real-world scenarios.	*Students will be able to independently use their learning to apply computational techniques to solve complex problems.*
	Understandings What specifically do you want students to understand? What inferences should they make?	
	Students will understand that the motion of an object is determined by the sum of the forces acting on it. *Students will understand that for any given object, a larger force causes a larger change in motion.*	*Students will understand that predictive algorithms analyze past data to make informed predictions about future outcomes.*
What AI competencies will this unit address? *2-C-ii: For each of these types of reasoning problems (classification, prediction, sequential decision making, combinatorial search, heuristic search, adversarial search, logical deduction, and statistical inference), list an algorithm that could be used to solve that problem.*	***Essential questions*** What thought-provoking questions will foster inquiry, meaning making, and transfer?	
	How do forces cause and affect motion?	*In what ways can predictive algorithms enhance our understanding of motion?*
	Acquisition What facts and basic concepts should students know and be able to recall? What discrete skills and processes should students be able to use?	
	Students will know Newton's laws of motion and their applications.	*Students will know the basic principles of predictive algorithms and how they are used in AI.*
	Students will be skilled at describing and analyzing the motion of an object in terms of position, time, velocity, and acceleration. *Students will be skilled at modeling the position of objects mathematically.* *Students will be skilled at collecting, graphing, and interpreting data for position vs. time to describe the motion of an object.*	*Students will be skilled at applying predictive algorithms to analyze motion data.*

RECOMMENDATION 2: DEVELOP CULTURAL COMPETENCY AND INCLUSIVENESS

Cultivate cultural competency and inclusiveness, deepening understanding of diverse cultural perspectives and their intersection with AI literacy

Lesson: Reexamining the U.S. Civil War

4.2

Perspectives and Interpretations

For High School

In this history lesson students analyze alternative viewpoints on the causes, outcomes, and legacies of the U.S. Civil War, considering the role of bias, perspective, and interpretation in historical analysis. The U.S. Civil War has been referred to as the War Between the States, War of the Rebellion (used by the Union army), the War of Secession, the War for Southern Independence (used by the Confederate Army), the War of Northern Aggression (used by some modern-day southerners) and the Freedom War (used by some African Americans) (CSTA & ISTE, 2015).

> Discipline/Indicator: History/Perspectives
>
> D2.His.5.9-12. Analyze how historical contexts shaped and continue to shape people's perspectives.
>
> D2.His.6.9-12. Analyze the ways in which the perspectives of those writing history shaped the history that they produced.
>
> Dimension 3: Evaluating sources and using evidence: Developing claims and using evidence
>
> D3.3.9-12. Identify evidence that draws information directly and substantively from multiple sources to detect inconsistencies in evidence to revise or strengthen claims.

As you design the tasks, consider different perspectives your students bring to this lesson depending on their family history. Find resources for students to explore various interpretations of the causes and outcomes of the war, including

- primary and secondary sources representing diverse perspectives on the U.S. Civil War (e.g., speeches, letters, diaries, articles)
- visual aids (maps, timelines, images)
- access to AI tools for historical research and analysis.

Let students explore how training algorithms on different datasets could lead to bias in interpretations of historical events.

RESOURCES

- Universal Design for Learning (Meyer et al., 2014) is a framework to improve and optimize teaching and learning for all people based on scientific insights into how humans learn. The website offers guidelines, online tools, tips, and free resources for designing inclusive learning experiences.

- Valuing student experiences: An introduction to culturally responsive education (CRE) blog (https://qrs.ly/lkgh0wx) provides various resources with concrete examples of CRE in action that can help teachers become more culturally responsive in their approach to student learning.

- MIT moral machine (https://www.moralmachine.net/) is a platform to examine ethical decisions made by intelligent machines. Use available scenarios (e.g., self-driving cars) or design your own.

RECOMMENDATION 3: DEEPEN UNDERSTANDING OF AI TECHNOLOGY

Continuously deepen understanding of AI concepts and their implications for education, staying updated on advancements in AI technology and its applications across disciplines

EXAMPLE 4.1

ISTE Artificial Intelligence in Education (https://iste.org/ai)

The International Society for Technology in Education (ISTE) offers multiple professional development opportunities for teachers to become comfortable teaching with and about AI. These resources include professional development courses, lesson plans, and toolkits that focus on how AI can enhance learning across various subjects. For example, you can

- sign up for "StretchAI: An AI Coach Just for Educators" to get tailored guidance to improve your teaching

- download "Hands-On AI Projects for the Classroom" guide with activities for teaching about AI

- enroll in an "AI Explorations for Educators" course to learn how to bring AI to your classroom.

RESOURCES

- Google AI (https://ai.google/) offers a series of simple explanations to help anyone understand what AI is, how it works, and how it's changing the world around us.

- AI for Education (https://www.aiforeducation.io/) offers webinars and courses for teachers, downloadable resources, and lessons to introduce AI to students.

RECOMMENDATION 4: INCORPORATE AI TECHNOLOGY INTO STUDENT TASKS

Actively incorporate digital tools and AI concepts into student tasks and activities, leveraging technology to enhance learning experiences and develop students' AI literacy skills

EXAMPLE 4.2

Interactive Classroom Experiences with WolframAlpha

Explore WolframAlpha, an AI-powered computational engine, that allows you to create interactive visualizations to support your teaching. Students can use this technology to explore the concepts in mathematics, science, and technology. Natural language processing allows users to input different queries and receive step-by-step solutions, visualizations, and explanations (Figure 4.1).

FIGURE 4.1 ● Example of WolframAlpha Output

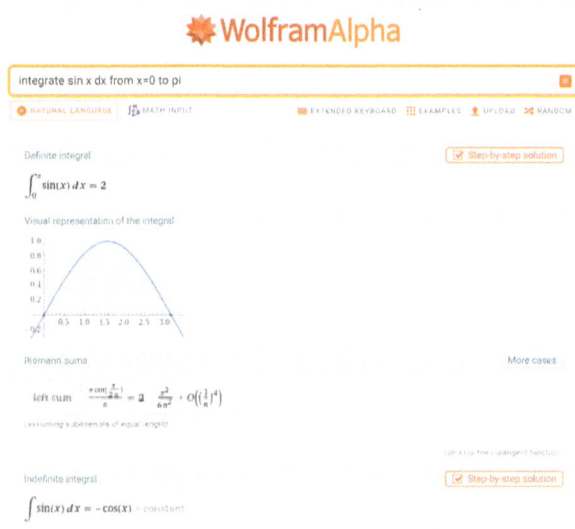

TIPS

Integrating AI tools

- Explore innovative ways to leverage technology to enhance learning experiences and develop students' AI literacy skills.

- Involve using AI-powered educational software, virtual simulations, or interactive online platforms to engage students in authentic learning experiences.

TIPS

Supporting student-centered teaching

- Encourage student autonomy and collaboration by guiding them through interactive and collaborative AI literacy experiences.

- Provide opportunities for students to explore, experiment, and problem solve with AI concepts in authentic contexts, fostering a deeper understanding of how AI affects their lives and society.

RESOURCES

- Day of AI (https://dayofai.org/) offers a list of free hands-on curriculum across disciplines to showcase how to integrate AI into daily teaching for K–12 students.

- PhET Interactive Simulations project at the University of Colorado Boulder (https://phet.colorado.edu/) offers free interactive simulations to engage students in discovery and inquiry-based explorations of K–16 topics in physics, mathematics, biology, and chemistry. In addition, the site offers free teaching resources and activities.

(Continued)

(Continued)

- HHMI Biointeractive (https://www.biointeractive.org/) is a platform for life science teachers that offers access to classroom resources, in particular, interactive media to engage students in explorations. In addition, the platform offers teaching tools and professional learning opportunities.

RECOMMENDATION 5: BECOME A FACILITATOR OF STUDENT LEARNING

Transition from a traditional teacher-centered approach to a facilitator role in the classroom, guiding students through interactive, collaborative, and authentic AI literacy experiences that reflect real-world applications of AI concepts

4.3 Lesson: Speech Recognition

(https://ai4k12.org/activities/)

For Middle School

This lesson supports development of the following core information communication technology (ICT) competencies (ISTE, 2024):

- 1.1 Empowered Learner: Students leverage technology to take an active role in choosing, achieving, and demonstrating competency in their learning goals, informed by the learning sciences.

- 1.3 Knowledge Constructor: Students critically curate a variety of resources using digital tools to construct knowledge, produce creative artifacts, and make meaningful learning experiences for themselves and others.

You can engage students in explorations of how the computer recognizes the audio-signal input, such as human speech, by letting them experiment with an online spectrogram (Touretzky, 2022). A spectrogram is a visual display of the sound pitch (frequency) in the audio signal, where color is used to show the amount of energy in each frequency band. High energy, shown as yellow or red in the display, means that this frequency contributes significantly to the mixture (Figure 4.2).

FIGURE 4.2 ● Spectrogram of the Phrase "AI for All" produced at https://spectrogram.sciencemusic.org/

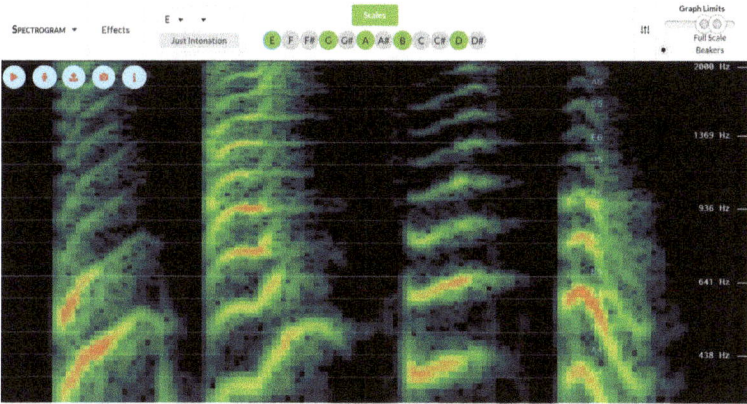

Source: Minces (2021)

Have students make their own spectrograms by using the computer microphone to sing, say different vowels, or speak a phrase. They can then analyze these spectrograms to observe the distinct patterns in frequency and intensity corresponding to different vocal sounds, providing hands-on experience with spectrogram interpretation and gaining insights into AI concepts of sensing and perceiving.

RESOURCES

- Visible learning means an enhanced role for teachers as they become evaluators of their own teaching. The Visible Learning website (https://visible-learning.org/) provides access to free online resources related to John Hattie's visible learning research (Hattie, 2012) with the goal to support teachers in a deeper understanding of the underlying concepts.

- AI4ALL (https://ai-4-all.org/resources/) offers an open learning curriculum and teacher resources to widen the access to AI education to students without computer science or mathematics backgrounds.

RECOMMENDATION 6. ENGAGE IN COLLABORATIVE REFLECTION

Take advantage of opportunities for collaborative reflection with other teachers to critically examine the successes and challenges encountered during the AI literacy integration

TIPS

Reflecting on professional experience

- Invest in professional learning opportunities that emphasize instructional design principles and effective classroom practices.

- Develop expertise in designing learning experiences that effectively integrate digital tools and AI concepts. This includes understanding how to scaffold learning experiences, differentiate instruction, and assess student understanding within the context of AI education.

EXAMPLE 4.3

Connect: ISTE + ASCD's Free Online Community (https://connect.iste.org/)

You can join Connect, a free online professional learning community that brings together educators from around the world to provide a collaborative space for educators to develop expertise in designing learning experiences that leverage AI to enhance problem solving and critical thinking skills, to tackle real-world challenges, and to improve student engagement and learning outcomes. After joining, you can select specific groups based on your interest, engage in conversations with colleagues, access a library of resources, and learn about various professional development opportunities.

TIPS

Assessing student learning

- Reflect on the extent to which students are actively participating in AI-related activities, demonstrating understanding of AI concepts, and applying their knowledge in authentic contexts.

- Evaluate the impact of AI-related tasks and activities on students' development of critical thinking, problem solving, and digital literacy skills.

- Consider collecting evidence of student learning through assessments, observations, and student feedback to inform future instructional decisions and improvements.

RESOURCES

- The Forum (https://forum.code.org/) is a professional learning community that provides a platform for teachers to engage in discussions on the impact of AI in the classroom, to stay informed about the latest advancements in AI, and to understand how to harness its potential for educational purposes. The code.org also provides curriculum resources and professional development opportunities for teachers of all disciplines.

- Stanford University d.school (https://dschool.stanford.edu/) provides teachers with a variety of professional learning opportunities, tools, and resources to use design principles in the classroom.

RECOMMENDATION 7: EVALUATE THE IMPACT OF AI ON STUDENT LEARNING

Evaluate the effectiveness of AI literacy integration in achieving desired learning outcomes, collecting evidence of student learning to inform future instructional decisions and improvements

Evaluating STEM Practices in AI-Related Tasks

Although researchers continue to push the boundaries in understanding STEM practices and students' development of 21st century skills, teachers often do not have access to user-friendly evaluation tools they need to effectively assess these skills. We recommend an instrument developed by MakeEval project (http://www.adammaltese .com/content/makeval/) that provides a tool for teachers to measure observable indicators of students engaged in STEM practices common to STEM professionals. There are a total of 11 practices included in the tool. Although this group developed the tool for evaluation of maker-specific tasks, we believe you will find this instrument useful in assessing AI-related tasks. Table 4.2 shows these practices, along with alignment with STEM disciplines standards of practice. The tool is available on our companion website at https://companion.corwin .com/courses/TeachingAILiteracy.

TABLE 4.2 ● Evaluation of STEM Practices

STEM PRACTICE	OBSERVABLE PERFORMANCE INDICATORS	STANDARDS ALIGNMENT[1]
Make Sense of Activity	• Explain the meaning of the activity • Decompose the activity into manageable subproblems • Analyze and explain constraints, given, unknowns, goals of the activity • Explain how different approaches (including those of peers) may be utilized in carrying out solutions to the activity	MP1 CSP3
Ask Questions, Define Problems	• Pose questions that require further (or new) investigation or research (e.g., How can I make my own solar eclipse glasses?); considered questions of high-cognitive demand • Develop/define a design problem that can be solved through the development of an object, tool, process, or system • Identify an interdisciplinary, real-world problem that can be solved computationally • Pose questions that seek clarification of a model/prototype, an engineering problem, an explanation, and/or an argument (e.g., What do you mean? How does adding this part help solve the problem?)	SEP1 CSP3

(Continued)

(Continued)

STEM PRACTICE	OBSERVABLE PERFORMANCE INDICATORS	STANDARDS ALIGNMENT[1]
Develop, Use Models, and Select Appropriate Tools	• Sketch/draw a model • Build a model/prototype • Practice technique before final design (e.g., practice a pop-up cut on a scrap sheet of paper) • Select appropriate tools for design solution and/or investigation (e.g., hot glue or tape)	SEP2 MP5
Plan Investigation	• Write down or verbally articulate sequence of steps for an activity or design process • Write down or verbally articulate needed material and tools to carry out activity or design • Brainstorm plans and ideas aloud with peer(s) • Select and use digital tools to plan and manage a design process that considers design constraints and calculated risks • Articulate goals/expectations in relation to the activity	SEP3 MP1 TP4 CSP5
Attend to Precision	• Use appropriate vocabulary and definitions in oral and/or written communication • Measure (e.g., length, weight) with precision • Label accurately when measuring, graphing, etc. • Express numerical answers with a degree of precision (e.g., rounding error) • Calculations are accurate	MP6
Document and Explain Activity	• Synthesize observational notes into an oral and/or written explanation or visual representation • Utilize prior experiences and/or prior knowledge to construct and/or support explanation (must be explicit) • Explain design solution, including constraints and criteria, and/or decisions made throughout the design or activity • Document failures and explain how failures led to changes in activity or design • Document process through photographs and/or video files	
Analyze and Interpret Data	• Construct a hypothesis or conjecture based on observations (e.g., I think the wheel is the problem because it keeps turning right instead of staying straight.) • Use digital tools to analyze data/information • "Testing" model/object/design (i.e., trials) and make changes to design based on "tests" (and can defend this change—informed decision making as opposed to uninformed decision making) • State and/or write "because" in relation to "tests" (e.g., This did not work because . . .") • Examine object or device (e.g., turning over in hand while "studying" object) • Persevere in solving problem	SEP4 CSP6

STEM PRACTICE	OBSERVABLE PERFORMANCE INDICATORS	STANDARDS ALIGNMENT[1]
Use Mathematics and Computational Thinking	• Develop visual representation(s) of observations or investigations (e.g., frequency chart, bar graph) to identify patterns • Apply mathematical concepts and/or processes (prior knowledge) to solve problems and/or investigations (e.g., indirect measurement, estimation, number sense, proportional reasoning, spatial reasoning) • Intuitive precision (e.g., "You've just built this tower with four toilet paper rolls and a flat piece of cardboard. Is the cardboard on the top flat? Why not?"; Are the four columns even?) • Create algorithms that a computer can execute • Recognize patterns and/or repeated sequences in data or code within activity	SEP5 MP4 TP5 CSP4
Engage in Constructive Feedback and Argumentation from Evidence	• Compare and critique at least two designs and analyze whether they meet the demands of the activity • Provide suggestions to peer(s) in how to improve and/or change design and/or activity using relevant evidence • Construct arguments and respond to the argument of others; explain flaws in own or peer's argument • Make conjectures, suggestions, and/or use counterexamples to support, improve, refute, and/or critique the argument and ideas of others • Defend how the mathematical results is warranted to reach goal(s) of activity	SEP7 MP3 CSP2
Obtain and Evaluate, and Communicate Information in a Responsible Manner	• Engage in positive, safe, legal, and ethical behavior when using technology, including online social interactions • Conduct research (e.g., books, Google) to inform design, investigation, interest, curiosities, etc. • Plan and employ effective research strategies to locate information and other resources for their intellectual or creative pursuits • Evaluate the accuracy, perspective, credibility, and relevance of information, media, data, or other resources	SEP8 TP2 TP3
Communicate/ Present Information	• Communicate/showcase final product, design solution, and/or investigation clearly (i.e., appropriate manner that audience can understand) • Explain the mathematical results within the context of the problem and/or investigation • Use technology to demonstrate their learning in a variety of ways (e.g., documentation, social media, portfolio) • Cites the work of online resources (e.g., images) • Creates original digital works • Repurpose or remix digital resources into a new creation	SEP8 MP4 TP1 TP6 CSP7

Source: Maltese & Simpson (2019)

[1]MP – CCSS Mathematical Practices (https://www.thecorestandards.org/Math/Practice/), SEP – NGSS Science and Engineering Practices (https://my.nsta.org/ngss/PracticesFull.aspx), CSP – K-12 Computer Science Framework Computer Science Practices (https://k12cs.org/), TP – ISTE Standards for Students Technology Practices (https://iste.org/standards/students)

Chapter Summary

This chapter guides teachers through the critical steps needed to thoughtfully and effectively integrate AI literacy across the curriculum. Using the Pedagogical Framework for AI Literacy, we identified seven recommendations to scaffold professional learning necessary to prepare for effective integration of AI literacy. The key points of these recommendations are:

- the importance of utilizing backward design—teachers must align AI literacy goals with overall curriculum standards and design authentic assessments that allow students to demonstrate mastery.

- developing teachers' own understanding of AI concepts, applications, and implications for education—teachers need to stay updated on the rapid advancements in AI technology across disciplines to design meaningful student-centered learning experiences.

- cultural competency—teachers must cultivate awareness of diverse cultural perspectives and how they intersect with the development and use of AI systems, exploring ethical issues like bias, fairness, and equity in AI as part of the instruction.

- collaboration among teachers—teachers need to engage in productive collaborative reflection to analyze successes, challenges.

Through reflection questions we ask teachers to consider how to implement these recommendations in a meaningful, contextual way for their specific classroom and students. The overall focus is on building teachers' capacity to make AI literacy an integrated, authentic part of student learning experience.

Wrap-Up Questions

- What AI literacy learning objectives are aligned to the standards in your content area? How can you apply the backward design process to plan authentic student-centered learning experiences to address these objectives?

- What are some specific strategies you plan to implement for continuously updating your own knowledge of AI concepts, applications, and implications for education?

- What challenges might you face in exploring cultural perspectives and ethical considerations around AI development/use with your students?

- How do you see your role in productive collaborative-reflection opportunities with colleagues around AI literacy integration?

- What challenges do you expect to encounter while integrating AI literacy into your teaching? How do you plan to address them?

PART II

Practical Applications

Chapter 5: AI Literacy in Science Education

Chapter 6: AI Literacy in Mathematics Education

Chapter 7: AI Literacy in Language Arts Education

Chapter 8: AI Literacy in Social Studies Education

AI Literacy in Science Education

In this chapter we'll

- Discuss connections between Five Big Ideas in AI and Next Generation Science Standards (NGSS)

- Suggest strategies for integrating AI literacy across different grade bands and science disciplines

- Demonstrate the application of the Pedagogical Framework for AI Literacy for designing a middle school life science unit that integrates AI's concept of datasets

So far, we focused mostly on AI concepts and essential understandings. You may be thinking: That's great, but I have a curriculum to teach. How do I integrate AI literacy in my subject specific curriculum? Do you have specific recommendations and examples for me? In Chapters 5–8, we'll tackle these questions. In this chapter we focus on how AI literacy can be integrated into the discipline of science. In subsequent chapters, we'll discuss other disciplines, so that you will see how AI can be integrated throughout the subjects.

We'll first look at how science standards (NGSS Lead States, 2013)—in particular, science and engineering practices—connect with core concepts of the Five Big Ideas in AI. Then for each big idea we outline a few short examples of science lessons that integrate core AI literacy concepts. These examples are really meant to spur your creativity rather than provide fully articulated lessons. Finally, the chapter concludes with an illustration of how the Pedagogical Framework for AI Literacy is applied to plan a complete middle school life science unit that integrates AI's concept of datasets.

• Science and engineering practices are what students DO to make sense of phenomena. They are a set of skills and knowledge to be internalized. The SEPs reflect the major practices that scientists and engineers use to investigate the world and design and build systems.

SCIENCE STANDARDS AND FIVE BIG IDEAS IN AI

- **Crosscutting concepts** are concepts that hold true across the natural and engineered world. Students can use them to make connections across seemingly disparate disciplines or situations, connect new learning to prior experiences, and more deeply engage with material across the other dimensions.

- **Disciplinary core ideas** have broad importance within or across science or engineering disciplines, provide a key tool for understanding or investigating complex ideas and solving problems, relate to societal or personal concerns.

- **Real-world phenomena** are events or processes that we observe either directly through our senses or indirectly through data.

As many of you know, the NGSS is a set of K–12 science education standards developed to improve science education in the United States. They were released in 2013 and are based on the Framework for K–12 Science Education developed by the National Research Council (NRC, 2012). Since their publication, the majority of states have adopted the NGSS or have education standards influenced by the Framework for K–12 Science Education and/or NGSS.

NGSS emphasizes three dimensions of learning: **Science and Engineering Practices (SEP)**, **Crosscutting Concepts (CC)**, and **Disciplinary Core Ideas (DCI)**. The practices outline the actions scientists take as they explore and develop models and theories about the natural world. They also encompass the key engineering practices engineers employ when designing and building models and systems. Crosscutting concepts unify the study of science and engineering through their common application across fields. Their purpose is to help students deepen their understanding of the disciplinary core ideas. The core ideas are fundamental ideas that are necessary for understanding a given science discipline. They are taught over multiple grades at progressive levels of depth and complexity (National Science Teaching Association [NSTA], n.d.). These dimensions work together to provide students with a deeper understanding of science concepts and how they relate to **real-world phenomena.**

Not surprisingly, NGSS science and engineering practices can be effectively connected with various AI literacy concepts, which provides us an opportunity to effectively integrate these concepts into teaching to support students' learning of science. To illustrate these connections through examples of science lessons we paired each of the Five Big Ideas in AI with one or two practices. Let's explore these connections (Table 5.1).

This table shows that introducing AI literacy can enrich students' understanding of the process of scientific inquiry, experimentation, and problem solving. Moreover, you can make these connections even without directly employing

TABLE 5.1 ● Examples of Illustrated Connections Between Science and Engineering Practices and Five Big Ideas in AI

BIG IDEAS IN AI	AI'S CORE CONCEPTS	SCIENCE AND ENGINEERING PRACTICES	CONNECTIONS BETWEEN BIS AND SEPS	LESSON EXAMPLES
BI1. Perception	Sensing Processing	SEP1. Asking questions and defining problems	Asking investigative questions is the starting point for collecting data and observations about a particular science phenomenon through senses and sensors. When applied to AI, perception and sensing involve gathering raw data inputs from the environment to build a model of understanding. In science the goal of using experiments is to explain scientific phenomena, which mirrors how AI perception models use training data to learn patterns and make predictions about new sensory inputs.	5.1. Renewable energy (Elementary school) (p. 86)
BI2. Representation and Reasoning	Representation Search	SEP3. Planning and carrying out investigations	Planning systematic investigations parallels designing representations and search spaces for AI problems. Clarifying what data is relevant aligns with carefully constructing feature representations from raw data. Identifying variables/parameters is similar to defining the search space of possibilities an AI agent explores.	5.2. Homeostasis and body control (High school) (p. 88)
	Reasoning	SEP6. Constructing explanations and designing solutions	Scientists seeking explanations and engineers creating solutions is like AI reasoning over knowledge representations to infer conclusions and search to identify optimal solutions to problems.	5.3. Natural selection and evolution (Middle school) (p. 89)

(Continued)

BIG IDEAS IN AI	AI'S CORE CONCEPTS	SCIENCE AND ENGINEERING PRACTICES	CONNECTIONS BETWEEN BIS AND SEPS	LESSON EXAMPLES
BI3. Learning	Nature of Learning	SEP2. Developing and using models	Scientists and engineers use and construct various models based on data to represent ideas and explanations about studied phenomena. Representing quantitative variables as data is the basis for machine learning datasets.	5.4. Atomic structure of matter (Middle school) (p. 91)
	Neural Networks Datasets	SEP5. Using mathematics and computational thinking	Neural networks themselves are complex mathematical models that learn to represent and explain patterns in data. Mathematics and computation are fundamental tools for representing physical variables and their relationships. Drawing a parallel to that, computer simulations provide a means to train and test learning models like neural networks.	5.5. Conservation of momentum (High school) (p. 93)
BI4. Natural Interaction	Commonsense Reasoning	SEP4. Analyzing and interpreting data	The practice of analyzing and interpreting data requires identifying meaningful patterns in complex datasets, which relies on the robust perception and commonsense reasoning capabilities that AI natural interaction models aim to emulate.	5.6. Earth's features (Elementary school) (p. 95)

BIG IDEAS IN AI	AI'S CORE CONCEPTS	SCIENCE AND ENGINEERING PRACTICES	CONNECTIONS BETWEEN BIS AND SEPS	LESSON EXAMPLES
	Natural Language Commonsense Reasoning Philosophy of Mind	SEP7. Engaging in argument from evidence	Engaging in argumentation requires many of the same cognitive skills that power effective human–AI interaction. Constructing logically coherent arguments and explanations remains an AI challenge. Bridging this gap by enhancing AI's multimodal perception, commonsense inference, and contextual language is a key for more natural human–AI interaction in the scientific argumentation processes.	5.7. How old is Earth (High school) (p. 96)
BI5. Societal Impact	Ethical AI AI and Culture AI and Economy AI for Social Good	SEP8. Obtaining, evaluating, and communicating information	The practice of clearly communicating ideas/ methods and critiquing them individually/ in groups is general for all scientists and engineers regardless of domain. We can draw connections for how rigorously applying this practice to the AI field becomes critical for understanding/ managing AI's social impacts, which is critical for responsibly navigating AI's societal, cultural, and economic impacts.	5.8. Genetic engineering and natural genetic variations (High school) (p. 97)

AI-powered tools, because AI literacy can be taught by drawing parallels between science and engineering practices and workings of AI systems, as you will see in lesson examples that follow. With these connections in mind, we can now explore strategies for integrating AI literacy to not only support science standards, but also truly enrich student science learning experiences.

REFLECTION QUESTIONS

- Consider the statement that AI literacy can be taught without directly employing AI tools. How might you effectively teach AI concepts through analogies and parallels to science and engineering practices in your classroom?

- In what ways can hands-on activities or projects that integrate science and AI concepts foster interdisciplinary learning and creativity among your students?

- Discuss potential collaboration opportunities with technology or computer science teachers to enhance students' understanding of AI concepts while reinforcing core scientific principles.

LESSON SUGGESTIONS

AI'S BIG IDEA #1: PERCEPTION

In this elementary school lesson students use sensors to collect data from solar panels to explore the AI's core concepts of sensing and processing.

5.1 Lesson: Renewable Energy

For Elementary School

SEP1. Asking questions and defining problems

A practice of science is to ask and refine questions that lead to descriptions and explanations of how the natural and designed world works and which can be empirically tested (NSTA, n.d.).

CC5: Energy and matter

Energy can be transferred in various ways and between objects.

DCI: PS3.A. Definitions of energy

4-PS3-2. Make observations to provide evidence that energy can be transferred from place to place by sound, light, heat, and electric currents.

Overview:

Provide students with a solar panel, a light source (to represent the sun), and a light bulb and let them explore how solar panels capture sunlight and convert it into electricity (Figure 5.1).

FIGURE 5.1 ● Experimental Setup to Explore Solar Energy (Experiment #2 from *Investigating Solar Energy*, qrs.ly/cgggxzx)

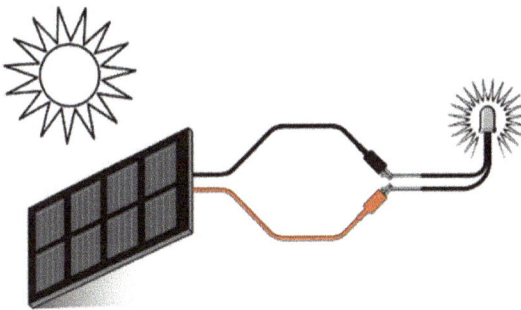

Source: Vernier Science Education

Based on their observations, students can generate questions related to energy transfer, for example,

- How efficient are solar panels in converting sun energy into usable electricity?
- What factors influence the energy transfer in this system?

Next, students can define problems based on their questions, such as:

- How to place the solar panel to capture the maximum amount of sunlight and optimize its energy production?

You can then provide students with sensors (e.g., light, voltage, temperature, energy) to collect data. Explain that the electrical signals generated by the sensor represent the data, which can be processed and analyzed using AI algorithms. AI can support sensing by integrating various sensor data from solar panels. Sensors on solar panels can measure factors like sunlight intensity, temperature, and voltage output. Discuss how AI algorithms can process and interpret this data to optimize the performance of the solar panel, such as adjusting its orientation to capture maximum sunlight or regulating its output based on changing light conditions.

AI'S BIG IDEA #2: REPRESENTATION AND REASONING

In this high school biology lesson students use virtual simulation to plan and carry out experiments to examine the effects of exercise and fitness level on their heart rate. They explore AI's concepts of representation and reasoning using AI data visualization tools.

5.2

Lesson: Homeostasis and Body Control

For High School

SEP3. Planning and carrying out investigations

> Scientists and engineers plan and carry out investigations in the field or laboratory, working collaboratively as well as individually. Their investigations are systematic and require clarifying what counts as data and identifying variables or parameters.

CC7: Stability and change

Feedback (negative or positive) can stabilize or destabilize a system.

DCI: LS1.A: Structure and Function

HS-LS1-3. Plan and conduct an investigation to provide evidence that feedback mechanisms maintain homeostasis.

Overview:

In this lesson students will plan and carry out an experiment to examine the effects of exercise and fitness level on their heart rate.

Recommendations:

- Incorporate interactive simulations or AI-driven modelling tools into the experiment-planning process. Allow students to simulate different scenarios, such as varying levels of exercise intensity, body parameters, fitness levels, diet, and so on and observe the predicted effects on heart rate.

  Here are two interactive simulations that students can use:

  o PhET Eating and Exercise (qrs.ly/2rggxzz)

  o PBS Body Control Center (qrs.ly/yzggy02/)

- After students complete the experiment, have them combine collected data into a class dataset and discuss the best visual representations of the data. This is a good place to introduce students to AI data visualization software, for example, Tableau (https://www.tableau.com/) or PowerBI (https://app.powerbi.com/)

- Demonstrate how students can use AI representations to create visualizations of their experimental data, such as graphs showing changes in heart rate over time for different fitness levels.

- Ask students to draw conclusions based on these representations. Provide examples of how AI systems use representation and reasoning to analyze data.

In this middle school lesson students use natural selection simulation to explain the changes in the population of rabbits depending on environmental factors. They draw parallels between their reasoning and predictions and how AI systems optimize solutions through data representation and reasoning.

Lesson: Natural Selection and Evolution

5.3

For Middle School

SEP6. Constructing explanations and designing solutions

The products of science are explanations and the products of engineering are solutions.

CC2: Cause and effect

Events have causes, sometimes simple, sometimes multifaceted. Deciphering causal relationships, and the mechanisms by which they are mediated, is a major activity of science and engineering.

DCI: LS4.B. Natural selection

MS-LS4-4. Construct an explanation based on evidence that describes how genetic variations of traits in a population increase some individuals' probability of surviving and reproducing in a specific environment.

Overview:

In this lesson we recommend using the PhET Natural Selection simulation (Figure 5.2). In this simulation students explore changes in the population of rabbits over time in different environments and explore how different traits can help an animal survive in an environment. Specifically, students

- determine which mutations are favored by the selection agents of predators and food variety and which mutations are neutral
- describe which traits change the survivability of rabbits in different environments
- make predictions about adaptations and environments that produce a stable population of rabbits, a population that dies out, and a population that takes over the world.

FIGURE 5.2 ● Natural Selection Lab by PhET Interactive Simulations (https://phet.colorado.edu/en/simulations/natural-selection)

Source: University of Colorado at Boulder

Here are some ways to integrate AI concepts of representation and reasoning into this lesson:

- Have students run simulations where they adjust parameters (such as predator or food availability) and observe the resulting changes in the rabbit population.
- Students can then apply AI concepts to analyze why certain traits or combinations of traits lead to better survival rates.
- Engage students in discussions about how the representation of genetic information and environmental factors influences the population dynamics they observe.
- Encourage them to apply reasoning skills to predict how changes in these factors might affect the rabbit population over time.
- Draw parallels between the natural selection observed in the simulation and how AI systems (like genetic algorithms) optimize solutions based on feedback from the environment or data.

AI'S BIG IDEA #3: LEARNING

In this middle school lesson students explore the AI core of nature of learning and datasets by drawing parallel between constructing molecular models based on known information about atomic structure and the principles of supervised machine learning (ML) that involves training a computer algorithm on labeled data.

Lesson: Atomic Structure of Matter

5.4

For Middle School

SEP2. Developing and using models

> A practice of both science and engineering is to use and construct models as helpful tools for representing ideas and explanations. These tools include diagrams, drawings, physical replicas, mathematical representations, analogies, and computer simulations.

CC3: Scale, proportion, and quantity

> In considering phenomena, it is critical to recognize what is relevant at different size, time, and energy scales, and to recognize proportional relationships between different quantities as scales change.

DCI: PS1.A. Structure and properties of matter

MS-PS1-1. Develop models to describe the atomic composition of simple molecules and extended structures.

Overview:

In this lesson you can draw a parallel between student-modeling activities and the principles of supervised ML. You can utilize a virtual lab, for students to build a collection of simple molecules from atoms (Figure 5.3).

FIGURE 5.3 ● Build a Molecule Lab by PhET Interactive
Simulations—Simple molecules screen (qrs.ly/ctggy0a)

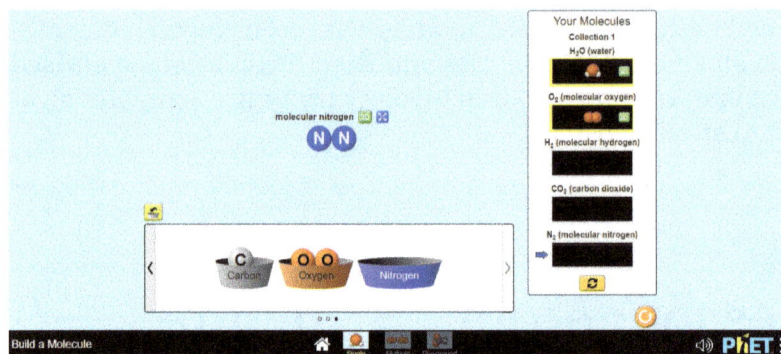

Source: University of Colorado at Boulder

As they use PhET simulation, they are learning to construct models of molecules based on known information about atomic structure, discover their molecular formulas and chemical names, and view their structures in 3D. Students may also start noticing some patterns in the types of bonds created by different elements. They then apply their learning to create collections of complex molecules in a playground (Figure 5.4).

FIGURE 5.4 ● Build a Molecule lab by PhET Interactive
Simulations—Playground screen (qrs.ly/acggy0c)

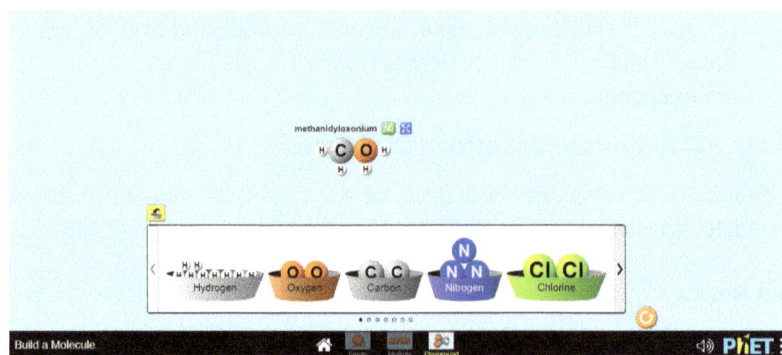

Source: University of Colorado at Boulder

At this point, you can draw analogies between the process of supervised ML and students' activities in modeling the atomic composition of molecules. Describe how supervised learning involves training a computer algorithm on labeled data (inputs and corresponding outputs) to predict the correct output for new, unseen inputs. Explain that, similar to how a computer algorithm learns from labeled data, students are learning to construct models of molecules based on known information about atomic structure (simple and multiple molecules screens in the simulation). Then, just like the algorithm predicts the correct output for new inputs after training, students' models on the playground screen should accurately represent the atomic composition of molecules based on their understanding of atomic structure.

In this high school physics lesson students explore AI concepts of nature of learning and datasets by drawing parallels between their process of developing a mathematical model of a total momentum from collision experimental data and training a supervised learning algorithm.

Lesson: Conservation of Momentum

5.5

SEP5. Using mathematics and computational thinking

For High School

In both science and engineering, mathematics and computation are fundamental tools for representing physical variables and their relationships. They are used for a range of tasks such as constructing simulations; statistically analyzing data; and recognizing, expressing, and applying quantitative relationships.

CC4: Systems and system models

A system is an organized group of related objects or components; models can be used for understanding and predicting the behavior of systems.

DCI: PS2.A. Forces and motion

HS-PS2-2. Use mathematical representations to support the claim that the total momentum of a system of objects is conserved when there is no net force on the system.

Overview:

Students can learn about ML using an analogy with their own learning of conservation of momentum. In this lesson students explore the collision of two carts, collecting data using digital tools. As they gain a deeper understanding of the underlying physics principles, they are also using mathematics and computation to represent physical variables and their relationships. Consider two possible scenarios of a collision experiment:

1. A physical experiment in which two carts are colliding on a track (Figure 5.5):

    - Students analyze motion data from sensors (e.g., distance, velocity, acceleration) and express quantitative relationships between them.

    - Students use statistical analysis to extract meaningful information from experimental data, for example, quantifying the amount of momentum transferred between the two carts.

FIGURE 5.5 ● Collision Experiment (Experiment #18 from Physics with Vernier, qrs.ly/ulggy0e)

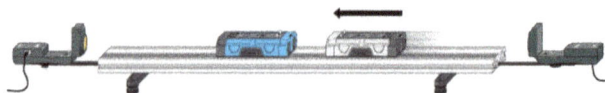

Source: Vernier Science Education

2. Simulated experiment with bumper carts (Figure 5.6)

    - Students use simulated experiments to collect data from the collision between the two bumper carts and predict the resulting transfer of momentum based on initial conditions.

    - Using such a simulation, students observe how the total momentum is conserved in different scenarios and develop mathematical relationships representing scientific phenomena.

FIGURE 5.6 ● CK12 Collision Simulation (ck12.co/3iUs)

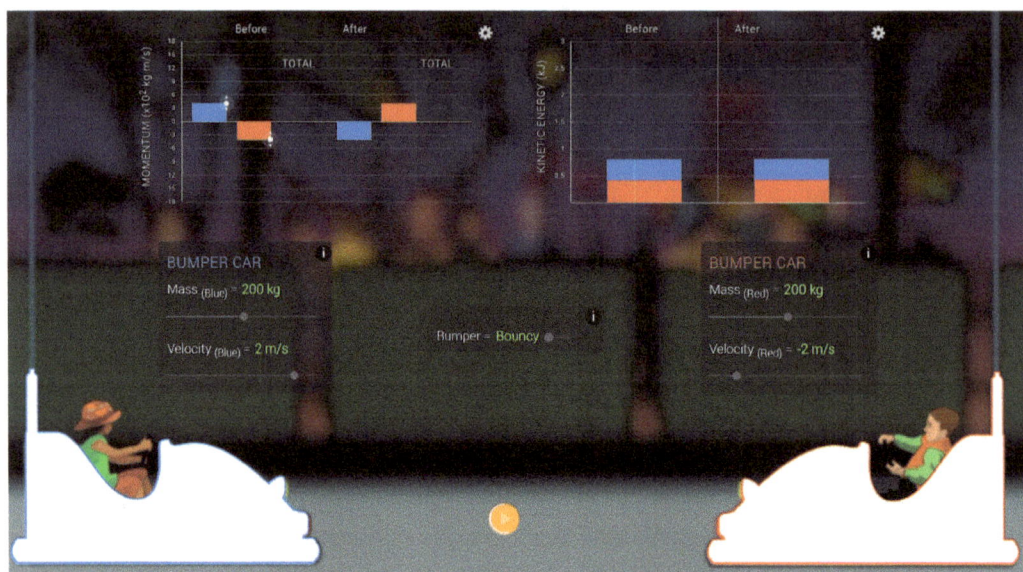

Source: cK-12 LICENSED UNDER CC License
© CK-12 Foundation · Visit us at ck12.org

Our recommendations for AI literacy integration:

- Draw a parallel between the students' process of developing mathematical relationships from experimental data to training a supervised learning algorithm. Explain that just like how a ML algorithm learns from examples to make predictions, students are using their data to derive mathematical equations that describe the relationship between variables in collisions.

- Discuss the importance of validation and evaluation in experimental science and ML. Just as ML models are tested on new data that were not used for training to assess their performance, students can validate their mathematical relationships by comparing predicted outcomes with experimental results from new collisions not used in the mathematical model development.

- Highlight the iterative nature of experimental science and ML. Just as ML models are refined and improved over multiple iterations, students can refine their mathematical relationships based on more experiments or further data analysis.

AI'S BIG IDEA #4: NATURAL INTERACTION

In this elementary school lesson students use simulation to explore how geological events affected Earth's different features. Students use commonsense reasoning about causal relationships between different features of Earth and events based on observed patterns. This approach directly parallels a significant challenge in developing AI with true commonsense reasoning.

Lesson: Earth's Features

5.6

SEP4. Analyzing and interpreting data

For Elementary School

Scientific investigations produce data that must be analyzed to derive meaning. Because data patterns and trends are not always obvious, scientists use a range of tools—including tabulation, graphical interpretation, visualization, and statistical analysis—to identify the significant features and patterns in the data. Scientists identify sources of error in the investigations and calculate the degree of certainty in the results. Modern technology makes the collection of large datasets much easier, providing secondary sources for analysis.

CC4: Systems and system models

> A system is an organized group of related objects or components; models can be used for understanding and predicting the behavior of systems.

DCI: ESS2.B. Plate tectonics and large-scale system interactions

4-ESS2-2. Analyze and interpret data from maps to describe patterns of Earth's features.

Overview:

In this lesson we suggest using EarthViewer (qrs.ly/5uggy0j)

This interactive module allows students to explore the Earth's history, from its formation 4.5 billion years ago to modern times. In particular, the simulation dynamically shows how continents grow and shift as students scroll through billions of years.

• Ill-defined problem
is a messy and complex situation with not enough information, so the situation requires inquiry, information gathering, and reflection (Thorp & Sage, 2002).

As students explore the changes in Earth's features over time, the simulation provides them with interactive visualization of the Earth's surface, helping them understand how geological events affected the different Earth's features, such as shape of continents, atmospheric composition, temperature, biodiversity, day length, and so on. Interactive tools also help students use commonsense reasoning about causal relationships between different features of the Earth and events based on observed patterns. This is a good place to discuss that computer scientists are working on extending AI's capabilities to use commonsense reasoning to solve **ill-defined problems**; however, this goal has not yet been achieved.

In this high school earth science lesson students use complex dataset to create graphical representations of data to reason about the Earth's age. They draw parallels between their reliance on commonsense reasoning and the need for AI to have commonsense or human-like reasoning to be able to solve ill-defined problems.

5.7 Lesson: How Old Is Earth

For High School

SEP7. Engaging in argument from evidence

> Argumentation is the process by which explanations and solutions are reached.

CC1: Patterns

Observed patterns in nature guide organization and classification and prompt questions about relationships and causes underlying them.

DCI: ESS1.C. The history of planet Earth

HS-ESS1-5. Evaluate evidence of the past and current movements of continental and oceanic crust and the theory of plate tectonics to explain the ages of crustal rocks.

Overview:

Biointeractive EarthViewer provides an excellent simulation to support student learning of the topic and engagement in arguments from evidence presented by the simulation. In addition to visualization, students can also have access to datasets used to create graphical representation of data. As students search for patterns in this complex dataset, draw their attention to the parallel between their reliance on commonsense reasoning and the need for AI natural interaction models to have this capability of human-like reasoning.

AI'S BIG IDEA #5: SOCIAL IMPACT

In this high school biology lesson students examine datasets representing genetic variations in a specific species to predict future genetic diversity. They discuss ethical implications of using AI to influence genetic variation addressing the concept of AI for a social good.

Lesson: Genetic Engineering and Natural Genetic Variations

5.8

For High School

SEP8. Obtaining, evaluating, and communicating information

Scientists and engineers must be able to communicate clearly and persuasively the ideas and methods they generate. Critiquing and communicating ideas individually and in groups is a critical professional activity.

CC2: Cause and effect

Events have causes, sometimes simple, sometimes multifaceted. Deciphering causal relationships, and the mechanisms by which they are mediated, is a major activity of science and engineering.

• Selective breeding is a process in which humans selectively breed organisms with desirable traits to produce offspring with those same desirable traits.

• Gene editing is a process of making precise changes to the DNA (genetic material) of an organism. It involves the alteration, addition, or deletion of specific nucleotides in the genome to modify the genetic information.

DCI: LS4.B. Natural Selection. LS4.C. Adaptation

HS-LS4-2. Construct an explanation based on evidence that the process of evolution primarily results from four factors: (1) the potential for a species to increase in number, (2) the heritable genetic variation of individuals in a species due to mutation and sexual reproduction, (3) competition for limited resources, and (4) the proliferation of those organisms that are better able to survive and reproduce in the environment.

Overview:

In this lesson provide students with datasets representing genetic variations in a specific species. Students can identify patterns in genetic variation, visualize changes in allele frequencies over generations, and predict potential future genetic diversity. Then, have students discuss how AI might influence genetic variation beyond natural processes:

- AI-augmented **selective breeding** programs
- AI-assisted **gene editing** techniques
- AI prediction of beneficial mutations for specific environments

Engage students in a discussion about the ethical implications of using AI to influence genetic variation, such as potential benefits (e.g., disease resistance, improved crop yields) and possible risks (e.g., reduced genetic diversity, unintended consequences).

REFLECTION QUESTIONS

- Reflect on your current teaching practices. In what ways do you already incorporate elements of scientific inquiry and experimentation that could be further enriched by integrating AI concepts?

- How can you integrate the core AI concepts into your existing science curriculum to enhance students' understanding of scientific inquiry and problem-solving processes?

- Can you think of other ways to effectively integrate AI concepts into your teaching to enhance students' understanding and engagement in science?

INTEGRATING AI CONCEPTS INTO MIDDLE SCHOOL UNIT ON ECOSYSTEMS

Now we are ready to demonstrate how you can use our template (Table 4.1) for Planning AI Literacy Integration to apply the Pedagogical Framework for AI Literacy to design an instructional unit in science. We use the topic of biodiversity taught within the unit about ecosystems in middle school life science for this purpose. At the same time, we want students to learn about features of different types of datasets and how the choice and labeling of **training dataset** shapes the way computers learn from data.

As you recall from Chapter 4, our Planning AI Literacy Integration template (available on our companion website at https://companion.corwin.com/courses/TeachingAILiteracy) is based on the principles of the backward design framework (Wiggins & McTighe, 1998)—in other words, we start instructional planning with the learning goals that embody the knowledge and skills we want our students to acquire in the instructional unit. Because the key elements of the Understanding by Design (UbD) framework—*transfer, understandings, essential questions,* and *performance tasks* (represented in Stages 1 and 2)—are too complex to be fully addressed within a single lesson, we follow recommendations from Association of Supervision and Curriculum Development (ASCD) to complete Stages 1 and 2 within a larger instructional unit. We then use developed key elements to complete Stage 3 for a single lesson within this unit. This decision is based on the fact that the teachers report that "Stages 1 and 2 sharpen their lesson planning, resulting in more purposeful teaching and improved learning" (ASCD, 2012, p. 7). After completing the template, we suggest resources and materials for the lesson.

• **Training dataset** is a subset of data used to train a machine learning model. The training dataset consists of examples, where each example typically includes input features (also known as predictors or independent variables) and their corresponding correct output (also known as labels or dependent variables).

STAGE 1: DESIRED RESULTS

The first stage of the template leads us through the process of establishing curricular priorities in the unit (Table 5.2). To identify the instructional goals we refer to subject-specific standards and AI learning objectives. In this example we use NGSS (NSTA, n.d.) to determine science standards (you might want to use your state standards to identify specific science standards if they differ from NGSS). The disciplinary core idea for our lesson is MS-LS2. Ecosystems: Interactions, Energy, and Dynamics. Specifically, we focus on a unit that is about changes in ecosystems. The science performance expectations that align with the goal of this unit are:

- Analyze and interpret data to provide evidence for the effects of resource availability on organisms and populations of organisms in an ecosystem (MS-LS2-1)
- Construct an explanation that predicts patterns of interactions among organisms across multiple ecosystems (MS-LS2-2)
- Construct an argument supported by empirical evidence that changes to physical or biological components of an ecosystem affect populations (MS-LS2-4)

For AI competencies we use learning objectives defined by the AI4K12 guidelines (AAAI & CSTA, n.d.). Because in this unit we are interested in integrating the AI core concepts of datasets and nature of learning, we are going to select the middle school learning objectives for the AI's Big Idea #3. Learning:

- Demonstrate how training data are labeled when using a machine learning tool (3-A-iv)
- Create a dataset for training a decision tree classifier or predictor and explore the impact that different feature encodings have on the decision tree (3-C-i)
- Examine features and labels of training data to detect potential sources of bias (3-C-iii)

After instructional goals are established, we need to decide:

- How will students *transfer* their science knowledge and understanding of AI core concepts gained from the unit and apply it outside the context of the class?
  - This question focuses on the larger purposes of learning a particular content, for example, what complex real-world tasks students will be able to tackle after mastering this content. In our case, we decided to select two authentic real-world tasks: (1) conservation efforts and preserving biodiversity and (2) exploration of datasets on human impact on student local environment or ecosystem.
- What are the big ideas and enduring *understandings* students will have when they complete the unit?
  - It is helpful to refer to the standards and curriculum guidelines that usually provide teachers with enduring understandings. For our unit we included reference codes for the essential understandings for science and AI concepts, so that you can readily see the overlaps.
- What are *essential questions* that will frame the lesson and that we expect students to answer if they accomplished the unit's goals?

- These are questions that cannot be answered with a brief sentence. The purpose of essential questions is to stimulate thinking, to provoke inquiry, and to inspire more questions including those from the students. At the same time, at the end answers to these questions should lead to stated instructional goals. In the planning template we included possible choices for the essential questions.

TABLE 5.2 ● Stage 1: Desired Results

STAGE 1 DESIRED RESULTS		
INSTRUCTIONAL GOALS	**SUBJECT-SPECIFIC**	**AI LITERACY**
What subject-specific content standards will this unit address?	*Transfer*	
	What kinds of long-term independent accomplishments are desired?	
NGSS Performance expectations:	Students will be able to independently use their learning to advocate for conservation efforts or participate in community projects aimed at preserving biodiversity.	Students will be able to independently use their learning to explore datasets on human activities affecting their local environment (e.g., waste production, energy consumption).
MS-LS2-1: Analyze and interpret data to provide evidence for the effects of resource availability on organisms and populations of organisms in an ecosystem.	*Understandings*	
	What specifically do you want students to understand?	
	What inferences should they make?	
	Students will understand that organisms, and populations of organisms, are dependent on their environmental interactions both with other living things and with nonliving factors. (MS-LS2-1)	In preparation for training a model, training data can be labeled by first defining the classes (the labels) and then adding examples for each class separately. After training, new data can be presented to the model, and it will predict the class, but the data are unlabeled so the model receives no feedback about the correctness of its class predictions. (3-A-iv)
MS-LS2-2: Construct an explanation that predicts patterns of interactions among organisms across multiple ecosystems.	Predatory interactions may reduce the number of organisms or eliminate whole populations of organisms. Mutually beneficial interactions, in contrast, may become so interdependent that each organism requires the other for survival. Although the species involved in these competitive, predatory, and mutually beneficial interactions vary across ecosystems, the patterns of interactions of organisms with their environments, both living and nonliving, are shared. (MS-LS2-2)	Students will understand that the choice of features to include, and the best encoding to use for these features, depends on the particular reasoning problem we are trying to solve. (3-C-i)
MS-LS2-4: Construct an argument supported by empirical evidence that changes to physical or biological components of an ecosystem affect populations.	Ecosystems are dynamic in nature; their characteristics can vary over time. Disruptions to any physical or biological component of an ecosystem can lead to shifts in all its populations. (MS-LS2-4)	Machine learning algorithms require a representative collection of data in order to build an accurate model. Training datasets drawn from historical data may reflect pre-existing human and societal biases. (3-C-iii)

(Continued)

(Continued)

STAGE 1 DESIRED RESULTS		
INSTRUCTIONAL GOALS	**SUBJECT-SPECIFIC**	**AI LITERACY**
What AI competencies will this unit address? **3-A-iv:** Demonstrate how training data are labeled when using a machine learning tool. **3-C-i:** Create a dataset for training a decision tree classifier or predictor and explore the impact that different feature encodings have on the decision tree. **3-C-iii:** Examine features and labels of training data to detect potential sources of bias.	***Essential questions*** What thought-provoking questions will foster inquiry, meaning making, and transfer?	
	How do changes in resource availability shape ecosystems and the organisms within them?	How does the way we represent data influence the decisions made by machine learning models?
	Acquisition What facts and basic concepts should students know and be able to recall? What discrete skills and processes should students be able to use?	
	Students will know • that ecosystems are composed of interconnected physical (abiotic) and biological (biotic) components. • that resource availability directly affects the survival, growth, and reproduction of organisms in an ecosystem. • how to interpret different types of data showing population changes in response to resource fluctuations. • the concept of carrying capacity and how it relates to resource limitations in an ecosystem.	Students will know • that feature labeling is the process of converting data into a format that can be effectively used by ML algorithms. • that different labeling methods can significantly affect the structure and performance of decision trees. • how to create a basic dataset and apply labeling techniques. • that training data used in scientific studies or models can contain biases due to factors such as sampling methods, study design, geographic or habitat preferences in data collection, and researcher biases.
	Students will be skilled at • analyzing and interpreting ecological data presented in various formats such as graphs, tables, and images. • identifying patterns and trends in population data that indicate changes in resource availability. • creating graphs and mathematical models to represent interactions in an ecosystem. • constructing logical arguments that connect specific changes in an ecosystem to observed impacts on populations.	Students will be skilled at • converting raw data into formats suitable for machine learning algorithms. • preparing datasets for use in decision tree models. • applying labeling techniques to different types of data. • evaluating the impact of different labeling methods on decision tree performance. • examining features and labels of training data critically to detect potential sources of bias.

- What are the key knowledge and skills students will *acquire* from the unit?

  - ○ The information that addresses this question could be the facts, concepts, principles, processes, strategies, and methods students should know when they leave the course.

  - ○ The targeted knowledge and skills can refer to "1) the building blocks for the desired understandings, 2) the knowledge and skills stated or implied in the goals, and 3) the "enabling" knowledge and skills needed to perform the complex assessment tasks identified in Stage 2" (Wiggins & McTighe, 1998, p. 57).

STAGE 2: ASSESSMENT EVIDENCE

Now that we've identified desired results, it is time to plan assessments (Table 5.3). At this stage it is important to consider a wide range of assessment methods to ensure that the type of assessment is aligned with the evidence of achieving desired results. The evidence can range from performance tasks that mirror complex real-world issues and challenges, academic open-ended tasks that require critical thinking, to simple content-focused tests and quizzes, and informal checks for understanding.

TIPS

Developing essential questions

- As you develop essential questions, keep in mind that these are broad in scope and should help students to inquire and make sense of the disciplinary core ideas.

- Moreover, essential questions are meant to be explored and revisited over time, not answered by the end of a single class period.

TABLE 5.3 ● Stage 2: Assessment Evidence

STAGE 2 ASSESSMENT EVIDENCE		
EVALUATIVE CRITERIA	**SUBJECT-SPECIFIC**	**AI LITERACY**
What criteria will be used in each assessment to evaluate attainment of the desired results?	***Performance Tasks*** How will students demonstrate their understanding (meaning making and transfer) through complex performance?	
• Interpret and describe the given dataset, and identify key variables and their relationships • Identify relationship between specific changes in the ecosystem, climate change and human	Taking the role of biologists and given an ecological dataset, students analyze changes in a given ecosystem due to climate change and human activities and make predictions about impact of these changes on biodiversity of the ecosystem.	Create a synthetic dataset for training a decision tree classifier to predict ecosystem health based on environmental variables and label them in various formats (numerical, categorical).

(Continued)

(Continued)

STAGE 2 ASSESSMENT EVIDENCE		
EVALUATIVE CRITERIA	**SUBJECT-SPECIFIC**	**AI LITERACY**
activities, and use appropriate statistical methods or visualizations to support findings • Demonstrate logical reasoning in making predictions and provide support for them based on evidence or literature • Demonstrate correct use and consistency of in labeling across the dataset • Includes sufficient details of relevant features to train a classifier		
Regardless of the format of the assessment, what qualities are most important? • Scientific reasoning • Data-handling skills • Connecting climate change, human activities, and biodiversity • Clear communication and critical thinking	**Other Evidence** What other evidence will you collect to determine whether Stage 1 goals were achieved? • Informal checks and observations—during group work and discussions • Semistructured class discussions—related to the topics of the lessons • Student online-reading reflections for the assigned reading materials such as case studies • Concepts maps demonstrating relationships between key elements of ecosystems virtual labs to simulate data collection in the fields • Virtual field trips to observe different ecosystems • Exit tickets in the form of quizzes, for example, given a variety of ecological data students will produce appropriate graphical representation for numerical data and label different types of data • Scientific report and presentation of the completed performance task	

The performance task should directly or indirectly require students to address the essential questions. Thus, we propose that in this unit groups of students take the role of biologists assessing changes in different ecosystems using real ecological data to analyze resource availability due to environmental factors such as climate change and human activities. Based on this analysis, students will produce a scientific report with predictions on how these changes will affect organisms and populations within the ecosystem and present their findings to local community leaders. Simultaneously, students will create a synthetic dataset for training a decision tree classifier to predict ecosystem health based on environmental variables. As students examine various ecological data sources, they will also analyze sampling methods used in studies, whether there is adequate representation of different habitats or geographic regions, and identify any biases introduced by the selection of study sites or species. This will require teachers to design appropriate scoring rubrics that relate specific task requirements to performance goals and define different degrees of understanding and proficiency.

Other types of evidence in this unit could include informal checks and observations, group and class discussions, reading reflections, concepts maps, quizzes, virtual labs and field trips. In a particular lesson that we explain in Stage 3, we focus on student skills to represent the ecological data visually (subject-specific evidence) and develop clear labels for different types of data (AI literacy).

STAGE 3: LEARNING PLAN

Stages 1 and 2 have established our learning goals and assessment criteria. With these in place, we can now focus on planning effective instructional strategies and learning activities that equip students with the resources and knowledge to achieve these goals (Table 5.4). Moreover, clear goals make the design of lesson tasks easier, because we now have a better idea of what we want the students to get out of these tasks.

TABLE 5.4 ● Stage 3: Learning Plan

STAGE 3 LEARNING PLAN		
LESSON STRUCTURE	**SUBJECT-SPECIFIC**	**AI LITERACY**
Does the learning plan reflect Pedagogical Framework for AI Literacy?	***Preassessment*** What preassessments will you use to check students' prior knowledge, preassessment skill levels, and potential misconceptions?	
	In small groups students discuss the following question: What types of data scientists collect when they study ecosystems and biodiversity? Each group shares their thoughts with the class.	
	Summary of Key Learning Events and Instruction Does the learning plan address instructional goals for disciplinary content and AI literacy? Is the plan likely to be engaging and effective for all students?	

(Continued)

(Continued)

STAGE 3 LEARNING PLAN		
LESSON STRUCTURE	**SUBJECT-SPECIFIC**	**AI LITERACY**
Design	At the *Empathize* step: • Video about biodiversity conservation efforts • Whole-class discussion of video • Analysis of case studies on the use of AI in biodiversity conservation At the *Define* step: • Small-group work with assigned ecosystem and corresponding dataset—exploring key variables and defining a problem statement for AI At the *Ideate* step: • Small-group work with assigned ecosystem and corresponding dataset—identifying types of data and brainstorming approaches to data analysis	
Create	At the *Prototype* step: • Small-group work with assigned ecosystem and corresponding dataset—creating initial training datasets At the *Test* step: • Gallery walk presentations of training datasets for peer feedback	
Reflect	Group discussions—on learning and on potential bias in data selection for AI training dataset	

As we mentioned earlier, here we focus on a single lesson about biodiversity within the instructional unit on ecosystems. As suggested by the UbD framework (Wiggins & McTighe, 1998) the lesson will start with a preassessment to see what our students already know about biodiversity and to identify any misconceptions they might have. We also want to see what students know about the AI core concept of datasets. We suggest a brief discussion about the types of data that scientists collect when they study ecosystems and biodiversity. You will be looking for students' knowledge of biodiversity, as well as to see whether they understand that the data can be numerical, categorical, and descriptive.

Our lesson will be structured as a DCR process according to the Pedagogical Framework for AI literacy (see Chapter 2). This also means that we plan the key learning activities that integrate disciplinary and AI literacy instructional goals, which is reflected in the fact that the template no longer separates these two aspects of the lesson.

During the *empathize* step of the design component (see p. xx), we want students to understand the challenges in conserving biodiversity in different ecosystems and learn how AI can help in these efforts by analyzing large datasets and making predictions. You can show students a video about conservation efforts followed by a whole-class discussion of challenges in preserving ecosystems and conserving biodiversity. During the discussion of the video, point students' attention to different types of data scientists collect to monitor biodiversity in the ecosystem. Introduce specific case studies where AI has been used in conservation efforts so students can learn how scientists can use AI machine learning to analyze large datasets and make predictions.

After this discussion, divide students into small groups and assign each group a different ecosystem and corresponding datasets. In these groups students identify key variables and relationships between specific changes in the ecosystem, climate change and human activities, and develop a clear definition of the problem that AI can solve, such as identifying trends in biodiversity data (*define* step). After the problem is defined, students brainstorm approaches for data selection, representation, and analysis necessary for development of their training datasets. This is also the time when students identify different types of data in their datasets, such as numerical data, images, texts, etc. (*ideate* step). They select and preprocess biodiversity data to create their initial dataset that could be used to train an AI model (*prototype* step). As a conclusion of this activity, each group shares their training datasets. This can be done as a **gallery walk**. Have each group present their ideas on a Post-It wall pad and post them around the classroom or write them on white boards. Give each student a regular Post-It notes or scrap paper and let them go around to review each other's work and leave comments to each other (*test* step). Leave some time at the end of the class for each group to reflect on their learning process, the challenges they faced, and the solutions they developed. Students should also *reflect* on how their choices of data for the training dataset might affect AI performance and why it is important to select a wide range of diverse data to allow for AI to make accurate decisions.

• **Gallery walk** is a teaching strategy in which students move around as they explore a range of documents, images, or student work displayed around the classroom.

Datasets

- Database of Global Data Sources for Biodiversity Conservation Monitoring (https://datasources. speciesmonitoring.org/)—access to data inventory of global databases of potential use in monitoring biodiversity states, pressures, and conservation responses at multiple levels.

- World Bank Data Catalog (https://qrs.ly/eqgtm5b)—public searchable datasets, with more than 7,000 datasets.
- Earth Engine Data Catalog (https://qrs.ly/zegh1hf)—public data archive of historical images and scientific datasets.

AI resources

- AI for Good (https://aiforgood.itu.int/)—resources to learn about practical applications of AI to advance the United Nations Sustainable Development Goals and scale those solutions for global impact.
- Biodiversity and AI (https://qrs.ly/bkgh1hh)—an article about AI potential in solving challenges in conserving biodiversity.
- AI in conservation (https://qrs.ly/jngh1hj)—Historical review and current trends in using AI for conservation

Organizations that have various resources for ecosystems and biodiversity

- Center for Biological Diversity (https://www.biologicaldiversity.org/)
- Nature and Culture International (https://www.natureandculture.org/)
- PBS Learning Media (https://www.pbslearningmedia.org/)

Teaching materials

- Types of ecosystems: qrs.ly/uygtm5l, qrs.ly/pzgh1hl
- Ecosystem lesson plan (qrs.ly/xngh1i9)—includes videos and interactive materials
- Ecosystem simulator (https://ecosimulator.netlify.app/)—virtual lab to observe changes in species populations, including effect of human intervention.
- Ecology lab (https://qrs.ly/ldgh1hn)—virtual lab related to food web
- CK-12 Ecosystems (https://qrs.ly/5egh1hr/)—various resources for teaching and learning the topic, including video, assessment
- Populations in balance unit plan (https://serpmedia.org/scigen/l1.html)—various teacher and student materials

Chapter Summary

Integrating AI literacy into science education is becoming not just beneficial but also essential. In this chapter we provided some strategies for teachers on how to incorporate Five Big Ideas in AI into standards-based science curricula across various disciplines and grade levels.

By integrating AI literacy into science education, we are equipping students with the knowledge and critical thinking skills they need to engage with and shape the future of science in an increasingly AI-driven world. By drawing parallels between human cognition and AI processes, we hope that we've demonstrated that teaching AI literacy doesn't always require the use of AI-powered tools. Instead, it can be achieved through thoughtful analogies, discussions, and critical thinking exercises that build upon fundamental scientific principles.

Wrap-Up Questions

- What are the potential benefits and challenges of integrating AI literacy into science education? How might these challenges be addressed in your classroom?

- How can connections between the Five Big Ideas in AI (perception, representation and reasoning, learning, natural interaction, and societal impact) and the NGSS science and engineering practices deepen students' understanding of AI concepts and scientific principles?

- Reflect on your own comfort level and familiarity with AI concepts. What steps could you take to further develop your own AI literacy and effectively teach these concepts to your students?

CHAPTER 6

AI Literacy in Mathematics Education

In this chapter we'll

- Discuss connections between Five Big Ideas in AI and Common Core State Standards for Mathematics

- Suggest strategies for integrating AI literacy across different grade bands and mathematics disciplines

- Demonstrate the application of the Pedagogical Framework for AI Literacy for designing a high school algebra lesson that integrates AI's concepts of representation and reasoning.

There is a natural connection between mathematics and Five Big Ideas in AI, which provides us with many opportunities to effectively integrate AI's concepts into mathematics teaching and learning. Mathematics serves as the language through which AI concepts are formulated, analyzed, and implemented. Concepts from linear algebra, calculus, probability theory, and statistics form the foundation of AI's algorithms. Vectors and matrices are used to represent AI features and parameters, whereas operations such as matrix multiplication, differentiation, and integration enable computations that drive machine learning (ML) and decision-making processes.

Much as we did in the Chapter 5, we first explore connections between the Five Big Ideas in AI and Common Core State Standards (CCSS) for Mathematics (MPs). We then illustrate these connections for each big idea using engaging and practical lesson ideas for K–12 mathematics topics. We conclude the chapter with an instructional plan for integrating AI concepts of representation and reasoning into an algebra unit about the structure of algebraic expressions.

MATHEMATICS STANDARDS AND FIVE BIG IDEAS IN AI

The development of the CCSS for Mathematics (National Governors Association Center for Best Practices & Council of Chief State School Officers, 2010) was a state-led effort to define the learning goals for what students should know and be able to do at each grade level. The standards were informed by the best state standards already in existence, the experience of teachers and content experts, and the feedback from the public, and were launched in the United States in 2009. As of 2020, 41 states, Washington, D.C., and four territories have adopted the CCSS for Mathematics. The content standards cover topics such as conceptual understanding, organizing principles, and mathematical understanding. The standards for mathematical practices (MPs) describe the expertise that students should develop, such as reasoning abstractly, constructing arguments, and using tools strategically.

• Procedural fluency is the ability to perform procedures flexibly, accurately, efficiently, and appropriately

• Productive disposition is a habitual tendency to view mathematics as sensible, useful, and worthwhile, along with a belief in one's diligence and efficacy

In this section we focus on the standards for MPs. These practices are based on critical "processes and proficiencies" that have been identified by the National Council of Teachers of Mathematics (NCTM) and the National Research Council (NRC) long before the MPs were developed. Specifically, the MPs include NCTM process standards such as problem solving, reasoning and proof, communication, representation, and connections (NCTM, 2000). They also encompass the strands of mathematical proficiency defined by the NRC report such as adaptive reasoning, strategic competence, conceptual understanding, **procedural fluency**, and **productive disposition** (NRC, 2001).

Connecting CCSS MPs with AI literacy concepts will enrich teaching and learning experiences. Our lesson examples illustrate these connections by aligning each of the Five Big Ideas in AI with specific MPs (Table 6.1).

These selected connections between MPs and Five Big Ideas in AI demonstrate how AI literacy can be integrated into mathematics classrooms as a tool to deepen students' mathematical understanding and problem-solving skills. With these connections in mind, we can now explore strategies for integrating AI literacy to not only support mathematics standards, but also truly enrich student mathematics learning experiences.

TABLE 6.1 ● Examples of Illustrated Connections Between Standards for Mathematics and Five Big Ideas in AI

BIG IDEAS IN AI	AI'S CORE CONCEPTS	MPS	CONNECTIONS BETWEEN BIG IDEAS AND MPS	LESSON EXAMPLES
BI1. Perception	Sensing Processing Domain knowledge	MP4. Model with mathematics.	In AI, perception involves translating real-world inputs into mathematical models for algorithmic processing. For instance, in computer vision, images are represented as matrices of pixels, enabling mathematical operations to extract features and identify patterns. This shows how mathematical modeling forms the basis for machines to perceive and interpret their surroundings.	6.1. Statistics in Digital Photography (Middle school) (p. 116)
BI2. Representation and reasoning	Representation Reasoning	MP2. Reason abstractly and quantitatively.	In AI, abstract concepts are represented quantitatively through data structures such as decision trees, graphs, or probabilistic models. For instance, in the weather prediction problem, students abstract the concept of conditional probability, then quantitatively apply it to calculate specific outcome probabilities. This process mirrors the mathematical practice of abstracting real-world scenarios into mathematical models and then using quantitative reasoning to make decisions or predictions.	Lesson 6.2. Probability Trees and Weather Prediction (High school algebra / precalculus) (p. 118)
		MP7. Look for and make use of structure.	In AI, the ability to represent knowledge efficiently and reason effectively relies heavily on identifying and leveraging underlying structures in data and problems. For instance, decision trees in AI embody a hierarchical structure that mirrors how humans might break down complex decisions into simpler, structured steps. Similarly, knowledge graphs in AI represent information as interconnected nodes, showcasing the relational structure of data. When students engage in MP7, they develop skills in recognizing these kinds of structures, which highlights how the mathematical skill of discerning structure directly informs the design and functionality of AI reasoning systems.	Lesson 6.3. Number Patterns (Elementary school) (p. 120)

(Continued)

BIG IDEAS IN AI	AI'S CORE CONCEPTS	MPS	CONNECTIONS BETWEEN BIG IDEAS AND MPS	LESSON EXAMPLES
BI3. Learning	Nature of learning Datasets	MP1. Make sense of problems and persevere in solving them.	Just as students analyze data, look for patterns, and adjust their approach based on new information, ML algorithms process large datasets to identify trends and make predictions. In a high school math class, students could explore this parallel by working on projects that involve collecting and analyzing data, then comparing their methods to simple ML models. This could include using technology to implement regression analyses or basic programming to develop classification algorithms, helping students understand both the mathematical foundations of these techniques and their real-world applications in AI.	Lesson 6.4. Line of Best Fit (High school algebra) (p. 122)
	Neural networks	MP8. Look for and express regularity in repeated reasoning.	In mathematical practice, students look for repeating patterns or structures in mathematical problems, using these observations to develop problem solutions. Similarly, in ML, algorithms analyze large datasets to identify recurring patterns and use these to make predictions or decisions. Both processes involve recognizing regularities in data or problem structures, generalizing from these observations, and applying the learned patterns to new situations. This parallel highlights how the cognitive processes students develop in mathematics directly relate to the computational methods used in AI, demonstrating the deep connection between human mathematical thinking and ML algorithms.	Lesson 6.5 Geometric Transformations and Tessellations (Middle school) (p. 124)
BI4. Natural interaction	Natural language Commonsense reasoning	MP3. Construct viable arguments and critique the reasoning of others.	The mathematical practice of constructing viable arguments and critiquing others' reasoning and the AI concepts of natural language and commonsense reasoning address the same goal of engaging in clear, logical communication and understanding and evaluating different perspectives. Just as students learn to articulate their mathematical thinking and assess the validity of their peers' arguments, AI systems designed for natural interaction must process and respond to human language, interpreting the logic and intent behind statements.	Lesson 6.6. Properties of Addition and Subtraction: True or False (Elementary school) (p. 127)

BIG IDEAS IN AI	AI'S CORE CONCEPTS	MPS	CONNECTIONS BETWEEN BIG IDEAS AND MPS	LESSON EXAMPLES
BI5. Societal impact	AI and the economy AI and culture AI for social good	MP5. Use appropriate tools strategically.	This practice involves choosing the right mathematical models, algorithms, and computational tools to solve mathematical problems. For example, selecting predictive models in healthcare to optimize treatment plans or in environmental science to predict climate change impacts requires strategic use of mathematical tools.	Lesson 6.7. Comparing Linear, Quadratic, and Exponential Models with Technology (High school algebra/precalculus) (p. 129)
	Ethical AI AI for social good	MP6. Attend to precision.	In math, we learn to be precise with our words, symbols, and calculations. This precision helps us communicate clearly and solve problems accurately. The precision we practice in math—using clear definitions, accurate calculations, and careful explanations—is crucial when developing and using AI in society. Just as math errors can lead to wrong answers, imprecise AI can cause unintended harm. By applying mathematical precision to AI, we can better address ethical concerns, such as fairness and bias. This careful approach helps ensure AI benefits everyone equally. Whether in math class or when creating AI systems, precision and ethical consideration go hand in hand, leading to more responsible and beneficial outcomes for society.	Lesson 6.8. AI for Social Good: Proportional Reasoning in Action (Middle school) (p. 131)

LESSON SUGGESTIONS

BIG IDEA #1: PERCEPTION

In this middle school lesson, students analyze a dataset of brightness values from a digital grayscale photograph, calculating measures of center and variability. They interpret these statistics to understand the image's overall brightness and contrast, mirroring how AI perceives and processes visual data.

6.1 Lesson: Statistics in Digital Photography

For Middle School

MP4. Model with mathematics.

Students who are mathematically proficient can apply the mathematics they know to solve problems arising in everyday life, society, and the workplace. Students who are mathematically proficient who can apply what they know are comfortable making assumptions and approximations to simplify a complicated situation, realizing that these may need revision later. They are able to identify important quantities in a practical situation and map their relationships using such tools as diagrams, two-way tables, graphs, flowcharts, and formulas. They can analyze those relationships mathematically to draw conclusions. They routinely interpret their mathematical results in the context of the situation and reflect on whether the results make sense, possibly improving the model if it has not served its purpose.

Grade 6: Statistics and Probability

6.SP.B. Summarize and describe distributions.

6.SP.B.5. Summarize numerical data sets in relation to their context.

Overview:

In this activity, students will work with a simple grayscale image and corresponding image data to understand how computers "see" images through numerical representation. Provide students with a simple pixelated image and a corresponding 5 × 5 grid. Each individual pixel in this 5 × 5 grid would have a grayscale value ranging from 0 to 255 (0 being *black*, 255 being *white*) (Figure 6.1). Explain that this grid is how a computer represents a simple grayscale image.

FIGURE 6.1 ● Digital (a) and Numerical (b) Representations of a Photograph of Stairs (c)

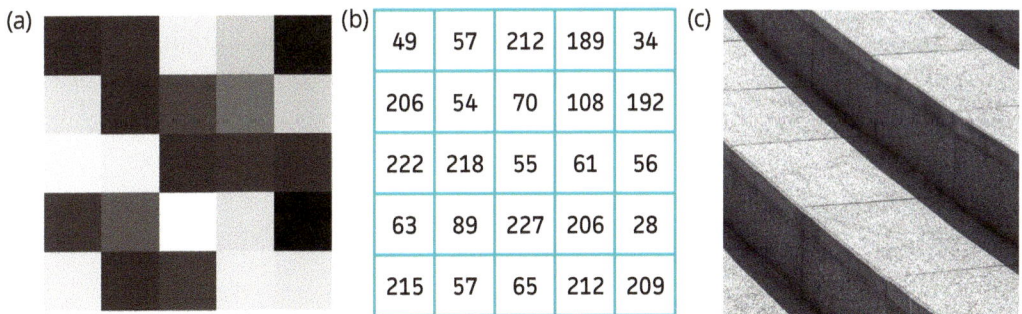

(a)

(b)

49	57	212	189	34
206	54	70	108	192
222	218	55	61	56
63	89	227	206	28
215	57	65	212	209

(c)

Source: Digital representation of stairs created with ChatGPT 4.0; photo of stairs image by istock.com/eugenesergeev

To analyze data students will

● Calculate the mean grayscale value of the entire image
● Find the median value
● Identify the mode (most common shade)
● Determine the range of values

Introduce students to the concept of thresholding in image processing to show how computers can make binary decisions based on continuous data, which is a fundamental concept in many AI algorithms. Students will choose a threshold value based on their analysis and convert their grayscale image to a binary image (black and white only) based on this threshold. You may want to suggest the students to

- Experiment with different thresholds and observe how it affects the resulting binary image.
- Consider the mean or median of their image data as potential thresholds.
- Think how the choice of threshold might depend on the goal of the image analysis (e.g., detecting light objects on a dark background or vice versa) and how it affects the system's perception of data.

Conclude the lesson with the discussion of how basic statistics relates to how a computer might "perceive" light and dark areas in an image.

BIG IDEA #2:
REPRESENTATION AND REASONING

In this high school algebra/precalculus lesson, students will explore how AI systems represent and reason about uncertain situations (like weather prediction) using probability trees, connecting the concepts of independence and conditional probability to quantitative decision making in AI.

6.2

Lesson: Probability Trees and Weather Prediction

For High School

MP2. Reason abstractly and quantitatively.

Students who are mathematically proficient make sense of quantities and their relationships in problem situations. They bring two complementary abilities to bear on problems involving quantitative relationships: the ability to decontextualize—to abstract a given situation and represent it symbolically and manipulate the representing symbols as if they have a life of their own, without necessarily attending to their referents—and the ability to contextualize, to pause as needed during the manipulation process to probe into the referents for the symbols involved.

Statistics and Probability: Conditional Probability & the Rules of Probability

HSS-C.P.A. Understand independence and conditional probability and use them to interpret data.

HSS-C.P.A.2. Understand that two events A and B are independent if the probability of A and B occurring together is the product of their probabilities, and use this characterization to determine if they are independent.

Overview:

Here is an example of a problem that you can give to the students:

An AI system is designed to predict whether it will rain tomorrow based on two factors: current cloudiness and humidity level. The system has the following information:

1. There's a 70% chance of significant cloudiness tomorrow.
2. If there's significant cloudiness, there's a 60% chance of high humidity.
3. If there's high humidity, there's an 80% chance of rain.

The AI needs to determine the probability of rain tomorrow based on this information, assuming there are two possible outcomes: it rains tomorrow or it doesn't rain tomorrow.

Recommendations:

- You can introduce this scenario at the beginning of the unit on independence and conditional probability, and use that as a jump-starting point for this topic, following the **problem-based learning (PBL)** approach.

- Alternatively, you can introduce the problem after students learned about independence and conditional probability as an application or assessment.

- After students solve the problem, discuss with them that this is an example of how AI systems represent knowledge and make decisions based on probabilistic information.

Solution steps:

1. Create a **probability tree**
2. Calculate probabilities for each path
3. Calculate the total probability of rain

• Problem-based learning (PBL) is a student-centered approach in which students learn about a subject by working in groups to solve an open-ended problem. This problem is what drives the motivation and the learning.

• Probability tree also known as tree diagram or decision tree is a tool that is used to give a visual representation of the probabilities as well as the outcomes of an event. A probability tree diagram consists of two parts—nodes and branches. A node is used to represent an event. A branch is used to denote the connection between an event and its outcome.

In this elementary school lesson, students will explore the number patterns and structures, relating this to how AI systems might recognize and use patterns in data.

Lesson: Number Patterns

6.3

MP7. Look for and make use of structure.

Students who are mathematically proficient look closely to discern a pattern or structure. Young students, for example, might notice that three and seven more is the same amount as seven and three more, or they may sort a collection of shapes according to how many sides the shapes have. Later, students will see 7 × 8 equals the well-remembered 7 × 5 + 7 × 3, in preparation for learning about the distributive property.

Grade 3: Operations & Algebraic Thinking

3.OA.D. Solve problems involving the four operations, and identify and explain patterns in arithmetic.

3.OA.D.9. Identify arithmetic patterns (including patterns in the addition table or multiplication table), and explain them using properties of operations.

Overview:

Start the activity by giving students several simple arithmetic sequences to explore and identify the rules behind each pattern, for example:

3, 6, 9, 12, . . . (multiples of 3)

2, 4, 8, 16, . . . (powers of 2)

Ask students to explain these patterns using properties of operations. Introduce the concept of "rule finding" as something humans and computers can do. Explain that AI systems look for patterns in large amounts of data.

You can then challenge students to look at the structures within numbers in more complex sequences, such as 1, 2, 4, 7, 11, 16, ... Let students make predictions of the next numbers in sequences, discussing their reasoning and strategies. Guide students to notice relationships, such as the growing differences between consecutive numbers. Discuss how recognizing this underlying structure helps predict future numbers in the sequence.

Suggested Extensions and AI Connections:

1. Use a 100 chart and have students shade the numbers in the sequence to observe visual patterns in arithmetic sequences. This approach creates visual structures that can help students to develop

deeper understanding of patterns and also make connections to AI representation and reasoning as following:

- The shaded patterns on the 100 chart can be seen as "features" of the number sequence. In AI, feature extraction is a crucial step where the system identifies key characteristics of the data. Students can discuss what features (like diagonals, steps, or jumps) they see in their shaded patterns.

- The 100 chart itself is a form of data representation, turning abstract number sequences into a structured, visual format. This is similar to how AI systems might represent complex data in structured ways to make it easier to process and analyze.

- After shading part of a sequence, students could predict how the pattern would continue beyond the 100 chart. This is similar to how AI systems use recognized patterns to make predictions.

- By observing the shaded patterns, students can infer the rules behind the sequences. This process is similar to how ML algorithms might infer rules or patterns from training data.

- The grid structure of the 100 chart allows for analysis of how patterns relate to tens and ones, showcasing how underlying mathematical structures can be revealed through appropriate representation—a crucial aspect of AI reasoning.

2. Introduce simple visual patterns (like growing arrangements of dots or shapes, see examples on Figure 6.2) and ask students to describe the structure they see.

- Students can observe and describe how a pattern grows from one step to the next, such as adding one more square or triangle each

FIGURE 6.2 ● Sample Visual Patterns for Structure Activity (created by the authors using GeoGebra, geogebra.org)

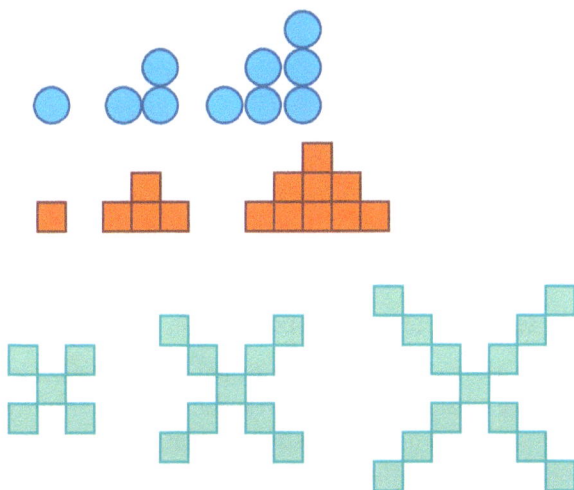

Source: Created with GeoGebra®, by Irina Lyublinskaya. GeoGebra® is a registered trademark of GeoGebra GmbH.

time. This idea of sequential patterns is fundamental to how AI systems learn to predict what comes next in a series.

- Students count the objects in each step of the pattern, discovering skip counting. This relates to how AI systems can be taught to recognize numerical patterns in data.

- Students identify and name the shapes used in the growing pattern, which mirrors basic shape recognition in computer vision, introducing the concept that computers can be taught to identify shapes just like students are learning to do.

Throughout the activity, students draw parallels to how computers, like the students, can be taught to recognize patterns in various types of data. This exploration not only reinforces the students' understanding of arithmetic patterns but also introduces them to AI's core concepts of representation and reasoning.

BIG IDEA #3: LEARNING

In this high school algebra lesson, students predict a person's shoe size based on their height. They collect and analyze height–shoe size data, make sense of the problem, plan solution pathways, and persevere through challenges in finding a line of best fit. By comparing their manual approach to calculator-generated linear regression, students experience how humans and machines can learn from data to make predictions.

6.4 Lesson: Line of Best Fit

For High School

MP1. Make sense of problems and persevere in solving them.

Students who are mathematically proficient start by explaining to themselves the meaning of a problem and looking for entry points to its solution. They analyze givens, constraints, relationships, and goals. They make conjectures about the form and meaning of the solution and plan a solution pathway rather than simply jumping into a solution attempt. They consider analogous problems and try special cases and simpler forms of the original problem to gain insight into its solution. They monitor and evaluate their progress and change course if necessary. Older students might, depending on the context of the problem, transform algebraic expressions or change the viewing window on their graphing calculator to get the information they need. Students who are mathematically proficient can explain correspondences between equations, verbal descriptions, tables, and graphs or draw diagrams of important features and relationships, graph data, and search for regularity or trends. Students who are mathematically proficient check their answers to problems using a different method and continually ask themselves, "Does this make sense?" They can understand the approaches of others to solving complex problems and identify correspondences between different approaches.

Statistics and Probability: Interpreting Categorical & Quantitative Data

HSS-ID.B. Summarize, represent, and interpret data on two categorical and quantitative variables.

HSS-ID.B.6. Represent data on two quantitative variables on a scatter plot and describe how the variables are related.

Overview:

For this lesson we suggest using measuring tapes and graphing calculators. Here is a possible outline for this lesson:

1. Data collection: In small groups students measure and record the height and shoe size of every person in their group. They then combine all class data in a single dataset.
2. Initial analysis: Students create a scatter plot of the data and discuss any visible patterns or relationships.
3. Manual prediction: Students use the built-in manual data-fit option of the graphing calculator to estimate the line of best fit and use it to make predictions for given heights.
4. Linear regression: Students use built-in linear regression of the graphing calculator to find the line of best fit and use it to make predictions for given heights.
5. Comparison and reflection: Students compare their manual predictions with the calculator-generated line and discuss accuracy and efficiency.
6. AI connections: Discuss how this relates to ML in broader contexts. If time allows, introduce the concept of training and test data sets.

DISCUSSION QUESTIONS

- In ML, we often split data into training and testing sets. How could we apply this concept to our height–shoe size data? What benefits might this approach offer in evaluating our model's performance?

(Continued)

(Continued)

- Besides height, what additional features could we create or collect to potentially improve our shoe-size prediction model? How might an AI system automatically discover useful features?

- AI systems often require large amounts of diverse data to make accurate predictions. How might the limitations of our classroom dataset affect our model's ability to generalize?

These questions incorporate AI terminology and concepts, encouraging students to draw parallels between their classroom activity and AI's core concepts of datasets and nature of learning.

In this middle school lesson, students apply their understanding of geometric transformations to explore geometric tessellations, identify patterns, and relate this to how AI systems are trained and learn to generate similar visual patterns.

Lesson: Geometric Transformations and Tessellations

6.5

For Middle School

MP8. Look for and express regularity in repeated reasoning.

Students who are mathematically proficient notice if calculations are repeated and look for general methods and for shortcuts. By paying attention to the calculation of slope as they repeatedly check whether points are on the line through (1, 2) with slope 3, middle school students might abstract the equation $(y - 2)/(x - 1) = 3$. As they work to solve a problem, students who are mathematically proficient maintain oversight of the process, while attending to the details. They continually evaluate the reasonableness of their intermediate results.

Grade 8: Geometry

8.G.A. Understand congruence and similarity using physical models, transparencies, or geometry software.

8.G.A.2. Understand that a two-dimensional figure is congruent to another if the second can be obtained from the first by a sequence of rotations, reflections, and translations; given two congruent figures, describe a sequence that exhibits the congruence between them.

Overview:

Provide students with examples of tessellations in architecture and in arts. Let students explore properties of tessellations and identify different geometric transformations in tessellations created using basic geometric shapes. Discuss how AI might "see" these patterns:

- Identifying basic shapes
- Recognizing repetition and orientation
- Breaking down images into recognizable components.

Show students incomplete tessellation patterns and let them complete the patterns, discussing their reasoning. Draw a parallel between their process of completing the patterns and AI pattern recognition.

Have students create a training dataset of tessellations for AI. Students can create five to seven simple tessellation patterns and list key characteristics of each pattern: shape(s) and transformations used (rotation, reflection, translation). Explain how these characteristics are similar to features AI might extract from images.

To simulate how AI learns from the training dataset, have student groups exchange their datasets. Each group now acts as an "AI model," analyzing the new dataset to generate two to three new tessellation patterns based on their analysis. Discuss how this simulates AI learning from data and generating new content.

DISCUSSION QUESTIONS

- How did analyzing multiple examples help in creating new patterns?
- How might real AI systems learn and generate tessellations?
- What are the similarities and differences between human and AI pattern recognition?

RESOURCES

GeoGebra book: *Exploring Tessellations* (qrs.ly/8dgtm5w) to explore tessellations created by basic geometric shapes, for example, square (Figure 6.3a), equilateral triangle (Figure 6.3b), regular hexagon (Figure 6.3c), kite (Fgure 6.3d), and to create new patterns.

(Continued)

FIGURE 6.3 ● Exploring Tessellations with GeoGebra

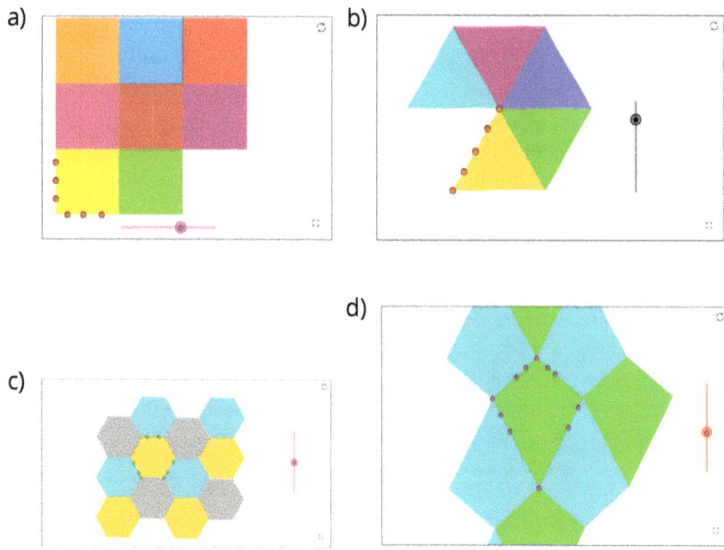

a)

b)

c)

d)

Credit: Created with GeoGebra®, by Steve Phelps. GeoGebra® is a registered trademark of GeoGebra GmbH.

By simulating AI processes, students gain insight into how machines learn patterns, simultaneously deepening their understanding of the geometric transformations in tessellations. This approach provides dddA   a rich, interdisciplinary learning experience that connects traditional geometry with AI concepts.

BIG IDEA #4: NATURAL INTERACTION

In this elementary school lesson, students explore properties of operations by creating and identifying true and false statements. They then train and test AI to recognize these properties, reinforcing their own understanding in the process.

Lesson: Properties of Operations

True or False

MP3. Construct viable arguments and critique the reasoning of others.

Students who are mathematically proficient understand and use stated assumptions, definitions, and previously established results in constructing arguments. They make conjectures and build a logical progression of statements to explore the truth of their conjectures. They are able to analyze situations by breaking them into cases and can recognize and use counterexamples. They justify their conclusions, communicate them to others, and respond to the arguments of others. They reason inductively about data, making plausible arguments that take into account the context from which the data arose. Students who are mathematically proficient are also able to compare the effectiveness of two plausible arguments, distinguish correct logic or reasoning from that which is flawed, and—if there is a flaw in an argument—explain what it is. Elementary students can construct arguments using concrete referents such as objects, drawings, diagrams, and actions. Such arguments can make sense and be correct, even though they are not generalized or made formal until later grades. Students at all grades can listen or read the arguments of others, decide whether they make sense, and ask useful questions to clarify or improve the arguments.

Grade 3: Operations & Algebraic Thinking

3.OA.B. Understand properties of multiplication and the relationship between multiplication and division.

3.OA.B.5. Apply properties of operations as strategies to multiply and divide.

Overview:

The lesson begins with students exploring properties of multiplication through hands-on activities and discussions. They discover how changing the order of factors doesn't affect the product (*commutative property*), how grouping factors in different ways leads to the same result (*associative property*), and how multiplying a number by a sum is equivalent to multiplying by each addend and then adding the products (*distributive property*). As they learn these concepts, students individually or in pairs develop verbal statements about multiplication, clearly labeling them as true or false. In the activity that follows, these verbal statements become a training dataset for AI to understand and apply the commutative, associative, and distributive properties of multiplication and to make decisions about the truth of mathematical statements. The lesson concludes with discussion that helps students to reflect on their learning process and how the AI context might have influenced their understanding, to think critically about mathematical communication and the precision required in both human and AI learning contexts, and to connect their experience to broader AI concepts and their own learning processes.

AI-related activity

We suggest two versions of this activity based on availability of resources:

1. Low-tech—The AI simulation process

   - Students take turns being the "AI" and the "trainer."

   - Trainer presents statements, AI decides if they're true or false.

   - Groups analyze their "AI's" performance to identify patterns in correct and incorrect responses.

   - Based on their analysis, groups create new rules to help their "AI" make better decisions and test the refined "AI" with new statements.

2. High-tech—The use of Machine Learning for Kids (https://qrs.ly/o7gh10y)—step-by-step instructions are available on our companion website at https://companion.corwin.com/courses/TeachingAILiteracy

   - Students create a new project in Machine Learning for Kids.

   - Students set up a text classification model with "true" and "false" labels.

   - Students use their true and false statements as training examples.

   - Students use the "Test" feature to see how well the model classifies new statements.

   - Based on test results, students add more training examples to improve accuracy, retest and discuss improvements.

Discussion Questions for Students

- How did your understanding of multiplication properties change after working with them in this AI-related activity?

- What was the most challenging part of creating true-and-false statements about multiplication? How do you think this relates to teaching math to others or to an AI?

- Based on our activity, how do you think AI systems learn and improve? Can you draw any parallels with how you learn math?

- Can you think of any real-world situations where an AI might need to understand multiplication properties? How might this be useful?

TIPS

Making decisions about number of examples to train AI

- Begin with a small dataset, as few as five to ten true-and-false statements each. This helps avoid overwhelming children and allows them to analyze limitations of ML with small training dataset.

- As students gain experience, gradually increase the number of examples. In this activity twenty-five to thirty true-and-false statements each is sufficient for the ML to be trained well.

- You can have students develop four to five true statements in small groups and then combine groups to get a larger training set.

- Emphasize the importance of high-quality data over a massive dataset. Ensure that the statements are clear and representative of the problem.

This lesson helps students reinforce and evaluate their understanding of properties of multiplication. At the same time, they also learn that natural language processing (NLP) is how computers understand and process human language, specifically, the AI is learning to "understand" mathematical statements written in everyday language, which is a core NLP task.

BIG IDEA #5: SOCIAL IMPACT

In this high school algebra/precalculus lesson, students will use technology to construct, compare, and analyze linear, quadratic, and exponential functions. They will apply their understanding of these functions to discuss the role of AI in model selection, analysis, and its broader societal implications.

Lesson: Comparing Linear, Quadratic, and Exponential Models With Technology

6.7

For High School

MP5. Use appropriate tools strategically.

Students who are mathematically proficient consider the available tools when solving a mathematical problem. These tools might include pencil and paper, concrete models, a ruler, a protractor, a calculator, a spreadsheet, a computer algebra system, a statistical package, or a dynamic geometry software. Students who are proficient are sufficiently familiar with tools appropriate for their grade or course to make sound decisions about when each of these tools might be helpful, recognizing the insight to be gained and their limitations. For example, high school students who are mathematically proficient analyze graphs of functions and solutions generated using a graphing calculator. They detect possible errors by strategically using estimation and other mathematical knowledge. When making mathematical models, they know that technology can enable them to visualize the results of varying assumptions, explore consequences, and compare predictions with data. Students who are mathematically proficient at various grade levels are able to identify relevant external mathematical resources, such as digital content located on a website, and use them to pose or solve problems. They are able to use technological tools to explore and deepen their understanding of concepts.

Functions: Linear, Quadratic, & Exponential Models

HSF-LE.A. Construct and compare linear, quadratic, and exponential models and solve problems.

HSF-LE.A.1. Distinguish between situations that can be modeled with linear functions and with exponential functions.

Overview:

For this lesson we suggest that you provide students with three datasets, one for each function type. We also recommend that the datasets are related to various societal issues, for example, income by education level, health risk factors by age, spread of viral content over time, and so on.

Without telling students which model is the best fit for each dataset, let students use graphing calculators, online tools, or spreadsheet software to plot data and fit models. For each dataset, ask students to compare and evaluate the fit of each model and the predictive power of each model within a specific context.

After students share their models and analysis, introduce an AI-powered data analysis tool (e.g., Tableau or GenAI) and demonstrate how AI can automatically select the best-fit model. Let students compare AI results with their results. The discussion could be guided by the following questions:

- How might AI-driven predictions affect decision making in societal issues?
- What are the potential benefits and risks of relying on AI predictions?
- What is the importance of understanding the underlying mathematics when using AI tools?
- What are potential biases in AI models and their real-world consequences?

RESOURCES

- World Inequality Database (https://wid.world/) provides open access to the most extensive available database on the historical evolution of the world distribution of income and wealth, within countries and between countries.

- Global Health Data Exchange (https://ghdx.healthdata.org/) provides comprehensive catalog of surveys, censuses, vital statistics, and other health-related data.

- Stanford Large Network Dataset Collection (https://snap.stanford.edu/data/) includes various datasets from multiple social media platforms for network analysis.

Although the lesson focuses on constructing and comparing linear, quadratic, and exponential models, this mathematical content is framed within the larger context of AI's growing role in data analysis and its societal implications.

The next lesson emphasizes the importance of mathematics precision in AI applications that affect communities. In this middle school lesson, students use proportional reasoning to analyze and optimize an AI-based system in a social context.

Lesson: AI for Social Good

Proportional Reasoning in Action

6.8

For Middle School

MP6. Attend to precision.

Students who are mathematically proficient try to communicate precisely to others. They try to use clear definitions in discussion with others and in their own reasoning. They state the meaning of the symbols they choose, including using the equal sign consistently and appropriately. They are careful about specifying units of measure and labeling axes to clarify the correspondence with quantities in a problem. They calculate accurately and efficiently, express numerical answers with a degree of precision appropriate for the problem context. In the elementary grades, students give carefully formulated explanations to each other. By the time they reach high school they have learned to examine claims and make explicit use of definitions.

Grade 7: Ratios & Proportional Relationships

7.RP.A. Analyze proportional relationships and use them to solve real-world and mathematical problems.

7.RP.A.2. Recognize and represent proportional relationships between quantities.

7.RP.A.3. Use proportional relationships to solve multistep ratio and percent problems.

Overview:

Explain the chosen social context and present relevant data related to the chosen topic. Have students

- Calculate current proportions in the system
- Solve proportional equations to determine optimal distributions or allocations
- Use proportional reasoning to predict outcomes of proposed changes
- Compare their solutions and discuss the implications of their findings.

Discuss how small changes in calculations could significantly affect outcomes, lead to potential biases, fairness issues, or unintended consequences of the AI system in the chosen context.

Conclude the lesson with recap of the connection between precise proportional reasoning and responsible AI development in social applications.

Suggested contexts, scenarios, and data types:

1. Social media content distribution

    TweenConnect, a new social media app for middle schoolers, uses AI to show users different types of content. But some kids feel they're seeing too many ads and not enough posts from their friends. Your class has been asked to help TweenConnect balance their content better.

    Data:

    - Percentages of current content types (e.g., friend posts, ads, suggested content, etc.)
    - User engagement rates for each content type
    - Total number of posts a user sees in an average session

2. Sustainable energy management in schools

    Our school just installed solar panels and a smart energy system. The AI-powered system needs to figure out how to use this new green energy along with regular electricity to power different parts of the school. Your class is challenged to help program the AI to make the school as eco friendly as possible.

    Data:

    - Energy consumption data for different school areas (classrooms, gym, cafeteria, etc.)
    - Solar panel energy production data (hourly or daily)
    - Regular electricity costs and solar energy savings
    - Peak usage times and amounts

3. Public transportation route optimization

   Our city is launching a new bus service for students, using AI to plan the routes. The system needs to balance the number of students picked up and the distance traveled. Your class has been invited to help the city planners make sure the new bus routes are fair for all students.

   Data:

   - Map of the city with student populations in different areas
   - Current bus routes and their capacities
   - Average travel times between key locations
   - Maximum allowed travel time for any student

4. Online learning resource allocation

   Your school district is creating an AI tutor to help students with after-school learning. The AI needs to figure out how to divide its time between different subjects and types of help (like videos, quizzes, or live chat). Your class gets to advise on how the AI tutor should split its resources.

   Data:

   - List of subjects and types of help offered (videos, quizzes, live chat, etc.)
   - Student performance data in different subjects

5. Community health resource distribution

   The local health department is using an AI system to decide where to send mobile health clinics in your county. These clinics offer check-ups, vaccinations, and health advice. Your class has been asked to help make sure the AI sends the clinics where they're needed most.

   Data:

   - Map of the county with population densities
   - Health statistics for different areas (e.g., vaccination rates, common health issues)
   - Number of mobile clinics available and their capacities
   - Travel times between different areas in the county

Teachers can adapt the lesson to any of the suggested topics or other contexts that fit their curriculum and student interests, while maintaining the focus on proportional reasoning and AI's social impact. The data should be simplified to be appropriate for middle school mathematics levels but detailed enough to allow for meaningful proportional reasoning tasks. Teachers might consider creating fictional but realistic datasets if actual data is not readily available or too complex.

INTEGRATING AI CONCEPTS INTO HIGH SCHOOL ALGEBRA UNIT ON STRUCTURE OF ALGEBRAIC EXPRESSIONS

Let's use our template for Planning AI Literacy Integration to apply the Pedagogical Framework for AI Literacy to design an instructional unit in algebra. We'll use the topic of multiplying polynomials taught within this unit to demonstrate planning of a single lesson. At the same time, we want students to learn about AI's core concepts of representation and reasoning. The connections between these core concepts and the mathematics topic of the unit are grounded in the following key insights from the Five Big Ideas in AI framework (AAAI & CSTA, n.d.):

- AI representations are data structures. The two major types of knowledge representations are symbolic and numerical representations.

- Reasoning methods are algorithms. Representations support reasoning; reasoning methods operate on representations.

- "Knowing" something means the ability to represent it and reason with it.

As you recall from Chapter 4, our Planning AI Literacy Integration Template (available on our companion website at https://companion.corwin.com/courses/TeachingAILiteracy) is based on the principles of the backward design framework (Wiggins & McTighe, 1998)—in other words, we start instructional planning with the learning goals that describe the knowledge and skills we want our students to acquire in the instructional unit. Similar to the approach we used in planning a science unit (Chapter 5), we complete Stages 1 and 2 within a larger instructional unit and then use developed key elements to complete Stage 3 for a single lesson within that unit. After completing the template, we suggest resources and materials for the lesson.

STAGE 1: DESIRED RESULTS

The first stage of the template leads us through the process of establishing curricular priorities in the unit (Table 6.2). To identify the instructional goals we refer to subject-specific standards and AI learning objectives. In this example we use CCSSM (National Governors Association Center for Best Practices & Council of Chief State School Officers, 2010) to determine mathematics standards (you might want to use your state standards to identify specific mathematics standards if they differ from CCSSM). The performance expectations that align with the goal of this unit are:

- Use the structure of an expression to identify ways to rewrite it. For example, see $x^4 - y^4$ as $(x^2)^2 - (y^2)^2$, thus recognizing it as a difference of squares that can be factored as $(x^2 - y^2)(x^2 + y^2)$. (HSA-SSE.A.2)

- Understand that polynomials form a system analogous to the integers, namely, they are closed under the operations of addition, subtraction, and multiplication; add, subtract, and multiply polynomials. (HSA-APR.A.1)

For AI competencies we use learning objectives defined by the AI4K12 guidelines (AAAI & CSTA, n.d.). Because in this unit we are interested in integrating the AI core concepts of representation and reasoning, we are going to select the high school learning objectives for the AI's Big Idea #2:

- Describe how to represent a concept as a schema. (2-A-i)

- Describe how schemas are used to structure information about people, places, or things in knowledge graphs. (2-A-iii)

- Categorize real-world problems as classification, prediction, sequential decision problems, logical deduction, or statistical inference. (2-C-i)

- For each of these types of reasoning problems (classification, prediction, sequential decision making, logical deduction, and statistical inference), list an algorithm that could be used to solve that problem. (2-C-ii)

After instructional goals are established, we need to decide:

- How will students *transfer* their mathematics knowledge and understanding of AI core concepts gained from the unit and apply it outside of the context of the class?

  This question focuses on the larger purposes of learning a particular content, for example, what complex real-world tasks students will be able to tackle after mastering this content. In our case, we decided to select the following authentic real-world tasks: 1) optimization problems in fields like finance, engineering, or supply chain management and 2) fraud detection, recommendation systems, or NLP applications.

- What are the big ideas and enduring *understandings* students will have when they complete the unit?

  It is helpful to refer to the standards and curriculum guidelines that usually provide teachers with enduring understandings and essential questions. For our unit we included reference codes for the essential understandings for science and AI concepts, so that you can readily see the overlaps.

- What are *essential questions* that will frame the unit and that we expect students to answer if they accomplished the unit's goals?

  These are questions that cannot be answered with a brief sentence. The purpose of essential questions is to stimulate thinking, to provoke inquiry, and to inspire more questions including those from the students. At the same time, at the end of the unit answers to these questions should lead to stated instructional goals. In the planning template we included possible choices for the essential questions.

TABLE 6.2 ● Stage 1: Desired Results

STAGE 1 DESIRED RESULTS		
INSTRUCTIONAL GOALS	**SUBJECT-SPECIFIC**	**AI LITERACY**
What subject-specific content standards will this unit address? *CCSSM Performance Expectations:*	***Transfer*** What kinds of long-term independent accomplishments are desired?	

STAGE 1 DESIRED RESULTS		
INSTRUCTIONAL GOALS	**SUBJECT-SPECIFIC**	**AI LITERACY**
A-SSE.A.2. Use the structure of an expression to identify ways to rewrite it. For example, see $x^4 - y^4$ as $(x^2)^2 - (y^2)^2$, thus recognizing it as a difference of squares that can be factored as $(x^2 - y^2)(x^2 + y^2)$.	*Students will be able to independently use their learning to manipulate algebraic expressions strategically to solve complex optimization problems in fields like finance, engineering, or supply chain management.*	*Students will be able to independently use their learning to develop and implement AI models for tasks such as fraud detection, recommendation systems, or NLP applications.*
	Understandings	
	What specifically do you want students to understand?	
	What inferences should they make?	
A-APR.A.1. Understand that polynomials form a system analogous to the integers, namely, they are closed under the operations of addition, subtraction, and multiplication; add, subtract, and multiply polynomials.	*The structure of an algebraic expression provides clues for rewriting it in different forms. Students should recognize and use the structure of an expression to identify ways to rewrite it. (A-SSE.A.2.)* *When polynomials are added, subtracted, or multiplied, the result is always another polynomial. This is analogous to the closure property of integers under addition, subtraction, and multiplication. (A-APR.A.1.)*	*A schema describes a concept by listing its superconcepts and defining its properties, some of which may be inherited from superconcepts. (2-A-i)* *A schema specifies the attributes of the concept being described, and its relationships to other concepts, for example, a fraud transaction schema might inherit properties from a more general financial transaction schema. (2-A-iii)* *Reasoning problems can be categorized based on the types of inputs supplied, the types of outputs to be produced, and the characteristics of the search space, if applicable. (2-C-i)* *AI includes a wide variety of reasoning algorithms for solving different types of reasoning problems. Some use symbolic representations (e.g., factoring polynomials) whereas others are numerical in nature (e.g., statistical models). (2-C-ii)*
What AI competencies will this unit address?	***Essential questions***	
	What thought-provoking questions will foster inquiry, meaning making, and transfer?	
2-A-i. Describe how to represent a concept as a schema.	*Why are the commutative, associative, and distributive properties so important in mathematics?*	*How do we effectively represent complex information to facilitate reasoning and problem solving?*
	Acquisition	
	What facts and basic concepts should students know and be able to recall?	
	What discrete skills and processes should students be able to use?	

(Continued)

STAGE 1 DESIRED RESULTS		
INSTRUCTIONAL GOALS	**SUBJECT-SPECIFIC**	**AI LITERACY**
2-A-iii. Describe how schemas are used to structure information about people, places, or things in knowledge graphs. *2-C-i. Categorize real-world problems as classification, prediction, sequential decision problems, logical deduction, or statistical inference.* *2-C-ii. For each of these types of reasoning problems (classification, prediction, sequential decision making, logical deduction, and statistical inference), list an algorithm that could be used to solve that problem.*	*Students will know* • *that two algebraic expressions are equivalent if we can convert one expression into the other by repeatedly applying the commutative, associative, and distributive properties and the properties of rational exponents* • *that there are analogies between the system of integers and the system of polynomials* • *that the sum or difference of two polynomials produces another polynomial* • *that the product of two polynomials produces another polynomial*	*Students will know* • *that millions of web sites use schema representations to make information intelligible to AI programs that utilize knowledge graphs.* • *a knowledge graph encodes information about things and the relationships between them.* • *selection of an algorithm depends on characteristics of the input data and the complexity of the decisions to be made.*
	Students will be skilled at • *using the structure of an expression to identify ways to rewrite it.* • *using the commutative, associative, and distributive property to recognize structure within expression prove equivalency of expressions.* • *adding, subtracting, and multiplying polynomials.*	*Students will be skilled at* • *identifying key attributes and relationships of a concept to create a schema, and iteratively improving it based on new information.* • *representing entities and their relationships as nodes and edges in a knowledge graph.* • *classifying real-world problems into appropriate AI problem types, such as classification, prediction, or decision making.* • *matching problem types with suitable algorithms, considering factors like data characteristics and desired output.*

STAGE 2: ASSESSMENT EVIDENCE

Now that we've identified desired results, it is time to plan assessments (Table 6.3). At this stage it is important to consider a wide range of assessment methods to ensure that the type of assessment is aligned with the evidence of achieving desired results. The evidence can range from performance tasks that mirror complex real-world issues and challenges, academic open-ended tasks that require critical thinking, to simple content-focused tests and quizzes, and informal checks for understanding.

TABLE 6.3 ● Stage 2: Assessment Evidence

STAGE 2 ASSESSMENT EVIDENCE		
EVALUATIVE CRITERIA	**SUBJECT-SPECIFIC**	**AI LITERACY**
What criteria will be used in each assessment to evaluate attainment of the desired results? • *Apply commutative, associative, and distributive properties to rewrite expressions.* • *Identify that polynomials are closed under addition, subtraction, and multiplication.* • *Correctly adds, subtracts, and multiplies polynomials using appropriate methods.* • *Create accurate schemas to represent complex information.* • *Model relationships between entities using a knowledge graph.* • *Categorize problems into appropriate AI problem types.*	***Performance Tasks*** How will students demonstrate their understanding (meaning making and transfer) through complex performance? *Assuming the role of transportation coordinators for a school district, students will optimize school bus routes to minimize transportation costs, fuel consumption, and student travel time.*	*Students will create detailed schemas and knowledge graphs to represent data in the school bus routing problem, explaining the reasoning behind their chosen representations, and justifying the connections between different data elements.*
Regardless of the format of the assessment, what qualities are most important? • *Using algebraic models to represent real-world situations* • *Effective communication of their mathematical thinking using multiple representations* • *Applying their knowledge to solve complex problems, make connections between different ideas, and justify their reasoning*	***Other Evidence*** What other evidence will you collect to determine whether Stage 1 goals were achieved? • *Informal checks and observations—during group work and discussions* • *Semistructured class discussions—related to the topics of the lessons* • *Student online reading reflections for the assigned reading materials such as case studies* • *Knowledge trees demonstrating relationships between key variables in the transportation problem* • *Completed worksheets for hands-on and technology investigations* • *Exit tickets in the form of quizzes* • *Report and group presentation of the completed performance task*	

TIPS

Developing Essential Questions

As you develop essential questions, keep in mind that these are broad in scope and should help students to inquire and make sense of the disciplinary core ideas. Moreover, essential questions are meant to be explored and revisited over time, not answered by the end of a single class period.

• What are the key knowledge and skills students will *acquire* from the unit?

  ○ The information that addresses this question could be the facts, concepts, principles, processes, strategies, and methods students should know when they leave the course.

  ○ The targeted knowledge and skills can refer to "1) the building blocks for the desired understandings, 2) the knowledge and skills stated or implied in the goals, and 3) the 'enabling' knowledge and skills needed to perform the complex assessment tasks identified in Stage 2" (Wiggins & Tighe, 1998, p. 57).

The performance task should directly or indirectly require students to address the essential questions. Thus, we propose that in this unit groups of students will assume the role of transportation coordinators for a school district. Their task will be to optimize school bus routes to minimize transportation costs, fuel consumption, and student travel time. This will require teachers to design appropriate scoring rubrics that relate specific task requirements to performance goals and define different degrees of understanding and proficiency.

Other types of evidence in this unit could include informal checks and observations, group and class discussions, gallery walks, reading reflections, concepts maps, quizzes, hands-on and technology investigations, and presentations. In a particular lesson that we explain in Stage 3, we focus on student skills to use polynomials to model relationships between variables, such as the cost function based on distance and fuel efficiency (subject-specific evidence) and to create a knowledge graph to represent bus stops, routes, and students (AI literacy).

STAGE 3: LEARNING PLAN

Stages 1 and 2 have established our learning goals and assessment criteria. With these in place, we can now focus on planning effective instructional strategies and learning activities that equip students with the resources and knowledge to achieve these goals (Table 6.4). Moreover, clear goals make the design of lesson tasks easier, because we now have a better idea of what we want the students to get out of these tasks.

TABLE 6.4 ● Stage 3: Learning Plan

STAGE 3 LEARNING PLAN		
LESSON STRUCTURE	**SUBJECT-SPECIFIC**	**AI LITERACY**
Does the learning plan reflect Pedagogical Framework for AI Literacy?	***Preassessment*** What preassessments will you use to check students' prior knowledge, preassessment skill levels, and potential misconceptions?	
	Students complete a quick multiple-choice assessment using your preferred online platform (e.g., Google Forms, Kahoot, etc.). The quiz will include two to three questions asking students to determine an expression equivalent to a given one, and two to three questions about AI data representation, data processing, and algorithms.	
	Summary of Key Learning Events and Instruction Does the learning plan address instructional goals for disciplinary content and AI literacy? Is the plan likely to be engaging and effective for all students?	

STAGE 3 LEARNING PLAN		
LESSON STRUCTURE	**SUBJECT-SPECIFIC**	**AI LITERACY**
Design	At the *Empathize* step: • In small groups students interview each other about their daily transportation challenges • As a whole class discuss how different factors in transportation can be represented by polynomial terms • Introduce knowledge graphs for representing transportation networks At the *Define* step: • Draw parallel between multiplying integers and polynomials, emphasizing closure property • Small group work—students synthesize interview findings to define key transportation issues and brainstorm about expressing routes as polynomials (e.g., $ax^2 + bx + c$, where a = travel time, b = travel distance, c = fixed cost) At the *Ideate* step: • In small groups students brainstorm ideas for an AI-powered routing system and create mind maps that they present to the class for peer feedback • Students use polynomial multiplication to calculate combined route costs • Discuss how AI could use these polynomial representations for classification and decision making • In small groups, students create a draft knowledge graph of their transportation network using polynomials as edge weights	

Create	At the *Prototype* step:
	• Groups develop
	   ○ a simple prototype of their AI routing system, using polynomials to represent different school bus routes
	   ○ basic algorithm for route classification based on their polynomials
	   ○ a visual representation of their system, showing how polynomial multiplication is used in decision making
	
	At the *Test* step:
	• Group oral presentations of AI routing system and knowledge graphs	

Reflect	Whole-class discussion with focus on how the closure property of polynomial multiplication ensures the AI system can always compute route costs	

As we mentioned earlier, here we focus on a single lesson about multiplying polynomials within the instructional unit on structure of algebraic expressions. As suggested by the Understanding by Design (UbD) framework (Wiggins & McTighe, 1998) the lesson will start with a preassessment to see what our students already know about polynomials and to identify any misconceptions they might have. You will be looking for incorrectly applied distributive property and misunderstanding of exponent rules. We also want to see what students know about the AI core concepts of representation and reasoning. We suggest a brief discussion about the difference between symbolic and numerical representations in AI and about data structures and algorithms types in AI.

Our lesson will be structured as a DCR process according to the Pedagogical Framework for AI Literacy (see Chapter 2). This also means that we plan the key learning activities that integrate disciplinary and AI literacy instructional goals, which is reflected in the fact that the template no longer separates these two aspects of the lesson.

• **Knowledge graph** is a data model that uses a network of interconnected nodes (like vehicles, locations, routes, and schedules) to represent complex relationships between different entities involved in transportation

During the *empathize* step of the design component, we want students to understand the challenges in optimizing the school bus routes to minimize transportation costs, fuel consumption, and student travel time. For that purpose, we suggest that you pair up students and let them interview each other about their experience traveling to school on a school bus. After these interviews, have a whole-class discussion about different factors that affect transportation and how these could be represented by polynomials. This would be a good time to introduce students to **knowledge graphs** used in transportation.

At the *define* step, start with introducing students to polynomial multiplication, for example by using an area model. Present side-by-side area model diagrams for multiplication of integers and for multiplication of polynomials (see Figure 6.4) and have students compare and contrast them.

FIGURE 6.4 • Geometric Diagram for Multiplication of Integers and Polynomials

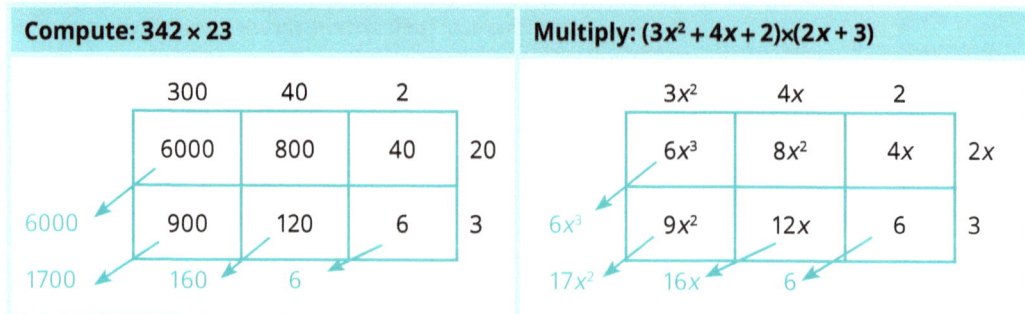

After this, divide students into small groups and based on their interview findings have them define key factors in the school bus transportation problem (e.g., travel time, distance, fixed cost, etc.) and how different school bus routes could be represented using polynomials. In the *ideate* step, the groups create mind maps about routing system for peer feedback, calculate combined route costs that will require use of polynomial multiplication, and create their draft knowledge graphs for the transportation network. This prepares them for the *prototype* step, where the groups prototype their AI routing system, using polynomials to represent different school bus routes, and develop algorithms for route classification. The product of this step is a visual representation of their transportation system, illustrating how they used polynomial multiplication in creating their prototype. Finally, they present their AI routing system and knowledge graphs to the class for feedback (*test* step). The lesson concludes with a whole-class discussion to reflect on student learning. It is important that throughout the lesson and during final reflection you emphasize these key points:

- How polynomial terms represent different factors in transportation problems
- The role of polynomial multiplication in combining and comparing routes
- How AI uses structures similar to polynomials for data representation and reasoning
- The connection between mathematical operations and AI decision-making processes

RESOURCES

- eMath instruction—Polynomials (https://qrs.ly/46gh18m)
- Khan Academy—Polynomial arithmetic (https://qrs.ly/2ugh18n)—provides instructional videos and practice problems on polynomial multiplication
- Free dynamic mathematics platforms:
    - Desmos (https://teacher.desmos.com/)—free digital lessons and lesson-building tools
    - GeoGebra (https://www.geogebra.org/)—a set of free digital tools to do mathematics
- GXWeb (https://qrs.ly/r4gh1ht)—free browser-based mathematical modeling platform
- Examples of AI-powered mathematics tools:
    - WolframAlpha (https://www.wolframalpha.com/)—a computational knowledge engine that uses NLP and

(Continued)

(Continued)

    can answer questions and solve problems in a variety of domains, including math, science, and engineering.

- ○ Mathway (https://www.mathway.com)—an online math solver that can solve a wide range of math problems, including algebra, calculus, trigonometry, and statistics.
- ○ PhotoMath (https://photomath.com/en)—a mobile app that can solve math problems by taking a picture of them.
- ○ Socratic (https://socratic.org/)—a mobile app that can help students with their math homework by providing step-by-step solutions and explanations.
- ○ Symbolab (https://www.symbolab.com/)—an online math solver that can solve problems in a variety of math subjects, including algebra, geometry, calculus, and physics.

- Wang and Johnson (2019) provide list of ideas how AI concepts can be connected to the high school mathematics topics

- Data visualization resources:

  - ○ Neo4j Bloom (https://neo4j.com/bloom/)—free version available for creating and visualizing knowledge graphs.
  - ○ Scratch (https://scratch.mit.edu/)—block-based programming language that can be used to create simple simulations of transportation systems.
  - ○ MIT App Inventor (https://appinventor.mit.edu/)—students can prototype a mobile app for their AI routing system.
  - ○ Tableau AI (qrs.ly/5qgtm6d)—students can create data story with the use of Generative AI.

Chapter Summary

The MPs provide a framework for developing mathematical thinking and problem-solving skills, which are crucial for understanding and developing AI systems. By integrating these practices, educators can help students not only excel in mathematics but also comprehend the fundamental concepts driving AI technologies and their impact on society. This alignment facilitates a deeper understanding of how mathematical principles underpin AI advancements and how AI systems can be ethically and responsibly developed and deployed.

Wrap-Up Questions

- What are the potential benefits and challenges of integrating AI literacy into mathematics education? How might these challenges be addressed in your classroom?

- How can connections between the Five Big Ideas in AI (perception, representation and reasoning, learning, natural interaction, and societal impact) and the MPs deepen students' understanding of AI and mathematics concepts?

- Reflect on your own comfort level and familiarity with AI concepts. What steps could you take to further develop your own AI literacy and effectively teach these concepts to your students?

CHAPTER 7

AI Literacy in Language Arts Education

In this chapter we'll

- Review connections between Five Big Ideas in AI and Common Core State Standards (CCSS) for English Language Arts (ELA)

- Suggest strategies for integrating AI literacy across different grade bands

- Demonstrate the application of the Pedagogical Framework for AI Literacy for designing a middle school ELA lesson that integrates the concept of AI for social good

There's an intrinsic link between ELA and AI's communication capabilities, which provides numerous opportunities to integrate AI concepts into ELA teaching and learning. Language serves as the primary medium through which AI interacts with humans, making ELA skills crucial for AI development and human–AI interaction. Concepts from linguistics, semantics, pragmatics, and discourse analysis form the foundation of natural language processing (NLP) algorithms. Vocabulary, syntax, and context are used to interpret and generate human-like text, whereas techniques such as **sentiment analysis**, **named entity recognition**, and text summarization enable AI to understand and respond to complex language inputs. This connection allows teachers to integrate AI's concepts of natural language and commonsense reasoning to support student development of reading, writing, speaking, and listening skills, enhancing their understanding of both fields.

Similar to Chapters 5 and 6, we first suggest connections between ELA strands such as reading, writing, speaking and listening, and language, and the Five Big Ideas in AI. Then, for each

• **Sentiment analysis** (also known as opinion mining or emotion AI) is the use of NLP, text analysis, computational linguistics, and biometrics to systematically identify, extract, quantify, and study affective states and subjective information. (https://qrs.ly/swgh18q)

• **Named entity recognition (NER)** (also known as [named] entity identification, entity chunking, and entity extraction) is a subtask of information extraction that seeks to locate and classify named entities mentioned in unstructured text into predefined categories such as person names, organizations, locations, medical codes, time expressions, quantities, monetary values, percentages, etc. (https://qrs.ly/npgh18y)

big idea, we illustrate these connections using examples that integrate core AI literacy concepts into K–12 ELA lessons. The chapter concludes with a middle school unit plan about power dynamics of creation in literature that integrates the concept of AI for social good.

ENGLISH LANGUAGE ARTS STANDARDS AND FIVE BIG IDEAS IN AI

The Common Core State Standards for English Language Arts ([CCSS for ELA]; National Governors Association Center for Best Practices & Council of Chief State School Officers, 2010) were developed simultaneously with CCSS mathematics standards to define a set of K–12 ELA education standards to ensure U.S. students are college and career ready by the end of high school.

The CCSS for ELA share a common goal with the standards set forth by the National Council of Teachers of English (NCTE, 1996): to foster strong literacy skills in students. However, their approaches and roles in education differ. The CCSS provides a detailed framework outlining specific knowledge and skills students should acquire at each grade level. The NCTE standards emphasize a holistic approach to literacy, focusing on broader concepts like critical thinking, creativity, and the ability to engage with diverse texts. Today, the CCSS serves as a national benchmark, guiding curriculum development and assessment in many states, whereas the NCTE standards are often used by the teachers to enrich their instruction, drawing on standards' emphasis on student-centered learning and engagement with authentic texts. Both sets of standards play a crucial role in shaping ELA education, aiming to equip students with the literacy skills necessary for success in college, career, and civic life. In this chapter we focus on CCSS for ELA standards.

The CCSS for ELA standards are divided into four major strands: Reading (with three substrands of literature, informational text, and foundational skills), Writing, Speaking and Listening, and Language. Each strand is headed by a strand-specific set of College and Career Readiness (CCR) Anchor Standards that is identical across all grades and content areas. The CCR Anchor Standards define general, cross-disciplinary literacy expectations of all students. The grade-specific standards provide additional details of what students should understand and be able to do by the end of each grade to develop and retain skills and understandings necessary for meeting the more general expectations described by the CCR standards.

ELA strands can be effectively connected with various AI concepts, providing an opportunity to integrate these concepts into ELA teaching and learning. Let's explore these connections (Table 7.1).

TABLE 7.1 ● Examples of Illustrated Connections between ELA Strands and Five Big Ideas in AI

BIG IDEAS IN AI	AI'S CORE CONCEPTS	ELA STRANDS	CONNECTIONS BETWEEN BIS AND ELA STRANDS	LESSON EXAMPLES
BI1. Perception	Processing	Reading: Literature	The AI's concept of processing involves the ability to take in raw sensory data and transform it into meaningful information. This parallels the act of reading literature, as readers absorb words and sentences, processing them to construct characters, settings, and plotlines. Both AI and readers engage in a form of pattern recognition, identifying recurring themes, motifs, or literary devices, and interpreting their significance within the context of the work.	7.1. Analyzing Character Development (Middle school) (p. 152)
	Sensing	Reading: Foundations Skills	Just as AI uses sensors to detect and interpret information, early readers use their senses to decode letters and words. This foundational skill, like AI's data processing, is essential for building higher-level comprehension in both humans and machines.	7.2. Phonics in Action: Decoding Complex Words (Elementary school) (p. 156)

(Continued)

(Continued)

BIG IDEAS IN AI	AI'S CORE CONCEPTS	ELA STRANDS	CONNECTIONS BETWEEN BIS AND ELA STRANDS	LESSON EXAMPLES
BI2. Representation and Reasoning	Representation Reasoning	Writing	Just as AI tools utilize representation and reasoning to generate coherent and logical text, the writing standards emphasize students' ability to develop clear arguments, support claims with evidence, and organize ideas in a structured manner. Both AI and student writers must consider audience and purpose, tailoring their language and style accordingly.	7.3. Mastering Evidence-Based Writing (High school) (p. 159)
BI3. Learning	Nature of Learning Datasets	Language	The ELA language standards emphasize students' continuous learning and refinement of language skills through exposure to diverse texts and vocabulary. This is similar to how AI learns and improves by analyzing large datasets. The ELA emphasis on grammar, vocabulary acquisition, and understanding nuances in language mirrors AI's focus on pattern recognition, semantic analysis, and language generation. Both aim to achieve increasingly sophisticated communication through a process of iterative learning and adaptation.	7.4. Identifying Words with Multiple Meanings (Elementary school) (p. 161)

BIG IDEAS IN AI	AI'S CORE CONCEPTS	ELA STRANDS	CONNECTIONS BETWEEN BIS AND ELA STRANDS	LESSON EXAMPLES
BI4. Natural Interaction	Commonsense Reasoning, Natural Language Philosophy of Mind	Speaking and Listening	AI models' ability to understand and generate natural language, while employing commonsense reasoning, aligns with the goals of the ELA listening and speaking standards. Just as AI uses contextual clues and background knowledge to make inferences, students are expected to analyze and interpret spoken language, utilizing their understanding of social cues and shared knowledge. Furthermore, both AI and students strive to adapt their communication styles to diverse audiences and situations.	7.5. Debating the Future of AI (High school) (p. 163)
BI5. Societal Impact	AI for Social Good	Reading: Informational Text	The goal of AI for Social Good is to harness technology to address societal challenges and promote positive change. Similarly, the ELA standard for reading informational texts equips students with the critical literacy skills needed to understand complex issues, evaluate evidence, and engage in informed civic discourse. Both emphasize the importance of analysis, evaluation, and synthesis of information to make informed decisions and take action.	7.6. Analyzing the Social Impact of Scientific Innovations (Middle school) (p. 166)

These selected connections between ELA Standards and the Five Big Ideas in AI demonstrate how AI literacy can be integrated into ELA classrooms to deepen students' understanding of texts, language, and communication. By aligning AI concepts with ELA standards, we can explore strategies for using AI to enrich students' learning experiences in analyzing literature, constructing arguments, and engaging in effective communication. This integration offers innovative ways to enhance students' analytical skills, critical thinking, and comprehension of complex texts through the lens of AI technologies.

REFLECTION QUESTIONS

- How can you use these connections between the ELA practices and the Five Big Ideas in AI to foster students' analytical and critical thinking skills, and comprehension of complex texts?

- What challenges do you anticipate in implementing AI-related activities into your ELA classroom, and how might these challenges be addressed?

- How can you integrate AI literacy in ELA instruction to meet the diverse needs of your students?

LESSON SUGGESTIONS

AI'S BIG IDEA #1: PERCEPTION

In this middle school lesson, students analyze character development in a novel and draw a parallel between this process and AI data processing.

7.1

Lesson: Analyzing Character Development

For Middle School

Reading: Literature » Grade 6

RL.6.3. Describe how a particular story's or drama's plot unfolds in a series of episodes and how the characters respond or change as the plot moves toward a resolution.

CCRA.R.3. Analyze how and why individuals, events, or ideas develop and interact over the course of a text.

Overview:

- Select a novel or a short story for students to read prior to the lesson (see our recommendations below or make your own selection).

RESOURCES

***The Giver* by Lois Lowry** (179 pages)

- Synopsis: Set in a society that at first appears to be utopian but is revealed to be dystopian as the story progresses. The novel follows Jonas, who is selected to inherit the position of Receiver of Memory, the person who stores all the past memories of the time before sameness.

- Character Focus: Students can examine Jonas's development from acceptance to questioning of his society's norms and how his experiences with the memories lead him to take drastic actions.

***Wonder* by R.J. Palacio** (315 pages)

- Synopsis: This inspiring tale follows August Pullman, a boy with facial differences who goes to public school for the first time in Grade 5. The novel is written from multiple perspectives, offering a comprehensive view of how Auggie's presence affects everyone around him.

- Character Focus: Analysis could focus on Auggie's resilience and growth in self-confidence, as well as the development of his peers in how they perceive differences and empathy.

***Percy Jackson & The Olympians: The Lightning Thief* by Rick Riordan** (380 pages)

- Synopsis: Percy Jackson discovers he is a demigod, the son of Poseidon, and is accused of stealing Zeus's lightning bolt. He embarks on a quest to prevent a war among the gods.

(Continued)

(Continued)

- Character Focus: Students can track Percy's evolution from a misunderstood kid to a hero, analyzing how his adventures and the revelation of his true identity influence his personal development and relationships.

Short stories (can be assigned a day before class):

- ***The Tell-Tale Heart* by Edgar Allan Poe** (4–5 pages)

- Synopsis: An unnamed narrator, obsessed with an old man's eye, meticulously plans and executes his murder. Driven by guilt and paranoia, the narrator's sanity unravels as he confesses to the crime.

- Character Focus:

  - The Narrator: Analysis can focus on his descent into madness, his unreliable narration, and the internal conflict between his guilt and his attempts to justify his actions.

  - The Old Man: Although a minor character, analysis can focus on his vulnerability and how he represents the narrator's fears and anxieties.

The Gift of the Magi by O. Henry (8–10 pages)

- Synopsis: Della and Jim, a young couple with limited means, sacrifice their most prized possessions to buy each other Christmas gifts. Ironically, their gifts render each other's sacrifices useless, but the story reveals the true spirit of love and giving.

- Character Focus: Della and Jim: Analysis can center on their selfless love, their willingness to sacrifice for each other, and the irony of their situation. The story also provides an opportunity to discuss the theme of material possessions versus the intangible value of love and sacrifice.

The Necklace by Guy de Maupassant (10–12 pages)

- Synopsis: Mathilde Loisel, dissatisfied with her middle-class life, borrows a diamond necklace to attend a prestigious ball. She loses the necklace and spends years working to replace it, only to discover it was a cheap imitation.

- Character Focus:

  o Mathilde Loisel: Analysis can focus on her vanity, her discontentment, and how her pursuit of material wealth leads to her downfall.

  o Monsieur Loisel: His character can be analyzed in terms of his devotion to his wife, his willingness to sacrifice, and his acceptance of their fate.

During the lesson students can create a timeline of key moments in the main character's development. If students have access to computers, this timeline could be completed online and students can develop visual annotations. Students will use Canva to create the digital timeline (link: https://qrs.ly/nogh193).

- These tasks are best completed individually followed by small-group discussion of their findings. Here are some questions you can ask to guide student discussion:

  o How do the main character's understanding of their world or themselves change throughout the story? How do the key events you identified contribute to the character's transformation?

  o What are the central themes of the story? Discuss how these themes are developed through the plot and characters. How do these themes relate to real-world issues or universal human experiences?

AI Connections:

Conclude the lesson with a discussion that compares student annotation process and AI data processing. Draw students' attention to the similarity between how the annotation process supported their understanding of character's development, and how AI gathers and processes data to understand and predict behavior. For your reference, we included a description of these connections (see Table 7.2).

TABLE 7.2 ● Comparison of Annotation Process and AI Data Processing

ANNOTATION PROCESS IN LITERATURE	AI DATA PROCESSING TECHNIQUE	EXPLANATION
Identifying and selecting key events	Data selection	By pinpointing critical events in the character's life, students learn to focus on significant data points, akin to how AI selects essential features from vast datasets to improve model accuracy.
Noting changes in character	Feature extraction	Students annotate specific changes in character's traits or reactions over the course of the story. This is similar to how AI extracts features from data to understand patterns or predict outcomes.
Linking causes and effects	Pattern recognition	By linking events to changes in character's behavior or emotions, students practice recognizing patterns—much like an AI system identifies correlations in data to predict future behavior.
Tracking emotional arcs	Sentiment analysis	Students track the emotional progression of the character through the story, which parallels how AI uses sentiment analysis to gauge emotions from text data.
Visualizing development	Data visualization	Creating an annotated timeline of character's development allows students to see a clear progression and regression at different moments, mirroring how AI visualizes data to make complex information more comprehensible and impactful.

In the following elementary school lesson, students identify and isolate individual sounds in words with common vowel teams and digraphs (e.g., *ai*, *ay*, *ea*, etc.), and draw parallels to how an AI perceives and interprets information.

7.2 Lesson: Phonics in Action

Decoding Complex Words

For Elementary School

Reading: Foundational Skills » Grade 2

RF.2.3.B. Know spelling-sound correspondences for additional common vowel teams.

CCRA.R.4. Interpret words and phrases as they are used in a text, including determining technical, connotative, and figurative meanings.

Overview:

- Start the lesson by engaging students in a conversation with an AI voice assistant (e.g., Alexa, Siri, etc.). Have students give the voice assistant simple commands, such as "play music," "tell a joke," or "spell a word."

- Discuss how these assistants use their "ears" (microphones) to listen and understand what we say. Explain that just like voice assistants "decode" our spoken words, we also decode written words using our eyes and brains.

- Use phonics cards (see Figure 7.1) to practice common vowel teams such as *ai* as in *rain*, *ay* as in *day*, *ea* as in *beach*, *ee* as in *seed*, *oa* as in *boat*, *ow* as in *snow*. Let students identify sounds and practice blending them to form words. After each student's attempt, activate the voice assistant and have it repeat the word or use it in a simple sentence.

FIGURE 7.1 ● Example of a Phonics Card

Source: istock.com/ jsabirova

- Select a text for students to read that includes words with practiced consonant blends. Students can use context to confirm or self-correct word recognition and understanding, rereading as necessary.

- Conclude the lesson with a brief reflection. Ask students how the voice assistant helped them understand phonics better. This reinforces learning and promotes metacognition. Recap how voice assistants use their "hearing" to understand us and how we use our decoding skills to understand written words.

Introducing AI
Voice Assistant

- Consider using visuals to represent how the voice assistant processes sound and how we decode words. This can help visual learners make the connection.

- Include a variety of phonics cards with different blends and digraphs to keep students engaged and challenge them appropriately.

- You can extend the lesson by having students try to "trick" the voice assistant with mispronounced words or nonsense words, further highlighting the importance of accurate decoding.

Lesson rationale:

- Using a voice assistant is a great hook to capture student interest and introduce the concept of AI sensing in a tangible way.

- Giving the assistant commands directly demonstrates how it "hears" and interprets spoken language, setting the stage for the connection to decoding written words.

- The discussion explicitly links the voice assistant's "decoding" of spoken words to the process of decoding written words.

- This analogy helps students understand that both processes involve breaking down information (sounds or letters) and making sense of it.

- Using phonics cards provides a concrete, interactive way for students to practice blending and identifying sounds.

- The voice assistant acts as immediate feedback, reinforcing correct pronunciation and providing a fun, engaging element.

AI'S BIG IDEA #2: REPRESENTATION AND REASONING

In this high school lesson, students will develop argumentation skills by crafting claims linking historical figures' views to contemporary issues, while also exploring how AI translates human language into symbolic representations (like logical notation). Students will also examine how reasoning and decision making occur in historical arguments and AI algorithms.

Lesson: Mastering Evidence-Based Writing

7.3

Writing » Grade 9–10

W.9-10.1.A. Introduce precise claim(s), distinguish the claim(s) from alternate or opposing claims, and create an organization that establishes clear relationships among claim(s), counterclaims, reasons, and evidence.

CCRA.W.1. Write arguments to support claims in an analysis of substantive topics or texts using valid reasoning and relevant and sufficient evidence.

Overview:

- Select a controversial topic substantive for research, for example, climate change, social media impact on mental health, or AI ethics. Discuss how AI might be used to address or analyze the issue.

- Have students research a historical figure with views relevant to the topic. Students could use the historical-figure guess game to explore topics (https://chronogram.chat/) and analyze how the figure's views are represented in different sources. Explore how AI might represent and understand this historical information, considering different data types and potential schemas.

- Students' task could:

  o Develop a claim connecting the historical figure's views to the contemporary issue and identify counterclaims and opposing views from historical and modern perspectives, considering how AI might generate or evaluate such arguments.

  o Organize findings into a structured argument, linking claims, counterclaims, reasons, and evidence. Discuss how AI systems use reasoning and search algorithms to solve problems and reach conclusions, comparing this to human reasoning processes.

  o Write a short essay and reflect on how historical perspectives, AI concepts, and contemporary debates intersect.

- Conclude the lesson with student reading of their essays. The following questions could be used to further probe student understanding:

  o How do the views of the historical figure you researched relate to the current debate on this topic? Are there any striking similarities or differences?

  o In what ways has the historical context shaped the figure's views, and how does that context compare to our current societal landscape?

  o How might AI systems represent or reason about the chosen topic differently than humans?

  o What are the potential benefits and risks of relying on AI to analyze and interpret information about complex issues?

More AI Connections:

- Point out how this case study demonstrates AI concepts like representation (how Lovelace's views are interpreted and applied today) and reasoning (the logical arguments and counterarguments presented).

- Include some questions that encourage students to delve deeper into the AI connections, such as: "How might an AI system represent Lovelace's views on the Analytical Engine? How would it reason about the ethical dilemmas posed by modern AI?"

AI'S BIG IDEA #3: LEARNING

In this elementary school lesson, students play a board game to identify meanings of words using context clues illustrating different situations. They relate that to AI core concepts of datasets and nature of learning.

Lesson: Identifying Words With Multiple Meanings

7.4

For Elementary School

Language » Grade 4

L.4.4.A. Use context (e.g., definitions, examples, or restatements in text) as a clue to the meaning of a word or phrase.

CCRA.L.4. Determine or clarify the meaning of unknown and multiple-meaning words and phrases by using context clues, analyzing meaningful word parts, and consulting general and specialized reference materials, as appropriate.

Overview:

- Design a board game for students to use the context clues to determine the meaning of multiple-meaning words.

- In the lesson, let the students play the game navigating a colorful board, drawing cards that challenge them to identify word meanings within context and match them to corresponding picture cards.
- Conclude the lesson with a comparison of the student process of understanding word meanings within context and how AI models analyze context to accurately interpret language and make sense of ambiguous words.

Game design:

- Create a simple board with a start and finish point, and a clear path for movement.
- Prepare a word wall displaying multiple-meaning words suitable for Grade 4 level, for example: *fan, shed, mold, fenced, scale, trunk, change.*
- Create sentence cards with blanks, each using a word from the word wall in a specific context. For the words above here are sample sentences:
  1. *I brought back a beautiful _____ from my trip to Japan.*
  2. *I am a big _____ of tennis.*
  3. *We store our garden tools in the _____ at the back of our garden.*
  4. *Trees _____ their leaves in the fall.*
  5. *The workers poured cement into a _____ for the curb.*
  6. *There's _____ on the bread.*
  7. *The two competitors _____ well in the match.*
  8. *They _____ off the playground to keep the kids safe from nearby traffic.*
  9. *We need to _____ and clean the fish before we cook them.*
  10. *The _____ of this measuring tape is in centimeters.*
  11. *She opened the _____ and found it empty.*
  12. *The elephant picked up the banana with his _____.*
  13. *Look at all the spare _____ we found inside the couch.*
  14. *Remember to bring a _____ of clothes for your sleepover!*
- Gather or create picture cards that visually represent the different meanings of the words on the word wall.
- Create a separate answer sheet that matches the sentence number with each picture.

Gameplay:

- Place students in groups of four to five. In each group select one student who will be checking the answers that other students provide in the game. Provide this student with the answer sheet.
- Students take turns drawing a sentence card and selecting a word from the word wall to fill in the blank. They then choose a picture card that matches the meaning of the word as used in the sentence.

- Correct choices allow them to roll the dice and move their token; incorrect choices result in losing a turn. The first player to reach the finish wins!

AI Connections:

- Students are essentially data labeling when they match a word to its correct picture card based on context. This highlights how AI systems rely on labeled data to learn and make predictions.

- The game mechanics mimic a supervised learning approach, where the correct picture card serves as the "**ground truth**" or label for the given word in context. Students receive immediate feedback (win or lose their turn), which reinforces the learning process, similar to how AI models learn from labeled data.

- The core of the game involves understanding word meanings within context. AI models also need to analyze context to accurately interpret language and make sense of ambiguous words.

- Students actively participate in the learning process by making choices and receiving immediate feedback. This aligns with reinforcement learning in AI, where models learn through trial and error, adjusting their strategies based on rewards or penalties.

• Ground truth refers to the reality you want to model with your supervised machine learning algorithm. Ground truth is also known as the target for training or validating the model with a labeled dataset.

AI'S BIG IDEA #4: NATURAL INTERACTION

In this high school lesson, students develop their debate and communication skills by exploring the complexities of human–machine interaction and the AI's potential of achieving natural language understanding.

Lesson: Debating the Future of AI

7.5

Speaking & Listening » Grade 11-12

For High School

SL.11-12.1 Initiate and participate effectively in a range of collaborative discussions (one-on-one, in groups, and teacher-led) with diverse partners on Grades 11-12 topics, texts, and issues, building on others' ideas and expressing their own clearly and persuasively.

• Mind map
is a visual diagram that organizes ideas and concepts around a central theme. It commonly uses a nonlinear layout with a central image and branches that radiate out.

• Argument map
is a box-and-line diagram that lays out visually reasoning and evidence for and against a statement or claim.

• The Lincoln–Douglas (LD)
debate is a type of one-on-one competitive debate primarily focused on values and philosophical questions. It's named after the famous series of debates between Abraham Lincoln and Stephen A. Douglas in 1858, which centered on the issue of slavery.

• Parliamentary
style debate is a formal framework for debate used in debating societies, academic debate events and competitive debate. It has its roots in parliamentary procedure and develops differently in different countries as a result.

CCRA.SL.1. Prepare for and participate effectively in a range of conversations and collaborations with diverse partners, building on others' ideas and expressing their own clearly and persuasively.

Overview:

1. Introduction

   • Start the lesson with a quick poll using a tool like Poll Everywhere (https://www.polleverywhere.com/) or Google Forms to gauge students' initial opinions on AI. This creates immediate engagement and highlights the diversity of viewpoints in the classroom.

   • Utilize an AI chatbot, image generator, or video-creation platform to present a thought-provoking text or visual related to AI's impact, sparking curiosity and setting the stage for the debate.

   • Briefly explain the goal of natural interaction in AI—to communicate with machines as seamlessly as with humans. Touch upon the philosophy of mind: Can machines truly "think" or "understand" like humans?

2. Research and argument construction

   • Divide students into two groups: One arguing that AI can achieve true natural interaction, potentially even consciousness. The other contending that AI, though sophisticated, will always lack the depth and nuance of human communication.

   • Encourage students to leverage AI-powered research assistants or search engines to gather diverse perspectives and analyze data efficiently. Discuss the benefits and limitations of relying on AI for research.

   • Have students use visual tools like **mind map** or **argument map** software to organize their research and clearly visualize the connections between claims, evidence, and counterarguments.

3. Debate preparation and presentation

   • Challenge students to use an AI debate chatbot (e.g., Chat GPT https://chatgpt.com) to generate potential counterarguments to their claims. This helps them anticipate opposing viewpoints and strengthen their rebuttals.

   • Encourage students to find examples of AI successes and failures in natural interaction.

   • Incorporate peer-review sessions where students provide constructive feedback on each other's arguments and presentation skills. This fosters collaboration and helps refine their arguments.

   • Conduct the debate, emphasizing active listening, respectful communication, and building on ideas. Consider incorporating different debate formats (e.g., **Lincoln–Douglas, Parliamentary**) to expose students to various styles and strategies.

4. Reflection

   - Guide students' reflection to how AI systems handle arguments and responses. Discussion points could include:

     ○ Comparing the structure and reasoning of human debates with AI-generated responses.

     ○ Analyzing how AI uses commonsense reasoning and patterns to engage in debate-like conversations.

     ○ Considering how clear communication and logical argumentation are crucial in human and AI contexts.

5. Philosophical discussion

   - Guide a discussion beyond the debate's outcome, delving into philosophical questions:

     ○ What does it mean to "understand" or be "conscious"?

     ○ Can a machine truly replicate human empathy or intuition?

     ○ What are the ethical implications of increasingly human-like AI interactions?

AI Connections:

- Natural interaction: The central theme of the debate, exploring its feasibility and implications.

- NLP: How AI understands and generates human language, and its limitations.

- Commonsense reasoning: The ability to understand the world and make inferences like humans do, a crucial aspect of natural interaction.

- Philosophy of mind: Touching upon the question of whether machines can possess consciousness or genuine understanding.

TIPS

Overall suggestions:

- Provide clear guidelines and examples for each stage of the lesson, especially for students who are new to debate or AI concepts.

- Offer choices in research topics and presentation formats to cater to diverse learning styles and interests.

- Highlight real-world examples of AI being used in debates, decision making, or communication to make the lesson more relevant.

AI'S BIG IDEA #5: SOCIETAL IMPACT

In this middle school lesson, students engage with informational texts and multimedia resources to identify and analyze the key concepts and societal benefits of AI-powered innovations, demonstrating their understanding through summaries and creative visual representations.

Lesson: Analyzing the Social Impact of Scientific Innovations

7.6

For Middle School

• **Think-Pair-Share** is a cooperative learning strategy that encourages individual thinking, paired discussion, and whole-class sharing. Instructors pose a question, students first THINK to themselves prior to being instructed to discuss their response with a person sitting near them (PAIR). Finally, the groups SHARE out what they discussed with their partner to the entire class and discussion continues. Students get time to think critically, creating a learning environment that encourages high quality responses (Lightner & Tomaswick, 2017).

Reading: Informational Text » Grade 7

RI.7.2. Determine two or more central ideas in a text and analyze their development over the course of the text; provide an objective summary of the text.

CCRA.R.7. Integrate and evaluate content presented in diverse media and formats, including visually and quantitatively, as well as in words.

Overview:

1. Start the lesson with a quick "**Think-Pair-Share**" activity by posing the following question: How can technology, specifically AI, be used to make a positive difference in the world?

2. Lead a class discussion on the concept of AI for social good. Discuss examples of AI-powered scientific innovations being used to address societal challenges and improve people's lives. Show a short video on AI for social good and facilitate a brief discussion about the video, emphasizing the potential of AI to create positive change.

3. Have students read the two selected informational texts on science innovations focused on AI for social good. Guide them in completing the Central Idea Organizer to identify and track the development of the central ideas in each text.

4. Divide students into groups. Assign each group a specific focus question or task related to how the information from different formats (text, infographic, chart) complements and enhances their understanding of the central ideas and the positive impact of AI in the texts. Have groups share their findings with the class.

5. Introduce the AI infographic/interactive art generator. Provide specific prompts or topics related to the AI for social good innovations discussed in the texts. Have groups use the tool to create visual representations that highlight the positive impact and potential of these innovations. Facilitate group presentations, emphasizing how the visual representations showcase the benefits of AI for social good.

6. Have students write an objective summary of each text, focusing on the central ideas, their development, and the positive impact of AI. Facilitate a class discussion on the reflection questions, including:

- How do different formats (text, infographic, chart) contribute to showcasing the positive impact of AI innovations?
- In what ways can analyzing scientific language help us appreciate the potential of AI for social good?
- How can we, as individuals and as a society, encourage and support the development of AI for social good initiatives?

Suggested lesson materials:

- Selected informational texts on science innovations focused on AI for social good (two texts on the same or related topics). Topic examples:
  - AI-powered tools for disaster relief and humanitarian aid
  - AI in education to personalize learning and provide accessibility
  - AI in healthcare for disease prediction and treatment optimization
  - AI for environmental conservation and sustainability
- Short video showcasing AI for social good (e.g., https://qrs.ly/ijgh1hw)
- Central Idea Organizer
- Social Impact Analysis Chart (adapted to focus on positive impacts and potential challenges)
- Access to the AI infographic/interactive art generator (e.g., https://qrs.ly/blgh198)

REFLECTION QUESTIONS

- How can AI-powered text analysis tools be utilized in your ELA curriculum to help students develop deeper skills in literary analysis and understanding complex narratives?

- In what ways could you incorporate AI-driven storytelling platforms to enhance creative writing exercises, and how might this influence students' engagement and creativity in writing tasks?

- What role can AI play in facilitating interactive reading sessions in your classroom, and how might this technology be used to adapt reading materials to individual students' learning styles and comprehension levels?

INTEGRATING AI CONCEPTS INTO MIDDLE SCHOOL ELA UNIT "MAN VS. MACHINE: EXAMINING THE POWER DYNAMICS OF CREATION IN LITERATURE"

Let's apply the Pedagogical Framework for AI Literacy to design an ELA instructional unit that delves into the question of literary representation of the power struggle between creators and their creations. At the same time, we want to deepen students' understanding of the core concept of ethical AI by using this literary lens to analyze the ethical dynamics between human and AI in modern society. The connections between this core concept and the ELA focus of the unit are grounded in the following key insights from the Five Big Ideas in AI framework (AAAI & CSTA, n.d.):

- Developing AI applications involves technical and ethical design decisions.

- AI systems that make decisions about people should be engineered to adhere to societal values such as fairness, transparency, and privacy.

  - AI is a disruptive technology that will not only affect the economy and employment but also shape social and cultural norms.

We continue using the same approach for planning this ELA unit as we used in a science unit (Chapter 5) and in a mathematics unit (Chapter 6). In other words, we use a backward design framework (Wiggins & McTighe, 1998) and use our Planning AI Literacy Integration Template (available on our companion website at https://companion.corwin.com/courses/TeachingAILiteracy), we complete Stages 1 and 2 within a larger instructional unit and then use developed key elements to complete Stage 3 for a single lesson within that unit. After completing the template, we suggest resources and materials for the lesson.

STAGE 1: DESIRED RESULTS

The first stage of the template focuses on curricular priorities in the instructional unit (Table 7.4). For this purpose, we use CCSS for ELA (National Governors Association Center for Best Practices & Council of Chief State School Officers, 2010). The performance expectations that align with the goal of this unit are:

- Write arguments to support claims with clear reasons and relevant evidence. (W.8.1)

- Write arguments to support claims in an analysis of substantive topics or texts using valid reasoning and relevant and sufficient evidence. (CCRA.W.1)

For AI competencies, we use learning objectives defined by the AI4K12 guidelines (AAAI & CSTA, n.d.). Because in this middle school unit we are interested in integrating the core concept of ethical AI, we select corresponding learning objectives:

- Evaluate the ways various stakeholders' goals and values influence the design of AI systems. (5-A-i)
- Evaluate ways that AI system designers can learn about and incorporate the values of their stakeholders into the design process. (5-A-iii)

After instructional goals are established, we need to decide

- How will students transfer their language skills and knowledge and understanding of ethical AI gained from the unit and apply it outside of the context of the class?

  This question focuses on the larger purposes of learning a particular content, for example, what complex real-world tasks students will be able to tackle after mastering this content. In the case of this unit, we want students to be prepared for developing written and oral evidence-based arguments for complex topics, in particular in evaluating and analyzing ethical issues of AI.

- What are the big ideas and enduring understandings students will have when they complete the unit?

  It is helpful to refer to the standards and curriculum guidelines that usually provide teachers with enduring understandings. In ELA standards, these are described in details of each standard. In AI guidelines these are clearly marked as enduring understandings. For our unit we included reference codes for the essential understandings for ELA writing standards and ethical AI concept.

- What are essential questions that will frame the unit and that we expect students to answer if they accomplished the unit's goals?

  These are questions that cannot be answered with a brief sentence. The purpose of essential questions is to stimulate thinking, to provoke inquiry, and to inspire more questions including those from the students. At the same time, at the end of the unit answers to these questions should lead to stated instructional goals. In the planning template we included possible choices for the essential questions.

TABLE 7.4 ● Stage 1: Desired Results

STAGE 1 DESIRED RESULTS		
INSTRUCTIONAL GOALS	**SUBJECT-SPECIFIC**	**AI LITERACY**
What subject-specific content standards will this unit address? CCSS for ELA & Literacy W8.1.Write arguments to support claims with clear reasons and relevant evidence. CCRA.W.1.Write arguments to support claims in an analysis of substantive topics or texts using valid reasoning and relevant and sufficient evidence	**Transfer** What kinds of long-term independent accomplishments are desired?	
	Students will be able to independently analyze and construct persuasive arguments in a variety of contexts, using evidence and logical reasoning to support their claims, enabling them to effectively communicate their ideas and engage in informed discussions on complex topics.	Students will be able to independently analyze and evaluate the impact of AI systems, considering the diverse perspectives and values of various stakeholders, leading to informed advocacy for responsible and ethical AI development that benefits society as a whole.
	Understandings What specifically do you want students to understand? What inferences should they make?	
	Introduce claim(s), acknowledge and distinguish the claim(s) from alternate or opposing claims, and organize the reasons and evidence logically. (W.8.1.A) Support claim(s) with logical reasoning and relevant evidence, using accurate, credible sources and demonstrating an understanding of the topic or text. (W.8.1.B) Use words, phrases, and clauses to create cohesion and clarify the relationships among claim(s), counterclaims, reasons, and evidence. (W.8.1.C)	The behavior of AI systems is determined by the choices of the designers, which may involve tradeoffs between conflicting goals and values. If other stakeholders' perspectives aren't given sufficient weight, there could be negative consequences for users. (5-A-i) AI systems need to align with the norms and values of the groups they aim to serve. Developers of AI systems need to understand that values vary across cultures and ensure these values inform the design of products they create. (5-A-iii)
What AI competencies will this unit address? 5-A-i: Evaluate the ways various stakeholders' goals and values influence the design of AI systems.	**Essential questions** What thought-provoking questions will foster inquiry, meaning making, and transfer?	
	How do authors use literary devices to portray the complex relationship between creators and their creations? What are the explicit and implicit messages about power, responsibility, and control conveyed in these texts?	How do the power dynamics between creators and their creations, as explored in literature, reflect or differ from the relationship between humans and AI? In what ways can literature help us understand and navigate the ethical complexities of AI development and its impact on society?

STAGE 1 DESIRED RESULTS		
INSTRUCTIONAL GOALS	**SUBJECT-SPECIFIC**	**AI LITERACY**
5-A-iii: Evaluate ways that AI system designers can learn about and incorporate the values of their stakeholders into the design process.	***Acquisition*** What facts and basic concepts should students know and be able to recall? What discrete skills and processes should students be able to use?	
	Students will know • *that argumentative writing relies on clear reasoning and relevant evidence to support claims, and the strength of an argument can often be improved by reevaluating and rearranging its components.* • *analogies between literary analysis and scientific methods, such as the way hypotheses are supported or refuted by evidence.* • *that the analysis of a text involves interpreting what the text says explicitly and drawing inferences, similar to constructing and deconstructing arguments using logical reasoning.* • *that the synthesis of multiple textual evidences forms a stronger, more coherent argument in literature and persuasive writing*	*Students will know* • *that AI systems often utilize ethical schemas to ensure that the technology aligns with human values and societal norms.* • *that a knowledge graph in AI encodes information about entities and the relationships between them, serving as a foundation for decision-making processes.* • *that selection of an AI algorithm depends on the characteristics of the input data, the complexity of the decisions to be made, and the ethical implications of the outcomes.* • *that ethical considerations in AI require understanding of and adherence to stakeholders' values, which influences system design and operation.*
	Students will be skilled at • *using textual evidence to construct and support claims in written arguments.* • *recognizing and interpreting explicit statements and inferences in texts.* • *constructing coherent arguments that are grounded in valid reasoning and sufficient evidence.* • *evaluating arguments in texts and speeches, distinguishing between strong and weak uses of evidence.*	*Students will be skilled at* • *identifying key attributes and relationships in AI ethics to create and refine ethical schemas.* • *representing ethical considerations and stakeholder values as elements in a decision-making framework.* • *classifying ethical dilemmas in AI into appropriate categories for analysis and resolution.* • *matching ethical challenges with suitable frameworks and algorithms, considering factors like stakeholder impact and societal norms.*

- What are the key knowledge and skills students will acquire from the unit?

  - The information that addresses this question could be the facts, concepts, principles, processes, strategies, and methods students should know when they leave the course.

  - The targeted knowledge and skills can refer to 1) the building blocks for the desired understandings, 2) the knowledge and skills stated or implied in the goals, and 3) the ability to unblock the knowledge and skills needed to perform the complex assessment tasks based on the material in Stage 2.

STAGE 2. ASSESSMENT EVIDENCE

After defining our goals, we need to plan assessments that accurately measure student progress toward those goals (Table 7.5). It's crucial to utilize a diverse range of assessment methods, ensuring each assessment aligns with the specific evidence needed to demonstrate mastery. This evidence should include complex, real-world performance tasks, open-ended academic tasks that demand critical thinking, or more straightforward content-focused reading quizzes, alongside informal checks for understanding.

TABLE 7.5 ● Stage 2: Assessment Evidence

STAGE 2 ASSESSMENT EVIDENCE		
EVALUATIVE CRITERIA	**SUBJECT-SPECIFIC**	**AI LITERACY**
What criteria will be used in each assessment to evaluate attainment of the desired results? • *Demonstrate knowledge of key concepts in AI ethics, argumentation, and textual analysis, and articulate connections between these areas.* • *Analyze AI scenarios and texts, identify key elements (ethical challenges, arguments, evidence), and synthesize information to construct coherent, well-supported arguments.* • *Evaluate and improve arguments, transfer understanding between different contexts, and construct persuasive arguments using evidence and reasoning.*	***Performance Tasks*** How will students demonstrate their understanding (meaning making and transfer) through complex performance? *Students will act as members of an Ethics Committee on AI Advancement, taking on the roles of AI developers, ethicists, or community representatives. They will delve into Mary Shelley's* Frankenstein *to analyze the power dynamics between creator and c'eation and connect these themes to the ethical complexities of AI development. Through collaborative research, persuasive presentations, creative storytelling, and formal writing, students will engage in a simulated committee hearing, ultimately producing a comprehensive report and individual essays that advocate for responsible AI advancement.*	

TIPS

Developing
Essential Questions

- As you develop essential questions, keep in mind that these are broad in scope and should help students to inquire and make sense of the disciplinary core ideas.

- Moreover, essential questions are meant to be explored and revisited over time, not answered by the end of a single class period.

STAGE 2 ASSESSMENT EVIDENCE		
EVALUATIVE CRITERIA	**SUBJECT-SPECIFIC**	**AI LITERACY**
Regardless of the format of the assessment, what qualities are most important? • *Argumentative reasoning* • *Ability to synthesize multiple textual evidences* • *Clear communication and critical thinking* • *Originality and creativity*	***Other Evidence*** What other evidence will you collect to determine whether Stage 1 goals were achieved? • *Debates related to AI ethics* • *Group and class discussions about the power dynamics in* Frankenstein • *Gallery walks to share research findings, analysis, and arguments and provide peer feedback* • *Reading critique related to implications for modern AI ethics* • *Concept maps to visually represent the relationships between key concepts, themes, and research findings* • *Presentations to report on the impact of AI systems on individuals and society*	

To integrate language arts skills with AI concepts, we propose a collaborative project, where students are assigned groups and produce a comprehensive report advocating for responsible AI advancement. Grounded in their analysis of the power dynamics between creators and their creations such as in Mary Shelley's novel *Frankenstein*, students will take on the roles of either an ethicist, a community representative, or an AI developer. Ensuring that each group includes all roles, the teams will then develop a comprehensive report, accompanied by individual essays, highlighting the potential impact of the AI system on individuals and society.

Mary Shelley's Frankenstein is a novel that explores the ethical responsibilities involved in creation and the consequences of that creation on the individual and society. Just as Frankenstein delves into the creation of the creature and the ethical dilemmas that arise, students will explore the parallels with the development of AI, examining the ethical considerations that should be involved in its creation.

Other activities that could also be used to further assess students' comprehension of AI ethics concepts include debates, group and class discussions, gallery walks, reading critiques, concept maps, and presentations. In a particular lesson that we explain in Stage 3, we focus on developing students' skills in crafting detailed literary analyses, making clear and debatable claims about the power dynamics in *Frankenstein* (subject-specific evidence) and drawing connections to ethical AI practices grounded in reasoning and textual evidence (AI literacy).

STAGE 3. LEARNING PLAN

Stages 1 and 2 have established our learning goals and assessment criteria. With these in place, we can now focus on planning effective instructional strategies and learning activities that equip students with the resources and knowledge to achieve these goals (Table 7.6). Moreover, clear goals make the design of lesson tasks easier because we now have a better idea of what we want the students to get out of these tasks.

TABLE 7.6 ● Stage 3: Learning Plan

STAGE 3 LEARNING PLAN		
LESSON STRUCTURE	**SUBJECT-SPECIFIC**	**AI LITERACY**
Does the learning plan reflect Pedagogical Framework for AI Literacy?	***Preassessment*** What preassessments will you use to check students' prior knowledge, preassessment skill levels, and potential misconceptions? *In three to four sentences, students describe how they can construct an argument to persuade their school to implement a policy on responsible use of AI. The writing should include a description of supporting evidence and address potential opposition.* ***Summary of Key Learning Events and Instruction*** Does the learning plan address instructional goals for disciplinary content and AI literacy? Is the plan likely to be engaging and effective for all students?	
Design	At the *Empathize* step: ● Character Hot Seat role-playing activity in small groups At the *Define* step: ● Small-group discussions about Mary Shelley's life, experiences, and connection between environmental influences and the novel's development At the *Ideate* step: ● Individual writing of a creative piece (a monologue, a short scene, or a series of letters) that illustrates the chapter's key themes and employs Generative AI tools	
Create	At the *Prototype* step: ● Students write an individual essay from the perspective of a selected character in *Frankenstein* At the *Test* step: ● Gallery walk for students to share their essays and provide feedback to each other	
Reflect	Whole-group discussion on the ethical implications of AI and its relevance in society by drawing parallels to *Frankenstein*	

In this lesson, we explore how Mary Shelley's personal experiences shaped her novel *Frankenstein*. Following the Understanding by Design (UbD) framework (Wiggins & McTighe, 1998), the lesson begins with a preassessment that gauges students' existing knowledge on constructing persuasive arguments. Specifically, students will be asked to outline how they would persuade school leadership to implement a policy on responsible use of AI, including the types of evidence they would use and how they would address opposition to their claim.

After completing the preassessment task, we proceed to the "writing arguments" task. This activity emphasizes the importance of clear reasoning and relevant evidence in supporting claims, reinforcing that the strength of an argument can often be improved by reevaluating and rearranging its components. Through this task, students will draw similarities between literary-analysis techniques and the utilization of the scientific method, recognizing that just how hypotheses in science are refuted by concrete evidence, claims made in literature are strengthened by contextual evidence. The writing arguments process will involve six key steps of a DCR process (see Chapter 2): *emphasize, define, ideate, prototype, test,* and *reflect*.

During the *emphasize* step, the goal is to equip students with the skills to analyze and interpret literary texts by engaging in role-play and discussing literary devices. We suggest dividing students into groups and assigning each student a character from *Frankenstein*. They can then prepare and perform character responses in a Character **Hot Seat,** role-playing activity. You can also introduce various literary devices, such as symbolism, dialogue, and motifs, to assist students in analyzing the themes in *Frankenstein*.

• Hot Seat is a drama-based instructional strategy in which a character or characters, played by the teacher or a student, are interviewed by the rest of the group.

In the *define* step, the goal is to help students develop skills in identifying overarching themes in *Frankenstein* through small-group discussions about Mary Shelley's life experiences. Students can discover the connections between environmental influences and author's intent, contextualizing the creation of the novel's theme. In small groups students can make predictions about the novel's development based on Shelley's life that included illness, loss, and the scientific advancements of her time.

Next, in the *ideate* step, ask students to create original works of fiction, such as a monologue, short scene, or series of letters, that reflects the novel's key themes. Students can use AI tools, such as text generation or image creation, to enhance their creative piece and explore the potential of AI in storytelling.

In the *prototype* step, the goal is for students to synthesize everything they have learned. During this step, students should be able to apply their knowledge of literary analysis, writing, and critical thinking to produce an individual essay from the perspective of any character in *Frankenstein*.

In the *test* step, the goal is for students to give and receive feedback, and then incorporate suggestions to improve their essays. You can organize a class exhibition where students present their essays in a gallery walk format.

Finally, in the *reflect* step, the goal is for students to critically reflect on the connections between themes they identified in through the literary analysis and parallels seen in AI creation. Students draw on their evaluation of themes they have identified in Mary Shelley's *Frankenstein*, to then engage in a whole-group discussion on the ethical implications of AI and its relevance in a modern society.

RESOURCES

- *Frankenstein* character map to explain the character relationship (https://qrs.ly/fcgh1hz).

- TechnoRomanticism (https://qrs.ly/62gh19d), which lists a wealth of teaching resources on the topic.

- Arizona State University | The Frankenstein Bicentennial Project (https://frankenstein.asu.edu/) that explores the legacy of *Frankenstein* in contemporary science, technology, and ethics discussions.

- *The New Republic* | "How Frankenstein's Monster Became Real" (https://qrs.ly/3xgh19j), which discusses modern AI and biotechnology parallels to Shelley's creation.

- *The Guardian* | "What Frankenstein Means Now" (qrs.ly/hhgtm4g) (qrs.ly/2cgh19n), which discusses the relevance of "Frankenstein" in modern AI and ethical debates.

- Alternative readings

  - "The Veldt" by Ray Bradbury that explores the dangers of AI-driven technology replacing human relationships and the ethical consequences of such dependence.

  - *Flowers for Algernon* by Daniel Keyes, which examines the moral implications of intelligence enhancement and the emotional cost of scientific experimentation on human dignity.

○ Excerpts from *I, Robot* by Isaac Asimov that introduces the ethical complexities of AI decision making through the Three Laws of Robotics.

- MIT Moral Machine (https://www.moralmachine.net/) is an interactive platform prompting reflection on AI's role in life-and-death decisions.

Chapter Summary

In this chapter, we provide strategies for you to incorporate the AI concepts into standards-based ELA curriculum across grade bands. This integration fosters creativity and innovation by deepening students' understanding of AI concepts in their reading, writing, speaking, and listening. We hope we demonstrated that teaching AI literacy does not always require the use of AI tools. Instead, it can be achieved through thoughtful analogies, discussions, and exercises that build upon reading and writing.

Wrap-Up Questions

- What are the potential benefits and challenges of integrating AI concepts into ELA education? How could you effectively address these challenges within your classroom setting?

- How can you connect the Five Big Ideas in AI (perception, representation and reasoning, learning, natural interaction, and societal impact) to key ELA concepts and practices?

- In your opinion, what opportunities exist for using AI concepts to create interactive and personalized reading and writing experiences that adapt to individual student levels and preferences in ELA?

- Reflecting on your current comfort level and familiarity with AI concepts, what steps would you undertake to enhance your own AI literacy to effectively incorporate these concepts into your teaching?

CHAPTER 8

AI Literacy in Social Studies Education

In this chapter we'll

- Discuss connections between the Five Big Ideas in AI and the College, Career, and Civic Life (C3) Framework for Social Studies State Standards

- Suggest strategies for integrating AI literacy across different grade bands and social studies disciplines

- Demonstrate the application of the Pedagogical Framework for AI Literacy by designing a middle school social studies lesson that integrates AI's concept of natural language

There is an obvious connection between social studies and the Five Big Ideas in AI, providing opportunities to effectively integrate AI concepts into various disciplines of social studies in K–12 education. The **Inquiry Arc** provides a structured process for students, starting with developing questions and planning inquiries, then moving to applying disciplinary concepts, evaluating sources, gathering evidence, and finally, communicating conclusions and making informed decisions.

• **An Inquiry Arc** guides students through a cyclical process of inquiry, involving question formulation, evidence evaluation, and informed action.

This cyclical process of inquiry mirrors how AI systems operate, where they begin with data collection (perception), apply reasoning to interpret and represent the data, learn from the information, and then interact with users or systems through natural language and interaction. This parallel between the Inquiry Arc and the Five Big Ideas of AI—perception, representation, reasoning, learning, natural interaction, and societal impact—highlights how both frameworks equip students to tackle real-world problems. By applying AI responsibly, students can use these structured approaches to critically analyze complex societal issues, make evidence-based decisions, and design AI solutions that consider ethical implications and societal impact.

In this chapter we focus on how AI literacy can be woven into the social studies curriculum. Similar to Chapters 5, 6, and 7, we begin by examining how social studies standards (National Council for Social Studies [NCSS], 2013)—specifically the Inquiry Arc, practices, and disciplinary concepts—align with the core concepts of the Five Big Ideas in AI. For each big idea we provide lesson suggestions to demonstrate various strategies for AI literacy integration. Finally, we conclude with a detailed example of how the Pedagogical Framework for AI Literacy can be applied to create a comprehensive middle school social studies unit that integrates AI's concept of natural language.

SOCIAL STUDIES STANDARDS AND FIVE BIG IDEAS IN AI

The development of social studies frameworks was a comprehensive effort to define the educational goals and learning objectives for students in the United States. These frameworks were collaboratively developed by key stakeholders, including state education departments, curriculum experts, and national organizations such as the National Council for the Social Studies (NCSS). Since its founding in 1921, the NCSS has played a significant role in shaping social studies education in the United States. It has guided the creation of comprehensive standards that address a wide array of topics, including history, geography, economics, and civics. The work of the NCSS reflects current academic research and best practices in education, ensuring that students develop factual knowledge and essential skills, such as critical thinking, civic responsibility, and the ability to engage with diverse perspectives (NCSS, 2010). In the late 20th and early 21st centuries, the NCSS spearheaded the development of the College, Career, and Civic Life (C3) Framework for Social Studies State Standards, a landmark advancement in social studies education (NCSS, 2013). Released in 2013, the C3 Framework emphasizes an inquiry-based approach to learning, encouraging students to engage with compelling and supporting questions, apply disciplinary concepts, evaluate sources, and take informed action.

The C3 Framework is organized around four key dimensions that form the foundation of inquiry-based learning and highlights the importance of using disciplinary concepts and tools across four key social studies disciplines (Table 8.1).

TABLE 8.1 ● C3 Framework Organization (NCSS, 2013)

DIMENSION 1: DEVELOPING QUESTIONS AND PLANNING INQUIRIES	DIMENSION 2: APPLYING DISCIPLINARY TOOLS AND CONCEPTS	DIMENSION 3: EVALUATING SOURCES AND USING EVIDENCE	DIMENSION 4: COMMUNICATING CONCLUSIONS AND TAKING INFORMED ACTION
Developing Questions and Planning Inquiries	Civics	Gathering and Evaluating Sources	Communicating and Critiquing Conclusions
	Economics		
	Geography	Developing Claims and Using Evidence	Taking Informed Action
	History		

The C3 dimensions are defined as following:

- *Dimension 1: Developing Questions and Planning Inquiries.* Students frame their research with compelling questions on broad issues and supporting questions for specific details, mirroring AI's process of gathering and analyzing data to frame inquiries.

- *Dimension 2: Applying Disciplinary Concepts and Tools.* Students utilize multidisciplinary tools and concepts to address their questions, mirroring AI's representation and reasoning, where systems employ structured knowledge and algorithms for problem solving.

- *Dimension 3: Evaluating Sources and Using Evidence.* Students critically evaluate sources and use evidence to build arguments, similar to AI's learning processes where systems analyze data to improve accuracy.

- *Dimension 4: Communicating Conclusions and Taking Informed Action.* Students communicate findings and make informed decisions, mirroring AI's interaction with users and its societal impact.

The Dimensions 1, 3, and 4 define social studies practices, whereas Dimension 2 provides an organizing mechanism for the foundational content and skills within each discipline. The C3 Framework as a whole emphasizes the development of critical skills that enable students to analyze historical events, civic issues, and societal changes with a deeper level of thought. By incorporating AI literacy concepts into these practices, students gain not only an understanding of social studies content but also insight into how AI systems function and interact with societal issues (see Table 8.2).

TABLE 8.2 ● Examples of Illustrated Connections between Social Studies Dimensions, Disciplines, and Five Big Ideas in AI

FIVE BIG IDEA IN AI	AI'S CORE CONCEPTS	SOCIAL STUDIES DIMENSION	CONNECTIONS BETWEEN BIS AND SOCIAL STUDIES DIMENSIONS	DISCIPLINE	LESSON EXAMPLES
BI1. Perception	Sensing, Processing	D3. Evaluating Sources and Using Evidence: Gathering and Evaluating Sources	In social studies: Students gather information from diverse sources, including primary documents, secondary texts, images, and oral histories. They evaluate the credibility and perspective of each source, considering its origin, purpose, and potential biases. In AI: AI systems perceive the world through sensors that collect data, such as cameras, microphones, and other sensors. They process this raw sensory data to extract meaningful information and make sense of their environment. Connection: Both involve the process of gathering and interpreting information from various sources, while critically evaluating the reliability and potential biases of those sources.	History	8.1. WWI The Battle of the Somme (Middle school) (p. 185)
BI2. Representation and Reasoning	Representation, Search, Reasoning	D3. Evaluating Sources and Using Evidence: Developing Claims and Using Evidence	In social studies: Students apply disciplinary tools like maps, timelines, and primary source analysis to understand historical events, geographic patterns, and social structures. They use these tools to interpret information and draw conclusions about the past and present. In AI: AI systems use various representations, such as graphs, trees, and logical rules, to organize and reason with information. They apply algorithms and logical reasoning to solve problems, make predictions, and draw inferences. Connection: Both involve using tools and conceptual frameworks to analyze information, make sense of complex phenomena, and draw conclusions based on evidence.	Geography	8.2. Along the Silk Road: A Journey of Global Exchange (Middle school) (p. 188)
BI3. Learning	Nature of Learning, Neural Networks, Datasets	D1. Developing Questions and Planning Inquiries	In social studies: Students develop questions to guide their inquiries, exploring different perspectives and identifying relevant sources of information. They learn to refine their questions as they gather new evidence and encounter different viewpoints.	Civics	8.3. Celebrating Together: Exploring Cultural Holidays in the United States (Elementary school) (p. 191)

FIVE BIG IDEA IN AI	AI'S CORE CONCEPTS	SOCIAL STUDIES DIMENSION	CONNECTIONS BETWEEN BIS AND SOCIAL STUDIES DIMENSIONS	DISCIPLINE	LESSON EXAMPLES
			In AI: Machine learning models learn by analyzing data and adjusting their parameters to improve their performance on a given task. They continuously refine their understanding of the data as they are exposed to more examples and feedback. Connection: Both emphasize the iterative process of inquiry and learning, where new information is used to refine understanding, generate new questions, and deepen knowledge.		
BI4. Natural Interaction	Natural Language	D4. Communicating Conclusions and Taking Informed Action: Communicating and Critique Solution	In social studies: Students communicate their findings and perspectives through various media, such as essays, presentations, and debates. They engage in constructive dialogue, critiquing different solutions to social problems and considering diverse viewpoints. In AI: AI systems are designed to interact with humans in a natural and intuitive way, using natural language processing and other techniques to understand and respond to human communication. Connection: Both focus on effective communication and the ability to engage in meaningful interactions, exchanging ideas, and providing feedback.	Civics	8.4. Understanding Political Parties and Voter Registration (High school) (p. 193)
BI5. Societal Impact	AI and Economy, AI for Social Good	D4. Communicating Conclusions and Taking Informed Action: Taking Informed Action	In social studies: Students apply their knowledge and skills to address real-world issues, taking informed action to promote positive change in their communities. They engage in civic discourse, advocate for policies, and participate in democratic processes. In AI: AI is transforming society in profound ways, impacting various sectors like healthcare, education, and transportation. It is essential to consider the ethical implications of AI and ensure its responsible development and use. Connection: Both emphasize the importance of applying knowledge to real-world situations, taking action to address challenges, and shaping a better future.	Economics	8.5. Bridging the Gap: An AI-Powered Approach to the Digital Divide (High school) (p. 195)

These examples of connections between social studies dimensions and the Five Big Ideas in AI provide a basis for integrating AI literacy into social studies disciplines to deepen students' understanding of historical, economic, civic, and geographic concepts. By aligning AI concepts with social studies standards, we can explore strategies for using AI to support students' learning experiences in exploring historical events, economic systems, and societal impacts. This integration offers innovative ways to enhance students' analytical skills, critical thinking, and understanding of complex societal issues, as highlighted in the Inquiry Arc.

REFLECTION QUESTIONS

- How can you use these connections between social studies and Five Big Ideas in AI to foster students' critical thinking and problem-solving skills?

- What challenges do you anticipate in implementing AI-related activities into teaching social studies? How might these challenges be addressed?

- How can you integrate AI literacy into teaching social studies to address the diverse needs of your students?

LESSON SUGGESTIONS

AI'S BIG IDEA #1: PERCEPTION

In this middle school lesson, students investigate the realities of trench warfare during the Battle of the Somme in World War I. They analyze photographs and AI-generated images of depicting the battle, learning to critically evaluate the credibility of different sources. By excluding unreliable sources and focusing on credible evidence, students connect historical documents and images to key events of the Battle of the Somme and construct a more accurate understanding of the battle's devastating impact. Students in this lesson act as "sensors" by observing historical materials and use their critical thinking skills to "process" and understand the information they gather about this pivotal event in modern warfare.

Lesson: World War I

The Battle of the Somme

Discipline/Indicator: History/Historical sources and evidence

D2.His.12.6-8. Use questions generated about multiple historical sources to identify further areas of inquiry and additional sources.

D2.His.13.6-8. Evaluate the relevancy and utility of a historical source based on information such as maker, date, place of origin, intended audience, and purpose.

Dimension 3: Evaluating sources and using evidence: Gathering and evaluating sources

D3.2.6-8. Evaluate the credibility of a source by determining its relevance and intended use.

Overview:

- Collect authentic photographs depicting key events of the Battle of the Somme, such as the initial advances, the long periods of stalemate, and the immense casualties on both sides.

- Generate AI images that depict scenes related to these events.

- Important: Include AI-generated images with subtle inaccuracies or inconsistencies to challenge students' evaluation skills (see Figure 8.1). Here, the Battle of the Somme was intentionally generated incorporating 20th-century tanks and weapons to create historical inaccuracies.

FIGURE 8.1 ● Battle of the Somme (generated with OpenAI, DALL-E 3, 2024 (https://openai.com/index/dall-e-3/)

Image generators
suggestions

Here are a few free AI
image generation tools
that teachers can use
to create photos that
have subtle inaccuracies
or inconsistencies, with
suggestions on prompts:

1. Craiyon (formerly
   DALL-E mini, https://
   www.craiyon
   .com/) allows you
   to generate images
   from text prompts.
   It's known for its
   quick generation
   time and often
   produces images
   with interesting
   quirks and
   inconsistencies due
   to its simplified
   model. Use prompts
   that are slightly
   ambiguous or
   contradictory to
   allow for more
   student discussion.

2. Bing Image Creator
   (https://www.bing
   .com/images/
   create) is a tool
   integrated with
   Microsoft Edge
   and Bing search.
   It is generally
   good at creating
   realistic images
   but can sometimes
   struggle with
   complex details.
   Provide prompts
   that require
   specific details
   or relationships
   between objects.

- Equip students with a graphic organizer or rubric specifically tailored to the historical context of the WWI The Battle of the Somme that prompts them to analyze sources with these questions in mind:
  - *Origin and Purpose:* Who created this image? Was it created by the Allies or the Central Powers?
  - *Historical Accuracy:* Does the image accurately reflect the realities of the Battle of the Somme?
  - *Perspective:* Whose viewpoint is represented? Are there voices or experiences missing?
  - *Consistency:* Are there any elements that conflict with known historical facts about the Battle of the Somme?

- Use a gallery walk to display students' analyzed images and graphic organizers around the classroom. Students can circulate and examine each other's work, noting similarities and differences in their analyses.

- Following that you can facilitate a whole-class discussion guided by the following questions:
  - What did you learn that challenged your prior knowledge?
  - How did different images portray the same events or issues differently?
  - Why is it crucial to evaluate the origin, purpose, and accuracy of historical sources, especially images?

- Guide students to develop questions for further inquiry based on their analysis. Encourage questions that explore specific aspects of the Battle of the Somme, connect the Battle of the Somme to the historical events that followed, like impact on soldiers' morale, German manpower crisis, and eventual Allied victory on the Western front.

Suggested AI Connections:

- AI as a "sensor" of data (this can be included after students analyzed the images):
  - Explain that just like our senses gather information about the world, AI algorithms "sense" data through inputs like images, text, and numbers. In this lesson, the AI model that generated the images "sensed" data from numerous historical sources to create its visual representations.
  - Just as our senses can be fooled (optical illusions, for example), AI can also misinterpret or be limited by the data it receives. This can lead to inaccuracies in the AI-generated images, highlighting the need for critical evaluation.
  - Have students brainstorm what types of data an AI model might have "sensed" to create the images they analyzed. Were

there limitations in the data? How might those limitations have affected the accuracy of the images?

- AI processing and interpretation (this can be included after the whole-class discussion):

  o Explain that once AI "senses" data, it processes it through complex algorithms to identify patterns, make predictions, and generate outputs (like the images in this lesson).

  o Compare this to how humans process information from their senses. We see an image, our brains process it, and we form an understanding of what we're seeing. AI does something similar, but with vast amounts of data and computational power.

  o Discuss how the AI might have "processed" information differently than a human artist creating an image of the same event. What might the AI prioritize or miss?

3. Canva Text to Image (https://www.canva.com/ai-image-generator/) is easy to use and offers a variety of styles. Although not as powerful as some other generators, it can still produce images with subtle errors. Experiment with prompts that involve multiple elements or specific actions.

RESOURCES

- The following websites could provide teaching resources for this topic. Although some resources require an account, you can find open materials such as texts and photographs.

  o The Battle of the Somme in the National Army Museum: https://qrs.ly/9pgh19p

  o The Battle of the Somme on History Channel: https://qrs.ly/bngh19r

  o The Somme timeline: qrs.ly/twgh1ax

- Resources for finding historic photographs:

  o National Archives has a collection of primary sources and online activities for teaching WWI (https://qrs.ly/mqgh1a0)

  o Library of Congress has a vast collection of photographs from the Battle of the Somme, many of which are available online. Search their Prints & Photographs Online Catalog (www.loc.gov/pictures/)

  o Getty Images is a commercial image archive but also has a significant historical collection. You can find photographs of from the Battle of the Somme by searching their website (www.gettyimages.com)

AI'S BIG IDEA #2: REPRESENTATION AND REASONING

In this middle school lesson students use maps, timelines, and primary sources to trace the **Silk Road** and analyze its impact on cultural diffusion, economic development, and technological innovation across different regions and time periods.

By exploring the Silk Road, students will draw parallels to how modern AI systems utilize vast networks and diverse data sources for representation, search, and reasoning to solve complex problems and facilitate global communication.

Lesson: Along the Silk Road

8.2

A Journey of Global Exchange

For Middle School

Discipline/Indicator: Geography/Spatial patterns and movements

D2.Geo.7.6-8. Explain how changes in transportation and communication technology influence the spatial connections among human settlements and affect the diffusion of ideas and cultural practices.

Dimension 3. Evaluating sources and using evidence: Developing claims and using evidence

D3.3.6-8. Identify evidence that draws information from multiple sources to support claims, noting evidentiary limitations.

Overview:

- Start the lesson with student discussion: Imagine a world without airplanes or the internet. How would people connect and share goods and ideas across vast distances?

- Briefly introduce the Silk Road and its historical significance as an ancient trade network that connected the East and West, facilitating trade and cultural, technological, and religious exchanges.

- Have students virtually "travel" along the Silk Road using an online interactive map (qrs.ly/iigtm4s), identifying key locations, geographical features, and trade goods associated with each region.

- During map exploration, discuss how AI uses geographic data for navigation and logistics, similar to how Silk Road travelers relied on maps and knowledge of terrain. Present students with a variety of primary sources related to the Silk Road, such as excerpts from travel journals, merchant records, or archaeological findings. Guide students in analyzing these sources, focusing on identifying key details, drawing inferences, and evaluating the reliability of the information.

  - After students complete analysis of primary sources, mention how AI can analyze text and images to extract information and identify patterns, much like historians do.

RESOURCES

- International Dunhuang Project (https://idp.bl.uk/) is a collaborative project that has digitized manuscripts, paintings, textiles, and artifacts found in Dunhuang and other Silk Road sites. Many of these are primary sources like letters, religious texts, and government documents.

- Silk Road Seattle (https://qrs.ly/sbgh1a2) is hosted by the University of Washington and provides a collection of historical texts related to the Silk Road, including traveler accounts and merchant records.

- Digital South Asia Library (https://dsal.uchicago.edu/) is a University of Chicago project that offers digitized books, newspapers, and political tracts, many related to India and Central Asia, which were key regions along the Silk Road.

- Divide students into small groups and provide each group with a set of events related to the Silk Road (e.g., the invention of paper, the spread of Buddhism, the rise of the Mongol Empire). Have each group collaboratively create an interactive digital timeline, placing the events in chronological order and annotating these events with summaries of their significance in the context of the Silk Road, images of artifacts, and links to key locations.

  - After students complete the map, highlight the parallels between student-created timelines and how AI represents temporal data. As a culminating activity, have students choose one aspect of the Silk Road (e.g., a specific trade good, cultural practice, or historical figure) and create a digital presentation to share their findings with the class.

Extension: Connecting lesson to students' interests

Assign students a mapping activity using online geospatial tools, for example, Google Earth (https://qrs.ly/mqgh1a3) to create their own maps that represent a global exchange of their choice (goods, people, ideas).

AI'S BIG IDEA #3: LEARNING

In this elementary school lesson, students inquire about the origins and traditions of various cultural holidays, comparing and contrasting how they are celebrated in different communities. They develop questions about the significance of these holidays and their impact on U.S. society. Just as AI systems learn and adapt through natural interaction and diverse datasets, students will engage with varied sources and perspectives to understand the rich tapestry of cultural holidays in the United States.

TIPS

Explaining idea of representation and reasoning

- AI systems use tools to organize and interpret vast amounts of data. AI technologies utilize representations such as graphs, trees, and logical rules to structure information and reason through complex problems.

- These representations allow AI to analyze patterns in data, solve problems, make predictions, and draw inferences. AI systems are particularly adept at processing large datasets that would be challenging for humans to analyze manually.

- AI systems use algorithms to reason about relationships between data points, which can be useful for understanding complex systems like global trade or cultural exchanges.

Lesson: Celebrating Together

Exploring Cultural Holidays in the United States

Discipline/Indicator: Civics/Participation and deliberation: Applying civic virtues and democratic principles

For Elementary School

D2.Civ.7.K-2. Apply civic virtues when participating in school settings.

Dimension 1: Developing questions and planning inquiries

D1.3.K-2. Identify facts and concepts associated with a supporting question.

D1.5.K-2. Determine the kinds of sources that will be helpful in answering compelling and supporting questions.

TIPS

Suggestions for classrooms that are less diverse

- If you do not have a lot of diversity among your students, you can create (or purchase) posters of different cultural holidays (see Figure 8.2).
- Divide students into groups and let each group pick one of the posters to explore that particular holiday.

FIGURE 8.2 ● Example of Cultural Holidays Posters Developed in Canva (https://www.canva.com/)

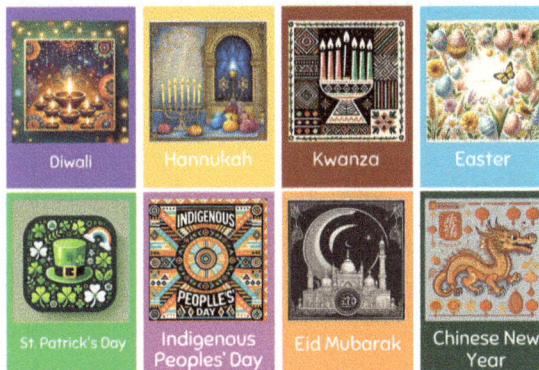

Source: OpenAI: Created with ChatGPT 4.0

Overview:

- Start with gathering information about special holidays that your students celebrate by asking: What are some special holidays that you celebrate with your family and friends?

- What are some ways that different families celebrate [holiday name]?

- What are some things that are the SAME about how people celebrate [holiday name], even if they come from different backgrounds?

- Why do you think people celebrate different holidays?

- How does learning about different cultural holidays help us understand each other better?

- Together as a whole class, create a list of different holidays that are celebrated by your students. Then ask students to select one holiday they want to learn more about and assign them to groups. Alternatively, divide students into small groups and select your preferred method to assign each group one holiday.

- Discuss the concept of holidays and their importance in different cultures. Introduce the idea that just like AI systems learn from diverse data, students will learn about different holidays by exploring various sources and perspectives, including learning from each other.

- Give each group one image representing that holiday. Let each group develop questions and plan how they want to explore the origin, traditions, and cultural significance of this specific holiday.

- Provide students with a variety of resources (books, articles, images, videos, websites) showcasing different cultural holidays in the United States. Have students create a presentation, artwork, or story to share their learning with the class. Encourage students to use different sources to gather information for their projects.

- As a whole class compare and contrast how different communities celebrate their holidays. Discuss how these similarities and differences reflect the diversity of U.S. society.

- Revisit the idea that AI systems learn through natural interaction and diverse datasets. Discuss how students' exploration of various resources mirrors the way AI gathers information. Emphasize that just as AI needs diverse data to learn effectively, understanding different cultures requires exploring diverse perspectives.

Materials:

- Books, articles, and images depicting various cultural holidays

- Online resources (videos, websites) showcasing diverse holiday celebrations (see suggestions below)

- Art supplies for creative activities

- Chart paper for brainstorming and note taking

RESOURCES

Public holidays in the United States Facts for Kids website (https://qrs.ly/vogh1a4) provides information about various holidays that you or students can use in this lesson.

- All About Holidays is a PBS collection that includes a variety of videos and documents about holidays (https://qrs.ly/uggh1a6).

- To create holiday posters, you can use free online platforms such as Canva (https://www.canva.com/). In particular, Canva also has text-to-image AI generators that can help you create images of different holidays.

AI'S BIG IDEA #4: NATURAL INTERACTION

In this high school lesson students research the platforms of different political parties, analyze their positions on key issues, and evaluate the effectiveness of various voter registration campaigns. Students communicate their findings through debates and presentations, critiquing different approaches to increasing civic participation. Students interact with an AI-powered chatbot that simulates conversations with voters from diverse backgrounds, allowing them to test their communication strategies and refine their arguments in a safe and interactive environment, while also learning about the concept of natural language processing (NLP).

Lesson: Understanding Political Parties and Voter Registration

8.4

For High School

Discipline/Indicator: Civics/Civic and political institutions

D2.Civ.4.9-12. Explain how the U.S. Constitution establishes a system of government that has powers, responsibilities, and limits that have changed over time and that are still contested.

Dimension 4: Communicating conclusions and taking informed action: Communicating and critiquing solution

D4.4.9-12. Critique the use of claims and evidence in arguments for credibility.

Overview:

- Introduce the concept of political parties and their role in representing diverse viewpoints.
  - ○ Highlight the dominance of the Democratic (qrs.ly/tkgtm6x) and Republican parties (e.g., https://gop.com/) in the U.S. political system but also introduce the other parties.
  - ○ Briefly discuss the role of political parties in a democracy and the importance of informed voting.

- Divide students into two groups and assign each group a major political party. Let students identify important issues that they care about. Have them research the party's platform, history, and stance on these key issues.

- Introduce the AI chatbot and explain its purpose: to simulate conversations with potential voters.

  - Briefly explain the concept of NLP and how it allows the chatbot to understand and respond to human language.

  - Discuss the potential benefits and limitations of using AI in this context.

- Provide students with the prepared prompts for training the AI to simulate different voter profiles (e.g., "Independent voter concerned about the economy," "Young voter passionate about climate change", etc.). Guide them on how to input these prompts and create diverse AI "voters."

For the next part of the lesson we suggest that you provide students with prompts that will "convert" AI chatbot into a potential voter. Here are examples of such prompts:

  - Independent voter concerned about the economy: "I don't identify with either party. I'm a small business owner struggling to keep my doors open. What is your party going to do to help me?"

  - Young voter passionate about climate change: "I'm 18 and this is my first election. I care about climate change and social justice."

  - Suburban parent, mid-forties, married with two children: "My kids are my top priority. I want them to have access to a good education and feel safe at school. But we're also getting squeezed by healthcare costs and rising taxes. How will your party address these issues and make life more affordable for families like mine?"

  - Retired senior citizen, living on a fixed income: "I worked hard my whole life and now I'm trying to enjoy my retirement. But it's getting harder to make ends meet with rising prices. How will your party ensure that seniors like me can afford a decent quality of life and protect the benefits we've earned?"

- Have each group interact with the AI voters they created, choosing different voter profiles (age, background, political leaning, etc.). Encourage them to try different communication strategies, tailoring their arguments to each voter's concerns and perspectives. Observe how the chatbot responds and discuss the challenges of communicating effectively with diverse audiences.

- Bring the class back together and discuss their experiences and learning.

AI'S BIG IDEA #5: SOCIETAL IMPACT

In this high school lesson, students investigate the causes and consequences of the Digital Divide in their communities, analyzing how unequal access to technology affects education, employment, and civic engagement. They take informed action by proposing AI-powered solutions to bridge the Digital Divide, such as advocating for affordable Internet access or organizing digital literacy workshops. By investigating the economic impact of the Digital Divide and proposing AI-driven solutions, students will analyze how AI can promote inclusive economic growth and reduce inequality.

Lesson: Bridging the Gap

8.5

An AI-Powered Approach to the Digital Divide

Discipline: Economics/Economic decision making

For High School

D2.Eco.2.9-12. Use marginal benefits and marginal costs to construct an argument for or against an approach or solution to an economic issue.

D4. Communicating conclusions and taking informed action: Taking informed action

D4.7.9-12. Assess options for individual and collective action to address local, regional, and global problems by engaging in self-reflection, strategy identification, and complex causal reasoning.

Overview:

We suggest that you start the lesson with a brief introduction of the concept of the Digital Divide and its connection to economic inequality. Divide students into small groups and assign each group a specific aspect of the Digital Divide to research (e.g., Internet affordability, digital literacy, access to technology, etc.). Students might need guidance to use data sources to analyze the extent of the Digital Divide in their community and globally.

Discussion questions:

- What are some specific ways AI can be used to bridge the Digital Divide in our community?

- How can we ensure that AI-powered educational tools are effective for students from diverse backgrounds and with varying learning styles?

- How can we ensure that AI algorithms used to address the Digital Divide are free from bias and treat everyone fairly?

- How can AI-powered solutions help stimulate economic growth in communities that are underserved?

- What are the potential costs associated with developing and implementing AI solutions for the Digital Divide?

- How can we ensure that the economic benefits of AI are shared equitably and don't further exacerbate existing inequalities?

RESOURCES

- National Telecommunications and Information Administration (https://www.ntia.gov/topics/data-central) conducts surveys and publishes reports on Internet use and access nationwide, often with breakdowns by demographics and geography. Data Explorer is a particularly useful tool.

- U.S. Census Bureau (https://www.census.gov/) collects data on various socioeconomic factors, including household income, educational attainment, and Internet access. Their American Community Survey (ACS) offers detailed information at the community level.

- Pew Research Center (https://www.pewresearch.org/tools-and-resources/) conducts extensive research on Internet and technology use, including studies on the Digital Divide and its impact on different communities.

- Have each group present their findings, highlighting the marginal costs and benefits associated with the lack of access to technology.

AI Connections:

Introduce the concept of AI and its potential to address social issues. Facilitate a brainstorming session on AI-powered solutions for bridging the Digital Divide (e.g., AI-powered tutoring platforms, personalized learning apps, AI-driven job training programs). Discuss the ethical considerations of using AI in this context (e.g., data privacy, algorithmic bias).

Extension

If time allows, assign each group an AI-powered solution to develop further. Let students research the feasibility, costs, and potential benefits of their chosen solution. Have students use data analysis to estimate the marginal costs and benefits of implementing their solution in the community. Students can then showcase their solutions to the class.

INTEGRATING AI CONCEPTS INTO ELEMENTARY SCHOOL UNIT "JOURNEYS OF HOPE: USING AI TO UNDERSTAND IMMIGRATION STORIES"

Similar to Chapters 5, 6, and 7, in this chapter we apply the Pedagogical Framework for AI Literacy to design a social studies instructional unit exploring how a variety of factors, including environmental features, cultural influences, and economic opportunities, shape migration patterns and the formation of communities. In this unit we also aim to deepen students' understanding of the core concept of natural language by encouraging students to train chatbots in this social context to share their experiences and cultures with the school community. The connections between this core concept and the social studies focus of the unit are grounded in the following key insight from the Five Big Ideas in AI framework (AAAI & CSTA, n.d.):

> Computers can use natural language to communicate factual information but struggle to understand nonliteral modes of expression such as metaphor, imagery, humor, and sarcasm.

We again use our Planning AI Literacy Integration Template (available on our companion website at https://companion.corwin.com/courses/TeachingAILiteracy) that is based on the principles of the backward design framework (Wiggins & McTighe, 1998). We complete Stages 1 and 2 within a larger instructional unit and then use developed key elements to complete Stage 3 for a single lesson within that unit. After completing the template, we suggest resources and materials for the lesson.

STAGE 1: DESIRED RESULTS

The template's first stage focuses on curricular priorities in the instructional unit (Table 8.3). Based on the C3 Framework for Social Studies (NCSS, 2010), the performance expectations that align with the goal of this unit are:

> Identify disciplinary concepts and ideas associated with a compelling question that are open to different interpretations. (D1.2.3-5)

> Explain how cultural and environmental characteristics affect the distribution and movement of people, goods, and ideas. (D2.Geo.7.3-5)

For AI competencies, we use learning objectives defined by the AI4K12 guidelines (AAAI & CSTA, n.d.). In this unit, we are interested in integrating AI core concepts of natural language, so we select corresponding learning objectives for Grades 3–5:

- Demonstrate some types of questions that a search engine or intelligent assistant can answer, and some types that it cannot answer. (4-a-iv)

After instructional goals are established, we need to decide:

- How will students *transfer* their social studies knowledge and understanding of natural language gained from the unit and apply that outside of the context of the school?

This question focuses on the larger purposes of learning a particular content, for example, what complex real-world tasks students will be able to tackle after mastering this content. In this unit we encourage students to explore immigration stories and connect them to geographical concepts and cultural understanding. Students will develop skills in analyzing information, interpreting different perspectives, and appreciating the diverse experiences of immigrants. They will also gain awareness of how AI can be used to understand and process language, opening doors for them to become citizens who are informed and empathetic in an increasingly interconnected world.

- What are the big ideas used in this section, and what enduring *understandings* will students have when completing the unit?

Referring to the standards and curriculum guidelines that usually provide teachers with enduring understandings and essential questions may be helpful. For our unit, we included reference codes for the essential understanding of social studies standards and the concepts of natural language and understanding emotions.

- What are *essential questions* we expect students to answer if they accomplish the unit's goals?

These are questions that cannot be answered with a brief sentence. The purpose of essential questions is to stimulate thinking, provoke inquiry, and inspire more questions from students. At the end of the unit, answers to these questions should lead to stated instructional goals. In the planning template, we included possible choices for the essential questions.

TABLE 8.3 ● Stage 1: Desired Results

STAGE 1 DESIRED RESULTS		
INSTRUCTIONAL GOALS	**SUBJECT-SPECIFIC**	**AI LITERACY**
What subject-specific content standards will this unit address? C3 Framework D1.2.3-5. Identify disciplinary concepts and ideas associated with a compelling question that are open to different interpretations.	***Transfer*** What kinds of long-term independent accomplishments are desired?	
	Students will be able to independently use maps and geographical tools to locate places, analyze the influence of environmental factors on migration patterns, and explain how geographical features can affect cultural development.	*Students will be able to independently identify how language can be used to express perspectives, and discuss the potential benefits and limitations of using AI to understand human communication.*
	Understandings What specifically do you want students to understand? What inferences should they make?	

(Continued)

(Continued)

STAGE 1 DESIRED RESULTS		
INSTRUCTIONAL GOALS	**SUBJECT-SPECIFIC**	**AI LITERACY**
D2.Geo.7.3-5. Explain how cultural and environmental characteristics affect the distribution and movement of people, goods, and ideas.	*Students should understand that big ideas and important concepts can be explored in many ways and might have different answers depending on who you ask. (D1.2.3-5)* *Students should understand that features like climate, natural resources, and landforms play a significant role in where people choose to settle and why they might migrate. (D2.Geo.7.3-5)* *Students should understand that cultural practices and beliefs influence how people adapt to and modify their environment. (D2.Geo.7.3-5)* *Students should understand that migration and trade introduce new cultural elements to different regions, leading to the blending and sharing of ideas, technologies, and traditions. (D2.Geo.7.3-5)*	*Students should understand that AI assistants are powerful tools for finding information, but they can't answer every question.* *Students should understand that some questions require human interaction or experiences to answer.* *Students should understand that the ability of AI assistants is constantly evolving.*
What AI competencies will this unit address? *4-a-iv. Demonstrate some types of questions that a search engine or intelligent assistant can answer, and some types that it cannot answer.*	**Essential questions** What thought-provoking questions will foster inquiry, meaning-making, and transfer?	
	Why do people move from one place to another, and how do their journeys change their lives and the places they go? *How are communities enriched by the contributions of immigrants?*	*How can AI help us understand the challenges and opportunities that people face as they immigrate and how they build new lives?*
	Acquisition What facts and basic concepts should students know and be able to recall? What discrete skills and processes should students be able to use?	
	Students will know that • *people experience and interpret events differently.* • *culture includes a wide range of elements, such as language, religion, food, clothing, music, and art.* • *people's beliefs and values can influence how they interact with their environment.* • *immigration is the movement of people from one place to another.* • *the movement of people, goods, and ideas can lead to cultural diffusion, which is the spread of cultural traits from one place to another.*	*Students will know that* • *AI assistants use information from huge databases and complex algorithms to answer questions and perform tasks.* • *AI assistants are good at answering factual questions, providing definitions, giving instructions, and completing simple tasks; but they struggle with questions that require opinions, beliefs, or complex reasoning.*

STAGE 1 DESIRED RESULTS		
INSTRUCTIONAL GOALS	**SUBJECT-SPECIFIC**	**AI LITERACY**
		• *questions about feelings, opinions, or physical sensations are best answered by people.* • *AI assistants are constantly learning and improving as they are exposed to more data and interactions.*
	Students will be skilled at • *considering different perspectives on immigration, recognizing that people may have diverse reasons for migrating and varying experiences in their new communities.* • *analyzing maps and data to identify the geographic factors that influence where people live and migrate.* • *identifying cultural traits that are reflected in different aspects of life, such as food, clothing, housing, and celebrations.* • *identifying examples of cultural diffusion in their own communities.*	*Students will be skilled at* • *organizing information in a way that AI chatbot can understand.* • *structuring information in a way that's suitable for AI chatbot training.* • *critically assessing the chatbot's responses.* • *refining their inputs to improve the chatbot's performance.*

- What are the key knowledge and skills students will *acquire* from the unit?

  o The information that addresses this question could be the facts, concepts, principles, processes, strategies, and methods students should know when they leave the course.

  o The targeted knowledge and skills can refer to "1) the building blocks for the desired understandings, 2) the knowledge and skills stated or implied in the goals, and 3) the "enabling" knowledge and skills needed to perform the complex assessment tasks identified in Stage 2" (Wiggins & Tighe, 1998, p. 57).

STAGE 2: ASSESSMENT EVIDENCE

Now that we've established the desired results for this unit, let's plan our assessment (Table 8.4). It's crucial to employ diverse assessment methods to align with the evidence of achieving

TIPS

Developing Essential Questions

As you develop essential questions, remember that these are broad in scope and should help students inquire and make sense of the disciplinary core ideas. Moreover, essential questions are meant to be explored and revisited over time, not answered by the end of a single class period.

the intended outcomes. This evidence should include complex, real-world performance tasks, open-ended academic tasks that demand critical thinking, or more straightforward content-focused reading quizzes, alongside informal checks for understanding.

TABLE 8.4 ● Stage 2: Assessment Evidence

STAGE 2 ASSESSMENT EVIDENCE		
Evaluative Criteria	**Subject-Specific**	**AI Literacy**
What criteria will be used in each assessment to evaluate attainment of the desired results? • *Gather accurate and relevant information about their assigned immigrant family's journey and experiences* • *Incorporate relevant historical events, cultural practices, and geographical details into their narrative* • *Accurately represent the journey's route, including starting point, key locations, and destination on a map* • *Accurately and respectfully portray the cultural background of the immigrant family* • *Explain the challenges and opportunities faced by immigrants* • *Effectively use the chatbot platform and its features to train their chatbot to share the story*	***Performance Tasks*** How will students demonstrate their understanding (meaning-making and transfer) through complex performance?	
	Students will become storytellers and technology creators, researching and mapping the journey of an assigned immigrant family to develop a compelling story. By training a chatbot to share this story, they'll demonstrate their understanding of AI and their ability to communicate complex information in an engaging way. Through this interactive exhibit, students will invite classmates to experience these journeys, fostering empathy and showcasing their mastery of geographical and cultural concepts.	
Regardless of the format of the assessment, what qualities are most important? *Present their ideas in a clear, organized, and logical manner* *Demonstrate creativity in their approach to the task* *Demonstrate ability to* • *link geographical concepts (like migration patterns and the impact of place) to cultural understanding (like traditions, values, and identity).* • *support ideas with evidence from reliable sources* • *analyze information.* • *show sensitivity and respect for various cultures and traditions.*	***Other Evidence*** What other evidence will you collect to determine whether Stage 1 goals were achieved? • *"Push and Pull" picture sorting: Students sort images representing reasons people might leave a place (push factors) and reasons they might choose a new place (pull factors).* • *"Two Worlds" Venn diagram: After reading or hearing an immigration story, students compare and contrast the immigrant's home country and new country.* • *Journal reflections: Students regularly reflect on their learning in a journal, responding to prompts related to immigration, geography, and cultural understanding.* • *Interactive mapping: Students create a digital or physical map of an immigrant family's journey, adding annotations and multimedia elements to tell their story.* • *Chatbot conversation simulation: Before training their own chatbot, students practice interacting with a chatbot trained by the teacher on a related topic.*	

STAGE 2 ASSESSMENT EVIDENCE		
Evaluative Criteria	**Subject-Specific**	**AI Literacy**
	• *"Expert panel" Q&A: One student from each group becomes a member of an expert panel to participate in an "expert panel" discussion, answering questions about immigration from the perspective of their assigned immigrant families.* • *Chalk talk: Students silently and reflectively engage with a central question or topic on the board, adding in writing their own thoughts and responding to others' contributions.* • *Cultural showcase: Students present information about a specific culture, including traditions, food, clothing, or art.*	

For the unit performance task, we suggest dividing students into groups of three to five, where each group will take the role of an immigrant's family assigned by the teacher. Using teacher-provided resources such as informational nonfiction, narrative nonfiction, and fiction texts that highlight the experiences of early and recent immigrants they'll dive into research, uncovering the reasons why their assigned families might have left their home countries and the challenges they faced along the way. They'll trace these journeys on the maps, plotting the routes taken and discovering the geographical features encountered. As they learn about different cultures and traditions, they'll develop a story of their assigned family's experience of moving and settling in the United States from a child's perspective (see an example of a story on our companion website at https://companion.corwin.com/courses/TeachingAILiteracy). Using their stories and a prompt provided by the teacher (also included on our companion website), students will train the chatbot to answer questions about the family's journey, allowing other students to interact with the chatbot and gain a deeper understanding of the immigrant experience.

This interactive approach brings culture and geography to life, fostering empathy and appreciation for the diverse journeys that shape our community.

Other activities to assess students' learning throughout this unit could include picture sorting, interactive mapping, chalk talks, journal reflections, vocabulary quizzes, chatbot conversation simulation, **"expert panel" Q&A**, and cultural showcases. In a specific lesson planned in Stage 3, students will combine their understanding of immigration journeys with AI technology.

TIPS

Finding immigrants' stories

• Learn about your students' families; some of them could be growing up in an immigrant family and can bring that story to the classroom. If you decide to do so, you may want to discuss your idea with the family first to avoid potential pain points. We also suggest that you supplement oral history with age-appropriate printed and online resources.

• Provide students with trade books and age-appropriate online resources that describe journeys of immigrants to the United States. We suggested some resources at the end of this chapter.

They will create interactive maps to visually represent the routes and locations from their stories (subject-specific evidence). Then, they will apply their knowledge of natural language to train AI chatbots to share these stories (AI literacy evidence). This lesson reinforces their understanding of subject-specific content and AI competencies.

STAGE 3: LEARNING PLAN

With our learning goals and assessment criteria in place, let's focus next on planning effective instructional strategies and learning activities that equip students with the resources and knowledge to achieve these goals (Table 8.5).

TABLE 8.5 ● Stage 3: Learning Plan

STAGE 3 LEARNING PLAN		
LESSON STRUCTURE	**SUBJECT-SPECIFIC**	**AI LITERACY**
Does the learning plan reflect Pedagogical Framework for AI Literacy?	**Preassessment** What preassessments will you use to check students' prior knowledge, preassessment skill levels, and potential misconceptions? • *True/false quiz about maps, using online tools for quick feedback* • *Whole-class "Show and Tell" about chatbots*	
	Summary of Key Learning Events and Instruction Does the learning plan address instructional goals for disciplinary content and AI literacy? Is the plan likely to be engaging and effective for all students?	
Design	At the *Empathize* Step: • "Expert Panel" Q&A about challenges and experiences during immigration journeys of different families At the *Define* Step: • Small-group discussions and research to define key events and geographic locations based on the story of immigrant family's journey At the *Ideate* Step: • Chatbot conversation simulation to practice interacting with a chatbot • Small-group brainstorming of strategies to train AI chatbot as a storyteller	

STAGE 3 LEARNING PLAN		
LESSON STRUCTURE	**SUBJECT-SPECIFIC**	**AI LITERACY**
Create	At the *Prototype* Step: • Develop interactive online maps to illustrate the immigrant family's journey • Create a story-specific training prompt for AI chatbot, train AI chatbot to respond to questions about the story At the *Test* Step: • Gallery walk to test all groups chatbots and learn about journeys of different immigrant families	
Reflect	At the *Reflect* Step: • Whole-class discussion to reflect on learning about immigrant families journeys and role of AI chatbot in their learning. • Exit ticket: Students write a diary entry from the perspective of an immigrant child, expressing their feelings and experiences.	

Before this lesson students completed their immigration stories and gathered all information that is needed for development of an interactive map of the family's journey. In this next lesson, students will finish the map using online MapMaker and train the AI chatbot (e.g., ChatGPT, Gemini, Co-Pilot) to become a storyteller of the family's journey. As suggested by the Understanding by Design (UbD) framework (Wiggins & McTighe, 1998), the lesson will start with a preassessment to see what students already know about geographic maps and to identify any misconception or difficulties that they might have. A simple true/false quiz can help identify these difficulties; see the tips we've included to help identify the issues.

Student prior knowledge about AI chatbots can be assessed via a quick show-and-tell. You can demonstrate a simple chatbot interaction and ask students whether they have seen something like this before and have them describe what they think is happening based on the interaction.

TIPS

Identifying common difficulties about geographic maps based on 2010 National Assessment of Educational Progress report for Grade 4 geography (National Center for Education Statistics, 2011):

Watch for difficulties:

• Estimating distances on a map using a scale

• Locating places on a map using grid systems (latitude and longitude)

• Misinterpreting symbols on maps

• Drawing a map based on written description of its features

• Determining elevation of a region on a physical map

Suggestions for
questions development:

- Structured
  information:
  Students might use
  a format that breaks
  down the journey
  into key stages with
  specific details for
  each (e.g., "When
  did the family leave
  their home country?
  Where did they go
  first? What were
  their reasons for
  leaving?"). This helps
  the AI understand
  the sequence
  of events.

- Keywords and
  concepts:
  Questions should
  include relevant
  keywords related
  to immigration,
  travel, challenges,
  and emotions to
  help the AI associate
  these concepts
  with the story (e.g.,
  "What were some of
  the difficulties the
  family faced during
  their journey? How
  did they feel when
  they arrived in their
  new home?").

- Contextualized
  questions: Students
  would learn to frame
  questions within
  the context of the
  story, providing
  background
  information to
  guide the AI's
  understanding (e.g.,
  "After leaving their
  home country, the
  family lived in a
  refugee camp. How

The lesson will start with students completing their interactive online maps of the immigrant family's journey based on the stories they wrote and research they conducted in the previous lessons. This prepares them for training a chatbot to become their immigrant family's storyteller. The chatbot training activity will follow a DCR process according to our Pedagogical Framework for AI Literacy (see Chapter 2). The design–create part represents the five steps of the design-thinking process: *empathize, define, ideate, prototype,* and *test,* and the lesson concludes with the *reflect* component. In this lesson we are also planning key learning activities that integrate disciplinary and AI literacy instructional goals.

In the *empathize* step, we want students to learn from each other about the complex emotions that people, especially immigrants, may experience during relocation. We suggest that you form an "expert panel" composed of one representative from each group who will be answering questions about immigration from the perspective of a child in that family. We also recommend that if a group is covering a region from which one of their classmates originates, that classmate becomes an expert on the panel, which will show respect for their culture. All other students will be asking questions about different families' experiences during their journeys.

In the *define* step, students define the key events and geographic locations of their immigrant family's journey to include on the map that will illustrate their written stories. Through research, they also identify multimedia elements that could be added to their maps.

In the *ideate* step, students first practice interacting with a chatbot on a related topic to get a sense of how AI can understand and respond to human language. Through this activity students can see the direct relationship between their input (questions or prompts) and the AI's output (responses). In small groups students brainstorm how to effectively communicate the written stories to an AI chatbot in a format the AI can understand. This process helps students recognize the differences between human language and the language AI understands.

In the *prototype* step, students complete two main tasks: 1) they create an interactive map using online MapMaker, adding annotations and multimedia elements to support their story, and 2) they develop a training prompt using the template provided by the teacher to teach their AI chatbot to become a storyteller and they train the chatbot to tell the story about the immigrant family's journey.

In the *test* step, the storytelling chatbots are tested by the whole class during a gallery walk. All students are actively interacting with different groups' chatbots asking questions and learning about diverse families' immigration journeys.

During the *reflect* part of the lesson, we suggest a whole-class discussion about the learning experience in geography and AI literacy. This is a good time to discuss with students how chatbots tell stories and how they might sometimes get things wrong. Encourage students to notice how a story might leave out important details or make things too simple. Conclude the lesson with a short assessment like an exit ticket, in which students write a short diary entry from the perspective of an immigrant child.

did this experience affect them?").

- Varied question types: To ensure the AI chatbot can handle different types of inquiries, students can ask a mix of factual questions ("When did the family immigrate?"), open-ended questions ("Can you describe the family's experience during the journey?"), and emotional reflection questions ("How did the family's children feel about leaving their friends behind?").

RESOURCES

- National Geographic MapMaker (https://qrs.ly/hygh1aa) provides simple and intuitive interface designed for classroom use with age-appropriate features.

- National Geographic Migration Resources (https://qrs.ly/l8gh1ab) offer interactive maps, articles, and videos on global migration patterns.

- UNESCO World Heritage (Migration and Cultural Integration) (https://qrs.ly/jngh1ae) global patterns of migration and how cultures mix over time, which will help enrich their chatbot storytelling.

- Picture books:

  ○ *Mango Moon: When Deportation Divides a Family* by Diane de Anda (2019)—A young girl's journey from Mexico to the United States (Grades P–3).

  ○ *All the Way to America: The Story of a Big Italian Family and a Little Shovel* by Dan Yaccarino (2014)—This story follows a family heirloom, a shovel, as it's passed down through generations of an Italian American family, symbolizing their journey and resilience (Grades K–3).

(Continued)

(Continued)

- *Islandborn* by Junot Díaz and Leo Espinosa (2018)—A story of Lola, a young girl who uses her imagination to reconnect with her homeland through stories and memories (Grades K–3).

- *Where Are You From?* by Yamile Saied Méndez (2019)—A story about a young girl asking her grandfather where she comes from (Grades K–3).

- Chapter books:

  - *Front Desk* by Kelly Yang (2019)—A young Chinese-American girl helps her immigrant parents run a motel, facing prejudice and challenges while finding strength in her family and community (Grades 5–7).

  - *Inside Out & Back Again* by Thanhha Lai (2013)—This novel tells the story of a young girl who flees Vietnam with her family during the war and adjusts to a new life in Alabama (Grades 3–7).

  - *Esperanza Rising* by Pam Muñoz Ryan (2002)—A historical fiction novel about a young girl who immigrates from Mexico to California during the Great Depression (Grades 4–7).

  - *Shooting Kabul* by N.H. Senzai (2001)—A story about a young boy who flees Afghanistan with his family and searches for his lost sister in a refugee camp (Grades 4–8).

Chapter Summary

In this chapter we explore the integration of AI literacy into social studies education. By connecting the Five Big Ideas in AI with the inquiry-based approach of the C3 Framework, the chapter illuminates how AI literacy can empower students to become informed, engaged, and responsible citizens in an increasingly AI-driven world.

We provide teachers with practical strategies for integrating AI literacy across different grade levels and social studies disciplines while emphasizing the importance of hands-on learning experiences and project-based activities that allow students to explore AI concepts through real-world applications. By fostering critical thinking, problem-solving, and ethical-reasoning skills, AI literacy in social studies also equips students with understanding the impact of AI on society.

Wrap-Up Questions

- What are the potential benefits and challenges of integrating AI literacy into social studies education? How might these challenges be addressed in your classroom?

- How can connections between the Five Big Ideas in AI (perception, representation and reasoning, learning, natural interaction, and societal impact) and the C3 Framework deepen students' understanding of AI and social studies practices?

- Reflect on your own comfort level and familiarity with AI concepts. What steps could you take to further develop your own AI literacy and effectively teach these concepts to your students?

PART III

Framework Revisited

Chapter 9 Assessment of AI Literacy Framework

Epilogue: How Will AI Transform K–12 Learning?

Assessment of AI Literacy Framework

In this chapter, we'll

- Briefly review current research on assessment of AI literacy
- Introduce an Assessment of AI Literacy Framework
- Provide overview of AI literacy assessment tools

As AI rapidly transforms various aspects of society, it becomes increasingly critical to cultivate AI literacy among learners of all ages. However, effectively evaluating an individual's understanding and competencies in AI presents unique challenges. In this chapter we address the pressing need for a comprehensive framework to assess AI literacy by introducing such framework that explicitly connects AI literacy competencies with learning outcomes. We designed this framework to guide educators in evaluating learners' knowledge, skills, and ethical considerations related to AI, specifically within the context of a DCR process. We hope that this framework can be used effectively for the development of assessment tasks and tools necessary to assess students' AI literacy.

CURRENT RESEARCH OVERVIEW

Effective assessment of AI literacy is essential for evaluating students' understanding of AI concepts, their ability to apply this knowledge practically, and their ethical reasoning. Since AI was introduced in education, multiple studies focused on assessment of various aspects of AI literacy, such as understanding of AI concepts, its capabilities, limitations, and societal implications; practical abilities to interact with and utilize AI effectively; and the attitudes, beliefs, and emotions students hold about AI. This research provides teachers with field-tested assessment strategies and tools that could be integrated into teaching and learning,

Let's start with strategies that have been proven to be effective in assessment of AI literacy. When it comes to assessment strategies, discussions and interviews that use open-response questions promote reflective and nuanced answers (Zhu & Van Brummelen, 2021). Although these strategies require more effort to evaluate, they offer richer insights into students' comprehension and reasoning abilities. They also enable students to articulate their ethical viewpoints and thought processes in real time (Park et al., 2021). Project-based tasks offer effective ways to assess how students apply their AI knowledge to real-world scenarios (Vartiainen et al., 2020). Such projects encourage practical problem solving and critical thinking, providing educators with a comprehensive view of students' capabilities beyond theoretical understanding. Finally, role-playing scenarios help students critically evaluate AI's societal impact, fostering ethical awareness through immersive engagement with ethical dilemmas (Lee et al., 2021). All these assessment strategies have been effectively used by researchers across diverse educational contexts.

Now, let's focus on assessment tools that have been used and validated in research and could be adapted for assessing student AI literacy in schools. For instance, AI competency rubrics provide clear criteria for evaluating open-response and project-based tasks, offering a structured and reliable approach to assess understanding of AI concepts, critical thinking, and problem-solving skills (Alturayeif et al., 2020; Zhang et al., 2025). Surveys are also valuable tools for assessing students' attitudes and ethical awareness regarding AI, tracking changes in their perceptions over time (Druga & Ko, 2021). Multiple-choice quizzes serve as standardized tools to measure students' factual understanding of AI concepts efficiently, offering objective insights into their knowledge (Lyu et al., 2022). Lastly, codebooks used in studies that analyze qualitative data from surveys and discussions can be adapted as rubrics for classroom use, enabling educators to systematically assess students' understanding of AI's ethical implications (Shamir & Levin, 2020).

Building on these existing research insights into AI literacy assessment strategies and tools, we'll next share our Assessment of AI Literacy Framework, which integrates the Pedagogical Framework for AI Literacy with Bloom's taxonomy (1969) of learning outcomes. This framework provides a structured approach to evaluating AI literacy, ensuring that learners develop a comprehensive understanding of AI concepts and their practical applications.

ASSESSMENT OF AI LITERACY FRAMEWORK

In Chapter 2, we introduced the Pedagogical Framework for AI Literacy, and in Chapter 3, we explored its practical application in teaching AI literacy effectively. In this chapter, we explain the Assessment of AI Literacy Framework that connects AI literacy competencies of the DCR process with learning outcomes. As such this framework can be used effectively for development of assessment tasks and tools necessary to assess students' AI literacy.

To effectively assess AI literacy, let's first recall the different types of learning that students may experience. Building upon Bloom's taxonomy (1969), we recognize that learning outcomes can be classified into three domains: cognitive, psychomotor, and affective. Within our Assessment of AI Literacy Framework, we prioritize cognitive learning outcomes, which emphasize mental skills and knowledge acquisition, encompassing activities such as remembering, understanding, applying, analyzing, evaluating, and creating. However, we recognize that holistic AI literacy development extends beyond the cognitive domain. It's equally important to acknowledge the roles of psychomotor outcomes, related to physical skills and coordination, and affective outcomes, focused on emotions and attitudes. These three domains intertwine to create a comprehensive understanding of AI and its implications.

This taxonomy allows us to determine specific types of learning outcomes for specific competencies identified in the

Pedagogical Framework for AI Literacy. Recall that the *design* component encompasses the first three steps of the design thinking process—empathize, define, and ideate—and the target competencies include *applying the design thinking process (D1) and evaluating AI applications (D2)*. Both competencies are relevant across all three design-thinking steps.

- The *empathize* step involves cognitive and affective learning outcomes. At this step students have to demonstrate understanding of user's needs, demonstrate empathy, conduct user research, and analyze user data.

- The *define* and *ideate* steps primarily focus on cognitive learning outcomes. Students first have to define the problem based on analysis of user research they gathered and set specific feasible goals for successful solutions. They then critically analyze AI technologies, develop a solid understanding of their functions, and generate creative and innovative ideas for real-world applications.

Although psychomotor outcomes are not explicitly listed for the *design* component, they become relevant in later steps of the design thinking process, particularly during prototyping and testing, which are steps in the *create* component. The *create* component builds on the design component by emphasizing hands-on application and the target competencies are *applying AI to solve real-world problems (C1)* and *decomposing complex problems into manageable parts (C2)*. Both competencies are highly relevant in the *prototype* and *test* steps.

- The *prototype* step involves cognitive and psychomotor outcomes, particularly when applying AI. At the *prototype* step students actively construct physical or digital prototypes to represent their ideas. They also apply cognitive skills to break down complex problems to devise solutions that can address real-world challenges.

- The *test* step primarily focuses on cognitive outcomes, though affective outcomes can also emerge when considering the broader impact of AI solutions. At this step students evaluate the effectiveness of the prototypes in meeting project goals and identify areas for improvement. This step also involves peer feedback and, therefore, willingness to accept positive criticism and iterate proposed solutions.

Finally, the process concludes with the *reflect* component, when students critically engage with the ethical implications of their AI applications, reflecting on *ethical awareness in AI (R1)* and the *responsible use of AI technologies (R2)*. Reflection encourages students to internalize their ethical responsibilities and motivates them to advocate for the responsible use of AI technologies, ensuring that their decisions prioritize human well-being and fairness. This component fosters a deeper emotional engagement and a sense of responsibility. Thus, both competencies are primarily focused on the affective outcomes, though cognitive outcomes are also crucial for understanding the complexities of AI ethics and making informed decisions. Psychomotor outcomes may be less directly relevant to these reflection competencies, though they could play a role in implementing responsible AI practices in future projects.

Based on these connections we developed the Assessment of AI Literacy Framework (Table 9.1) that explains the relationships between the learning outcomes and the components of the Pedagogical Framework for AI Literacy. In this table the learning outcomes for each component of the pedagogical framework are classified according to the learning domains and linked to corresponding competencies.

TABLE 9.1 ● Assessment of AI Literacy Framework

COMPONENTS OF THE PEDAGOGICAL FRAMEWORK FOR AI LITERACY AND STEPS OF DESIGN-THINKING PROCESS	LEARNING OUTCOMES		
	COGNITIVE OUTCOMES	PSYCHOMOTOR OUTCOMES	AFFECTIVE OUTCOMES
Design *Empathize*	• Gathering and analyzing information about the problem and users. (D1-C) • Understanding the context and potential use cases for AI applications. (D2-C)		• Developing empathy and understanding for users' needs and perspectives. (D1-A) • Considering the potential impact of AI applications on users and society. (D2-A)

(Continued)

(Continued)

COMPONENTS OF THE PEDAGOGICAL FRAMEWORK FOR AI LITERACY AND STEPS OF DESIGN-THINKING PROCESS	LEARNING OUTCOMES		
	COGNITIVE OUTCOMES	PSYCHOMOTOR OUTCOMES	AFFECTIVE OUTCOMES
Define	• Synthesizing information to clearly articulate the problem and define the desired outcomes. (D1-C) • Identifying criteria for evaluating the effectiveness and suitability of AI applications. (D2-C)		
Ideate	• Generating a wide range of creative and innovative ideas to address the defined problem. (D1-C) • Brainstorming potential AI applications and their potential benefits and drawbacks. (D2-C)		
Create *Prototype*	• Selecting and implementing appropriate AI techniques or tools to address the identified problem. (C1-C) • Breaking down the complex problem into smaller, more manageable components that can be addressed with AI. (C2-C)	• Developing and refining AI-powered prototypes or solutions. (C1-P)	

COMPONENTS OF THE PEDAGOGICAL FRAMEWORK FOR AI LITERACY AND STEPS OF DESIGN-THINKING PROCESS	LEARNING OUTCOMES		
	COGNITIVE OUTCOMES	PSYCHOMOTOR OUTCOMES	AFFECTIVE OUTCOMES
Test	• Evaluating the effectiveness of the AI-powered solution in addressing the real-world problem. (C1-C) • Analyzing the results of testing each component and identifying areas for improvement or further decomposition. (C2-C)		• Reflecting on the ethical and societal implications of the AI solution. (C1-A)
Reflect	• Identifying and analyzing ethical dilemmas and challenges associated with AI development and deployment. (R1-C) • Understanding the potential biases and unintended consequences of AI systems. (R1-C) • Evaluating the ethical implications of different AI design choices and applications. (R1-C) • Understanding the potential risks and limitations of AI technologies. (R2-C) • Applying ethical guidelines and principles to the use of AI. (R2-C) • Making informed decisions about the appropriate use of AI in different contexts. (R2-C)		• Developing a sense of responsibility and accountability for the ethical implications of AI. (R1-A) • Recognizing and valuing diverse perspectives on AI ethics. (R1-A) • Cultivating empathy and understanding for the potential impact of AI on individuals and society. (R1-A) • Demonstrating a commitment to using AI technologies in a responsible and ethical manner. (R2-A) • Recognizing the importance of transparency and accountability in AI development and use. (R2-A)

Icon sources: istock.com/ bakhtiar_zein; istock.com/ PeterSnow

ASSESSMENT OF AI LITERACY RESOURCES

Most research-based AI literacy assessment instruments draw from similar conceptualizations of AI literacy, often rooted in the work of Long and Magerko (2020). These instruments generally cover core areas of AI literacy, such as understanding AI (cognitive outcomes), using AI (psychomotor outcomes), evaluating AI (cognitive outcomes), and understanding ethical implications (affective outcomes). The majority of these instruments use multiple-choice questions as the primary assessment format. These instruments have undergone rigorous validation processes, demonstrating strong evidence for their structural validity, internal consistency, and construct validity.

Some of these instruments are designed for specific populations, such as higher education students, middle school students, or the general population. The content of the instruments varies depending on the specific areas of AI literacy being assessed. Some focus on technical knowledge, whereas others emphasize ethical considerations or practical applications. For example, the AI Literacy Test is a performance-based scale assessing AI-related knowledge using thirty multiple-choice questions, each with a single correct option, and includes one sorting question (Hornberger et al., 2023). Another example is the AI Literacy Concept Inventory for middle school students aims to evaluate AI-related knowledge using twenty multiple-choice questions (Zhang et al., 2025).

We'll offer more detailed descriptions of these instruments in the next section, aligned to the learning outcomes of the Assessment of AI Literacy Framework (Table 9.1). In addition to these research-based instruments, we also included descriptions of author-developed AI literacy assessment instruments provided on our website at https://companion.corwin.com/courses/TeachingAILiteracy.

OVERVIEW OF ASSESSMENT OF AI LITERACY RESOURCES

Reference Table 9.2 for research-based instruments and how they correspond to assessed learning outcomes; and Table 9.3 for instruments we have developed, along with how they correspond to assessed learning outcomes.

TABLE 9.2 ● Research-Based Instruments

INSTRUMENT DESCRIPTION	ASSESSED LEARNING OUTCOMES
AI-CI (AI Literacy Concept Inventory Assessment): This assessment evaluates individuals' understanding of fundamental AI concepts. It typically includes questions that probe knowledge of machine learning algorithms, neural networks, datasets, and ethical implications of AI (Zhang et al., 2025).	D2-C, R1-C, R1-A, R2-A
AILQ (AI Literacy Questionnaire): The AILQ is a broader survey that explores individuals' attitudes, beliefs, and perceptions about AI. It may delve into topics such as trust in AI, concerns about job displacement, and AI technology's potential benefits and risks (Ng et al., 2024).	R1-C, R2-C, R1-A, R2-A
Artificial Intelligence Literacy Scale for Middle School Students: This scale is specifically tailored to assess AI literacy among young learners. It focuses on measuring students' knowledge of AI concepts, their ability to identify AI applications in everyday life, and their understanding of AI's ethical considerations (Kim & Lee, 2022).	D2-C, R1-C, R1-A, R2-A
AI Literacy Test: This is a validated multiple-choice survey designed to assess university students' understanding of AI. It focuses on key AI competencies such as recognizing AI, decision-making processes, and ethical considerations. The test aims to capture technical knowledge and misconceptions about AI, making it an objective tool for evaluating students' AI literacy across disciplines (Hornberger et al., 2023).	D2-C, R1-C, R1-A, R2-A

TABLE 9.3 ● Author-Developed Instruments (available at https://companion.corwin.com/courses/TeachingAILiteracy)

INSTRUMENT DESCRIPTION	ASSESSED LEARNING OUTCOMES
Understanding AI Perception (Grades 6–8) rubric is an example rubric that evaluates middle school students' understanding of AI perception. It's based on the learning objectives defined by Big Idea #1 in AI for Grades 6–8, as outlined by AI4K12.org. Teachers can use this rubric as a starting point to develop their own assessment tools for evaluating student understanding of other Five Big Ideas in AI and for different grade levels.	D2-C, D1-C, D2-C, C1-C, C2-C
Assessing AI Literacy within Other Disciplines rubric assesses student performance across three key dimensions: knowledge & understanding, skills & abilities, and attitudes & values. Each dimension is further broken down into specific criteria according to the competencies defined by the Assessment of AI Literacy Framework, with performance levels ranging from "beginning" to "exemplary."	D1-A, D2-A, D1-C, D2-C, C1-C, C2-C, R1-C, R2-C
Five Big Ideas Quiz (High school level) is designed to assess high school students' basic understanding of Big Five Ideas in AI based on AI4K12.org. It includes four multiple-choice questions for each big idea.	R1-A, R2-A, R1-C, R2-C, C1-A, C1-C, C2-C, D2-A
Ethical AI survey is designed to assess students' understanding of key ethical principles related to AI. This survey gauges students' awareness of fairness, privacy, bias, and responsibility in the design and use of AI systems.	R1-A, R2-A, R1-C, R2-C
Ethical Reflection on AI (Upper elementary school) is designed to evaluate upper elementary students' reflections on the social impacts of AI, with a focus on the ethical responsibilities of developers, users, and society as a whole.	R1-C, R2-C, D2-A, C1-A, R1-A, R2-A
AI Ethics Debate rubric assesses students' ability to debate the social impacts of AI, explore ethical considerations, and evaluate how AI technologies influence society and human relationships.	R1-C, R2-C, D2-A, C1-A, R1-A, R2-A

Chapter Summary

In this chapter we suggest an approach to assessing AI literacy by introducing an Assessment of AI Literacy Framework. The framework integrates research-based effective assessment strategies with the design–create–reflect process of the Pedagogical Framework for AI Literacy (Chapter 2), emphasizing the cognitive, psychomotor, and affective domains of learning. Cognitive outcomes prioritize acquisition of knowledge about AI concepts, whereas psychomotor outcomes focus on physical skills in developing AI-powered solutions, and affective outcomes emphasize awareness of AI's ethical and societal implications. We suggest using this framework as a basis for design and/or selection of appropriate instruments to assess students' AI literacy across different competencies and learning domains.

Wrap-Up Questions

- How can the Assessment of AI Literacy Framework help ensure a balanced evaluation of students' technical knowledge and ethical understanding of AI applications?

- In what ways can project-based and role-playing assessments help students demonstrate their understanding of AI's ethical and societal impact?

- How can the DCR process be effectively integrated into assessments to evaluate students' problem-solving and decision-making skills in AI?

- What are the potential challenges in assessing psychomotor outcomes in AI literacy, and how can these be addressed?

- How can educators assess reflection activities that promote deeper ethical awareness of AI's implications among students?

Epilogue

How Will AI Transform K–12 Learning?

As we wrap up this exploration of integrating AI literacy across the curriculum, let's revisit a few key takeaways. This book isn't just about exploring AI concepts; we want to enable students to develop AI literacy to support their learning while equipping them to be critical thinkers and responsible users in a world shaped by AI. That means understanding how AI works, how to evaluate its outputs, and how to use it ethically and effectively. Through the lesson examples across different disciplines, we aim to demonstrate how AI literacy empowers students to analyze information, solve problems, and even create their own AI solutions. But it also requires us to address the potential biases and societal impacts of AI.

Imagine a classroom filled with students engaged in personalized learning, orchestrated by a teacher who expertly guides their exploration. AI tutors provide individualized support, adapting to each student's pace and learning style, while the teacher, freed from routine tasks, can provide more focused attention where it's needed most. Interactive simulations bring complex concepts to life, and intelligent tools offer real-time feedback, allowing for immediate adjustments and deeper understanding. In this dynamic environment, teachers become learning facilitators, fostering collaboration, critical thinking, and creativity. This isn't a far-off fantasy; it's the potential of AI to unlock a new era of learning where every student thrives.

This AI-powered future we're envisioning brings exciting opportunities and important responsibilities. Although AI can personalize learning and provide incredible support, we need to be mindful of potential pitfalls. For instance,

- How do we ensure these tools are accessible to students in schools that are underfunded or those with disabilities?

- How do we prevent AI from reinforcing existing biases, especially in areas like assessment and grading?
- And how can we best prepare teachers to use these technologies effectively and ethically?

These questions demand careful consideration and collaborative solutions.

We need to establish clear guidelines for data privacy, develop strategies to address algorithmic bias, and invest in professional development that empowers educators to navigate this evolving landscape.

As educators, we stand at the forefront of this exciting transformation. We are not just preparing students for an AI-powered world; we are shaping that world alongside them. This requires us to be more than just teachers; we must become guides, mentors, and colearners on this journey. Think about the skills our students will need in the future. Not only will they need to understand how AI works, but they'll also need to be creative problem solvers, ethical thinkers, and adaptable learners. They'll need to collaborate effectively with others, not just in their local communities but across the globe. And they'll need to embrace lifelong learning, because the only constant in this landscape is change. This is where the teacher's role becomes truly vital. We need to foster a classroom culture that values curiosity, critical thinking, and collaboration. We need to provide opportunities for students to explore AI ethically, to experiment with its potential, and to grapple with its challenges. And we need to model these values ourselves, by staying informed about AI developments, engaging in professional learning, and embracing our own growth as educators. In essence, we are not just preparing students for the jobs of tomorrow; we are empowering them to be citizens who are informed, engaged, and ethical in an AI-driven world. This is our responsibility, our opportunity, and our privilege.

To sum up, we don't know the future of AI in education. It's a future that we, as educators, will shape alongside our students. We hope that it's a future where technology and humanity intersect, where creativity and critical thinking flourish, and where every student has the opportunity to thrive. Let's embrace the challenge of integrating AI literacy across our curricula, not with fear or hesitation, but with enthusiasm and a sense of purpose. Let's empower our students to be more than just users of AI; let's empower them to be creators, innovators, and ethical leaders in a world driven by AI. The good news here is that you are not alone. You are part of a community of educators passionate about shaping a better future for our students. Let's collaborate, share our experiences, and support each other in navigating this exciting new landscape. Let's make it a future where AI serves humanity, and where education empowers all.

—Irina Lyublinskaya and Xiaoxue Du

References

AAAI & CSTA. (n.d.). *Artificial intelligence for K-12 initiative.* https://ai4k12.org/

ASCD. (2012). *Understanding by design® framework* [White paper]. https://files.ascd.org/staticfiles/ascd/pdf/siteASCD/publications/UbD_WhitePaper0312.pdf

Asimov, I. (2004). *I, Robot.* Bantam Books.

Bloom, B. S. (1969). *Taxonomy of educational objectives: The classification of educational goals.* David McKay Company.

Bradbury, R. (2012). The Veldt. In R. Bradbury (Ed.), *The illustrated man* (pp. 13–23). Simon & Schuster.

Brezina, C. (2020). *Artificial intelligence and you.* Rosen.

Cantú-Ortiz, F. J., Galeano Sánchez, N., Garrido, L., Terashima-Marin, H., & Brena, R. F. (2020). An artificial intelligence educational strategy for the digital transformation. *International Journal on Interactive Design and Manufacturing, 14*(4), 1195–1209. https://doi.org/10.1007/s12008-020-00702-8

Casal-Otero, L., Catala, A., Fernández-Morante, C., Taboada, M., Cebreiro, B., & Barro, S. (2023). AI literacy in K-12: A systematic literature review. *International Journal of STEM Education, 10*(1), 29. https://doi.org/10.1186/s40594-023-00418-7

Castro-Alonso, J. C., Wong, R. M., Adesope, O. O., & Paas, F. (2021). Effectiveness of multimedia pedagogical agents predicted by diverse theories: A meta-analysis. *Educational Psychology Review, 33*(3), 989–1015. https://doi.org/10.1007/s10648-020-09587-1

Chang, Y., Wong, S. F., & Park, M. C. (2014). A three-tier ICT access model for intention to participate online: A comparison of developed and developing countries. *Information Development, 32*(3), 226–242. https://doi.org/10.1177/0266666914529294

Chiu, T. K., Ahmad, Z., Ismailov, M., & Sanusi, I. T. (2024). What are artificial intelligence literacy and competency? A comprehensive framework to support them. *Computers and Education Open, 6,* 100171. https://doi.org/10.1016/j.caeo.2024.100171

Chiu, T. K., & Chai, C.-S. (2020). Sustainable curriculum planning for artificial intelligence education: A self-determination theory perspective. *Sustainability, 12*(14), 5568. https://doi.org/10.3390/su12145568

CSTA & ISTE. (2015). *Computational thinking teacher resources* (2nd ed.). https://cdn.iste.org/www-root/2020-10/ISTE_CT_Teacher_Resources_2ed.pdf

Darling-Hammond, L., Flook, L., Cook-Harvey, C., Barron, B., & Osher, D. (2020). Implications for educational practice of the science of learning and development. *Applied Developmental Science, 24*(2), 97–140. https://doi.org/10.1080/10888691.2018.1537791

Darling-Hammond, L., Flook, L., Schachner, A., & Wojcikiewicz, S. (2022). *Educator learning to enact the science of learning and development.* Learning Policy Institute.

de Anda, D. (2019). *Mango moon: When deportation divides a family.* Simon & Schuster.

Díaz, J., & Espinosa, L. (2018). *Islandborn.* Dial Books for Young Readers.

Druga, S., & Ko, A. J. (2021, June 24–30). How do children's perceptions of machine intelligence change when training and coding smart programs? [Conference session]. Proceedings of the 20th Annual ACM Interaction Design and Children Conference, Athens, Greece (pp. 49–61). Association for Computing Machinery. https://dl.acm.org/doi/10.1145/3459990.3460712

Du, X., & Breazeal, C. (2022). Engage teacher leaders to design inclusive and inquiry-based practices: Rethinking the use of Artificial Intelligence. In C. Webb & A. Lindner (Eds.), *Preparing pre-service teachers to integrate technology in K-12* classrooms: *Standards and best practices* (pp. 93–113). IGI Global. https://doi.org/10.4018/978-1-6684-5478-7.ch006

Fullan, M. (2015). *The new meaning of educational change* (5th ed.). Routledge.

Gerrish, S. (2019). *How smart machines think.* MIT Press.

Griffey, J. (2019). Artificial intelligence and machine learning in libraries [Special issue]. *Library Technology Reports, 55*(1), 5–10. https://doi.org/10.5860/ltr.55n1

Gutiérrez-Fallas, L., & Henriques, A. (2020). Prospective mathematics teachers' TPACK in a context of a teacher education experiment. *Revista Latinoamericana De Investigación En Matemática Educativa, 23*(2), 175–202. https://doi.org/10.12802/relime.20.2322

Hattie, J. (2012). *Visible learning for teachers: Maximizing impact on learning.* Routledge/Taylor & Francis Group.

Hornberger, M., Bewersdorff, A., & Nerdel, C. (2023). What do university students know about artificial intelligence? Development and validation of an AI literacy test. *Computers and Education: Artificial Intelligence, 5,* 100165. https://doi.org/10.1016/j.caeai.2023.100165

IDEO. (2015). *The field guide to human-centered design.* https://www.designkit.org/

International Society for Technology in Education (ISTE). (2024). *ISTE standards for students.* https://iste.org/standards/students

Kahn, K., & Winters, N. (2021). Constructionism and AI: A history and possible futures. *British Journal of Educational Technology, 52*(3), 1130–1142. https://doi.org/10.1111/bjet.13088

Keyes, D. (2004). *Flowers for Algernon.* Harcourt Brace Jovanovich.

Kim, S. W., & Lee, Y. (2022). The artificial intelligence literacy scale for middle school students. *Journal of the Korea Society of Computer and Information, 27*(3), 225–238. https://doi.org/10.9708/jksci.2022.27.03.225

Kong, S. C., Korte, S. M., Burton, S., Keskitalo, P., Turunen, T., Smith, D., Wang, L., Lee, J. C.-K., & Beaton, M. C. (2024). Artificial Intelligence (AI) literacy–An argument for AI literacy in education. *Innovations in Education and Teaching International, 62*(2), 477–483. https://doi.org/10.1080/14703297.2024.2332744

Lai, T. (2013). *Inside out & back again.* HarperCollins.

Laupichler, M. C., Aster, A., Schirch, J., & Raupach, T. (2022). Artificial intelligence literacy in higher and adult education: A scoping literature review. *Computers and Education: Artificial Intelligence, 3,* 100–101. https://doi.org/10.1016/j.caeai.2022.100101

Lee, I., Ali, S., Zhang, H., Dipaola, D., & Breazeal, C. (2021, March 13–20). *Developing middle school students' AI literacy* [Conference session]. SIGCSE '21: Proceedings of the 52nd ACM Technical Symposium on Computer Science Education, Virtual Event (pp. 191–197). Association for Computing Machinery. https://dl.acm.org/doi/10.1145/3408877.3432513

Lightner, J., & Tomaswick, L. (2017). *Active learning – Think, pair, share.* Kent State University Center for Teaching and Learning. https://www.kent.edu/ctl/think-pair-share

Lin, P., & Van Brummele, J. (2021, May 8–13). *Engaging teachers to co-design integrated AI curriculum for K-12 classrooms* [Conference session]. Proceedings of the 2021 CHI Conference on Human Factors in Computing Systems, Yokohama, Japan (Article No. 239, pp. 1–12). https://dl.acm.org/doi/10.1145/3411764.3445377

Liu, G., Du, X., & Blumofe, N. (2023). Designing AI recommender system curriculum to innovate pedagogical practices. In E. Langran, P. Christensen, & J. Sanson (Eds.), *Proceedings of society for information technology & teacher education international conference* (pp. 2140–2148). Association for the Advancement of Computing in Education (AACE).

Long, D., & Magerko, B. (2020, April 25–30). *What is AI literacy? Competencies and design considerations* [Conference session]. Proceedings of the 2020 CHI Conference on Human Factors in Computing Systems, Honolulu, HI, USA (pp. 1–16). https://doi.org/10.1145/3313831.3376727

Lyu, Z., Ali, S., & Breazeal, C. (2022, June). *Introducing variational autoencoders to high school students* [Conference session]. Proceedings of the AAAI Conference on Artificial Intelligence, (Vol. 36, No. 11, pp. 12801–12809). https://doi.org/10.48550/arXiv.2111.07036

Maltese, A. V. & Simpson, A. (2019). Evaluation of STEM practices (standards alignment). *Part of the STEM Practices Tool for the MakEval Project.* http://www.adammaltese.com/content/makeval

Méndez, Y. S. (2019). *Where are you from?* HarperCollins.

Meyer, A., Rose, D. H., & Gordon, D. (2014). *Universal design for learning: Theory and practice.* CAST Professional Publishing.

Micheuz, P. (2020). Approaches to artificial intelligence as a subject in school education. In T. Brinda, D. Passey, & T. Keane (Eds.), *Empowering teaching for digital equity and agency. OCCE 2020. IFIP advances in information and communication technology,* 595 (pp. 3–13). Springer. https://doi.org/10.1007/978-3-030-59847-1_1

Milliken, A., Cody, C., Catete, V., & Barnes, T. (2019, July 15–17). *Effective computer science teacher professional development: Beauty and joy of computing 2018* [Conference session]. Proceedings of the 2019 ACM Conference on Innovation and Technology in Computer Science Education, Aberdeen, Scotland UK (pp. 271–277). Association for Computing Machinery. https://dl.acm.org/doi/10.1145/3304221.3319779

Minces, V. H. (2021, July). *Developing and popularizing STEM online tools: The case of 'listening to waves' tools for the science of music.* Paper presented at 2021 ASEE Virtual Annual Conference Content Access, Virtual Conference. https://doi.org/10.18260/1-2--36938

Mitchell, M. (2020). *Artificial intelligence: A guide for thinking humans.* Picador.

Mogavi, R. H., Deng, C., Kim, J. J., Zhou, P., Kwon, Y. D., Metwally, A. H. S., Tlili, A., Bassanelli, S., Bucchiarone, A., Gujar, S., Nacke, L. E., & Hui, P. (2024). ChatGPT in education: A blessing or a curse? A qualitative study exploring early adopters' utilization and perceptions. *Computers in Human Behavior: Artificial Humans,* 2(1), 100027. https://doi.org/10.1016/j.chbah.2023.100027

National Academies of Sciences, Engineering, and Medicine. (2018). *How people learn II: Learners, contexts, and cultures.* National Academies Press.

National Center for Education Statistics. (2011). *The nation's report card: Geography 2010.* U.S. Department of Education.

National Council for Social Studies (NCSS). (2010). *National curriculum standards for social studies: A framework for teaching, learning, and assessment.* Author.

National Council for Social Studies (NCSS). (2013). *College, career, and civic life (C3) Framework for social studies state standards.* Author.

National Council of Teachers of English (NCTE). (1996). *Standards for the English language arts.* Author.

National Council of Teachers of Mathematics (NCTM). (2000). *Principles and standards for school mathematics.* Author.

National Governors Association Center for Best Practices & Council of Chief State School Officers. (2010). *Common core state standards for English language arts/literacy.* Authors. https://www.thecorestandards.org/ELA-Literacy/

National Governors Association Center for Best Practices & Council of Chief State School Officers. (2010). *Common core state standards for mathematics.* Authors. https://www.thecorestandards.org/Math/

National Research Council (NRC). (2001). *Adding it up: Helping children learn mathematics.* National Academies Press.

National Research Council (NRC). (2012). *A framework for K-12 science education: Practices, crosscutting concepts, and core ideas.* National Academies Press.

National Science Teaching Association (NSTA). (n.d.). *Science standards.* https://www.nsta.org/science-standards

Nazaretsky, T., Ariely, M., Cukurova, M., & Alexandron, G. (2022). Teachers' trust in AI-powered educational technology and a professional development program to improve it. *British Journal of Educational Technology, 53*(4), 914–931. https://doi.org/10.1111/bjet.13232

Ng, D. T. K., Wu, W., Leung, J. K. L., Chiu, T. K. F., & Chu, S. K. W. (2024). Design and validation of the AI literacy questionnaire: The affective, behavioural, cognitive and ethical approach. *British Journal of Educational Technology, 55*(3), 1082–1104. https://doi.org/10.1111/bjet.13411

NGSS Lead States. (2013). *Next generation science standards: For states, by states.* The National Academies Press.

Park, K., Mott, B., Lee, S., Glazewski, K., Scribner, J. A., Ottenbreit-Leftwich, A., Hmelo-Silver, C. E., & Lester, J. (2021, October 10–13). *Designing a visual interface for elementary students to formulate AI planning tasks* [Conference session]. 2021 IEEE Symposium on Visual Languages and Human-Centric Computing (VL/HCC), St Louis, MO, USA (pp. 1–9). IEEE. https://doi.org/10.1109/VL/HCC51201.2021.9576163

Pedro, F., Subosa, M., Rivas, A., & Valverde, P. (2019). *Artificial intelligence in education: Challenges and opportunities for sustainable development* (Working Papers on Education Policy, Vol. 7, No. 17). https://unesdoc.unesco.org/ark:/48223/pf0000366994.locale=en

Roshanaei, M., Olivares, H., & Lopez, R. R. (2023). Harnessing AI to foster equity in education: Opportunities, challenges, and emerging strategies. *Journal of Intelligent Learning Systems and Applications, 15*(4), 123–143. https://doi.org/10.4236/jilsa.2023.154009

Ryan, P. M. (2002). *Esperanza rising.* Scholastic.

Senzai, N. H. (2001). *Shooting Kabul.* Simon & Schuster Books for Young Readers.

Shamir, G., & Levin, I. (2020, July 6–7). *Transformations of computational thinking practices in elementary school on the base of artificial intelligence technologies* [Conference session]. EDULEARN20 Proceedings: 12th International Conference on Education and New Learning Technologies, Online Conference (pp. 1596–1605). IATED. https://doi.org/10.21125/edulearn.2020.0521

Shelley, M. (2012). *Frankenstein.* Penguin.

Southworth, J., Migliaccio, K., Glover, J., Reed, D., McCarty, C., Brendemuhl, J., & Thomas, A. (2023). Developing a model for AI Across the curriculum: Transforming the higher education landscape via innovation in AI literacy. *Computers and Education: Artificial Intelligence, 4,* 100127. https://doi.org/10.1016/j.caeai.2023.100127

Sperling, K., Stenberg, C. J., McGrath, C., Åkerfeldt, A., Heintz, F., & Stenliden, L. (2024). In search of Artificial Intelligence (AI) literacy in teacher education: A scoping review. *Computers and Education Open, 6,* 100169. https://doi.org/10.1016/j.caeo.2024.100169

Su, J., Zhong, Y., & Ng, D. T. K. (2022). A meta-review of literature on educational approaches for teaching AI at the K-12 levels in the Asia-Pacific region. *Computers and Education: Artificial Intelligence, 3,* 100065. https://doi.org/10.1016/j.caeai.2022.100065

Taylor, T., & Dorin, A. (2020). *Rise of the self-replicators: Early visions of machines, AI and robots that can reproduce and evolve.* Springer.

Tissenbaum, M., Sheldon, J., & Abelson, H. (2019). From computational thinking to computational action. *Communications of the ACM, 62*(3), 34–36. https://doi.org/10.1145/3265747

Thorp, L., & Sage, S. (2002). *Problems as possibilities: Problem-based learning for K-16 education.* ASCD.

Touretzky, D. (2022). *Waveforms and spectrograms. Activity guide.* AI4K12. https://ai4k12.org/activities/

Touretzky, D., Gardner-McCune, C., Martin, F., & Seehorn, D. (2019). Envisioning AI for K-12: What should every child know about AI? *Proceedings of the AAAI Conference on Artificial Intelligence, 33*(1), 9795–9799. https://doi.org/10.1609/aaai.v33i01.33019795

Touretzky, D., Gardner-McCune, C., & Seehorn, D. (2023). Machine learning and the five big ideas in AI. *International Journal of Artificial Intelligence in Education, 33*(2), 233–266. https://doi.org/10.1007/s40593-022-00314-1

UNESCO. (2022). *K-12 AI curricula: A mapping of government-endorsed AI* curricula. https://unesdoc.unesco.org/ark:/48223/pf0000380602

Vartiainen, H., Toivonen, T., Jormanainen, I., Kahila, J., Tedre, M., & Valtonen, T. (2020, October 21–24). *Machine learning for middle-schoolers: Children as designers of machine-learning apps* [Conference session]. 2020 IEEE Frontiers in Education Conference (FIE), Uppsala, Sweden (pp. 1–9). IEEE. https://ieeexplore.ieee.org/document/9273981

Wang, N., & Johnson, M. (2019). *AI education for K-12: Connecting AI concepts to the high school math curriculum.* https://par.nsf.gov/servlets/purl/10440200

Wei, Q., Li, M., Xiang, K., & Qiu, X. (2020). *Analysis and strategies of the professional development of information technology teachers under the vision of artificial intelligence* [Conference session]. 2020 15th International Conference on Computer Science & Education (ICCSE), Delft, Netherlands (pp. 716–721). IEEE. https://doi.org/10.1109/ICCSE49874.2020.9201652

Wiggins, G., & McTighe, J. (1998). *Understanding by design.* ASCD.

Wu, D., Zhou, C., Meng, C., & Chen, M. (2020). Identifying multilevel factors influencing ICT self-efficacy of k-12 teachers in China. In *Blended Learning. Education in a Smart Learning Environment: 13th International Conference, ICBL 2020* (pp. 303–314). Springer International Publishing. https://doi.org/10.1007/978-3-030-51968-1

Xiao, C., & Chan, W. F. (2022). Nurturing global problem solvers: An action research approach to instructional design. In D. Johnston & I. Lopez (Eds.), *The Wiley handbook of collaborative online learning and global engagement* (pp. 230–245). Wiley.

Yaccarino, D. (2014). *All the way to America: The story of a big Italian family and a little shovel.* Alfred A. Knopf.

Yang, K. (2019). *Front desk.* Arthur A. Levine Books.

Yue, M., Dai, Y., Siu-Yung, M., & Chai, C.-S. (2021). An analysis of k-12 artificial intelligence curricula in eight countries. In M. Mercedes, T. Rodrigo, S. Iyer, & A. Mitrovic (Eds.), *Proceedings of the 29th International conference on computers in education* (pp. 22–26). Asia-Pacific Society for Computers in Education.

Zhang, H., Perry, A., & Lee, I. (2025). Developing and validating the artificial intelligence literacy concept inventory: An instrument to assess artificial intelligence literacy among middle school students. *International Journal of Artificial Intelligence in Education, 35*(1), 398–438. https://doi.org/10.1007/s40593-024-00398-x

Zhu, J., & Van Brummelen, J. (2021, October 10–15). *Teaching students about conversational AI using convo, a conversational programming agent* [Conference session]. 2021 IEEE Symposium on Visual Languages and Human-Centric Computing (VL/HCC), St Louis, MO, USA (pp. 1–5). IEEE. https://ieeexplore.ieee.org/document/9576290

Index

accessibility sensor, 40, 44–45
accountability, 3, 6, 52, 57, 160, 219
advancements, 20, 62, 68, 72, 144, 172–73
affective, 215, 217–19
affective learning outcomes, 20, 216
affective outcomes, 215–17, 220, 223
agents, 23–24, 52, 54–55, 57, 83
agent sprite, 53–56
AI-generated images, 184–86
AI-Grader, 21
AI-powered educational platforms, 14–15
AI-powered learning platform, 5–6
AI-powered solutions, 195–96, 219
AI-related knowledge, 220
algorithms
   computer, 91–92
   machine learning, 101–2, 221
   supervised learning, 93, 95
alignment, 73–75, 144
annotation process, 155–56
applying disciplinary concepts, 179, 181
argument map, 164
Artificial Intelligence Literacy Scale for
   Middle School Students, 221
ASCD (Association of Supervision and
   Curriculum Development), 99
Assessment Evidence, 103–4, 138–39,
   172–73, 201–3
assessment strategies, 214
assessment tools, 214, 222
assistants, 200–201
Association of Supervision and
   Curriculum Development (ASCD), 99
atomic composition, 91–93
atomic structure, 91–93
autonomous agents, 40, 52–53, 55–57
   designing, 52, 57

backward design, 62, 64, 77
backward design framework, 99, 134,
   168, 198
backward design methodology, 61–62, 64
battle, 182–87
best fit, 114, 122–23, 130

biases
   algorithmic, 3, 43, 52, 196, 226
   cultural, 51
Big Ideas, 22–23, 35–36, 39, 44, 46, 49, 52,
   100, 135, 222
biodiversity, 96, 99, 103–8
block-based program, 52, 55
bridge, 14, 29–32, 195–96

calculations, 74, 115, 124, 132, 160
Canva, 155, 191–92
capabilities, 36, 45, 50, 96–97, 213–14
career, 148, 179–80
carts, 26, 93–94
causal relationships, 89, 95–97
CCSS (Common Core State Standards),
   111–12, 147–48, 168, 170
celebrate, 191–92
Character Focus, 153–55
characters, 149, 152, 155–56, 175–76
character's development, 155–56
chart, 120–21, 166–67, 192
chatbot, 10, 20, 41, 164, 194, 201–7
chatbot storytelling, 207
civics, 180, 182–83
Civil War, 66–67
classification, 65, 97, 135, 138, 141
climate change, 46–47, 49, 103–4, 107,
   159, 194
codesign workshops, 21
cognitive learning outcomes, 215–16
collaboration, 17, 28, 35, 53–56, 60, 69, 77,
   164, 225–26
college, 148, 179–80
collisions, 54, 93–95
Common Core State Standards. See CCSS
communities, professional learning,
   63, 72
complex concepts, 20, 225
complex problems, 13, 35–36, 46, 65, 123,
   139, 188, 190, 216, 218
complex systems, 35–36, 190
components, biological, 100–101
computer programs, 19, 52

computer science teachers, 20, 86
concepts maps, 104–5, 140, 173
conceptual understanding, 112
conservation, 84, 93, 108
conservation efforts, 100–101, 107
constraints, 30–32, 73–74, 122
content types, 132
context clues, 161
continuous learning, 49, 60, 150
control category, 53–54
costs, 29–30, 196
    marginal, 195–96
counterclaims, 159–60, 170
creators, 8, 37, 168, 170, 172–73, 226
critique, 75, 114, 127, 173, 193
cultural competency, 62, 66, 77
cultural understanding, 197–98, 202
curricula, 16, 20, 226
curriculum goals, 61–64
cyclical process, 179

databases, 107, 130, 200
data privacy, 6–7, 196, 226
data representation, 44, 89, 121, 140, 143
data security, 3, 5–6, 37, 49
data selection, 106–7, 156
datasets
    complex, 84, 96–97
    large, 49, 95, 107, 114, 150, 190
    machine learning, 84
    synthetic, 103, 105
data types, 132, 159
DCI, 82, 87–89, 91, 93, 96–98
decision trees, 100, 102, 113, 119
decoding, 149, 158
design, art, 51–52
design component, 34, 36, 107, 142, 216
design concepts, 30
    initial, 50
design process, 34, 40, 74, 169, 171
design solution, 74–75
design thinking process, 216
design-thinking process, 29, 31, 34–38,
    44–45, 206, 217–19
    five-steps, 28
design-thinking steps, 36, 216
developmental relationships, positive,
    32, 37
development of critical thinking and
    ethical reasoning skills, 58
devices, 24–25, 44, 74
    literary, 149, 170, 175

Digital Divide, 3, 8, 14, 183, 195–96
digital literacy, 20, 195
digital tools, 19, 62, 68, 70–71, 74, 76,
    93, 155
Dimension, 67, 82, 181–85, 188, 191,
    193, 222
disabilities, 20, 44, 225
disciplinary concepts, 180, 198
discrimination, 3–4, 6, 35, 37, 57
distributive properties, 120, 127, 137–39

Earth, 84–85, 95–96
ecosystems, 8, 47, 99–108
    assigned, 106
educational goals, 180
educational goals and learning objectives
    for students, 180
educational practices, 3, 60
effectiveness, 35, 60, 63, 72, 127, 193, 216,
    218–19
elementary school lesson, 120, 126, 156,
    161, 190
empathy, 28–29, 51–52, 153, 202–3,
    216–17, 219
energy, 70, 83, 87, 99
engineering practices, 75, 81–83, 85–86
equity, 6, 8, 11, 14–15, 37, 76–77
Essential Questions, 139, 172, 201
ethical awareness, 11, 17, 35, 214, 217, 223
ethical challenges, 4, 16, 171–72
evaluative criteria, 103–4, 139, 172–73,
    202–3
experiment, 31, 69–70, 83, 87–88, 94–95,
    118, 187, 226
experimental data, 89, 93–95
experimental science, 95
·expert panel, 203, 206

factual questions, 200, 207
families, 47, 191, 194, 203–4, 206–8
family's journey, immigrant, 202, 204–7
fitness levels, 88–89
formats, 102–4, 139, 164, 166–67, 173, 176,
    202, 206
foundational skills, 11–13, 148–49, 156
foundations, 16–17, 38, 40–41, 45, 53–56,
    111, 147, 149, 171, 180
framework
    conceptual, 22, 182–83
    educational, 11, 17
Frankenstein, 172–76
frequency, 8, 70–71

GenAI (Generative AI), 19–20, 40, 49–51, 130, 144, 174
GenAI technologies, 51–52
Generative AI. *See* GenAI
genetic variations, 89, 97–98
GeoGebra, 121, 125–26, 143
geographical concepts, 198, 202
Global Perspectives, 5, 7, 9, 11, 13, 15, 17
graphing calculators, 123, 129–30

HCD (Human-centered design), 22, 28, 34–35
heart rate, 5, 88–89
heights, 122–24
high school algebra lesson, 111, 122
high school algebra/precalculus lesson, 118, 129
high school lesson, 158, 163, 195
historical data, 4, 57, 101
historical sources, 185–86
history, 67, 97, 160, 180–83, 194
history lesson students, 66
holidays, 190–92
cultural, 190–92
human activities, 101, 103–4, 107
Human-centered design. *See* HCD

ICT (information communication technology), 39, 70
identities, 47, 202
Identity Wheel, 46–47
images
binary, 118
grayscale, 117–18
immigrants, 198, 200, 202–3, 206
immigration, 200–203, 206
inconsistencies, 67, 185–86
independence, 118–19
informational texts, 148, 151, 165–66
information communication technology (ICT), 39, 70
informed action, 179–81, 183, 193, 195
innovations, 12, 28, 35, 37, 50–51, 151, 160, 166–67, 177
input data, 138, 171
Inquiry Arc, 179–80, 184
inquiry-based learning, 59, 180
instructional goals, 65, 99–101, 105–6, 135–36, 140, 142, 169, 174, 198–99, 204, 206
instructional unit, 99, 106, 134–35, 141, 168, 197–98

instruments, 73, 220–23
literacy assessment, 220–21
research-based, 221
integers, 135, 137–38, 142
International Society, 39–40, 68
internet, 188, 195–96
interviews, 21, 142, 214–15

journeys, 182–83, 188, 197, 202–3, 205–7, 226

Key Learning Events, 105, 140, 174, 204
knowledge development, 32
knowledge graphs, 113, 135, 138–43, 171
knowledge representations, 83, 134

labels, 74, 99–104, 163
learning domains, 217, 223
learning environments, 6, 20, 166
inclusive, 10, 16
safe, 37–38
student-centered, 22
learning experience, 14, 35, 207
authentic, 35, 38
learning outcomes, 9, 35, 63–64, 72, 213–15, 217–19, 221
learning plan, 105–6, 140–41, 174, 204–5
learning styles, 165, 167, 196, 225
lesson examples, 85, 112–15, 182–83, 225
lesson tasks, 105, 140, 174
Lifelong Kindergarten Group, 53–56
lifelong learning, 60, 226
literacy assessment strategies, 214
literacy assessment strategies and tools, 214
literacy assessment tools, 213
literacy competencies, 58, 76, 213, 215
Literacy Concept Inventory Assessment, 221
literacy concepts, 81–82, 112, 148, 181
literacy curricula, 20–21
literacy evidence, 204
literacy integration, 63–65, 71–72, 95, 99, 134, 180
Literacy Integration Template, 64, 134, 168, 198
literacy learning objectives, 61–64, 77
Literacy Questionnaire, 221
literacy skills, 62, 68–69, 148
digital, 16, 72, 76
strong, 148
Literacy Test, 220–21
literary analysis, 167, 171, 173, 176
literary concepts, 8
literary texts, 8, 175

literature, 104, 148–49, 152, 156, 168, 170–71, 175
logical deduction, 65, 135, 138
logical reasoning, 170–71, 182–83
Lovelace, Ada, 160–61

machine learning, 25–26, 46–47, 107, 128
machines, 19, 24, 26, 50, 113, 122, 126, 149, 160, 164–65, 168
manual prediction, 123
maps, 67, 96, 117, 133, 182–83, 188–90, 199, 201–6
mathematical models, 93, 102, 113, 129
mathematical practices. See MPs
mathematical problems, 114–15, 129, 131
mathematical relationships, 65, 94–95
mathematical understanding, 112
mathematics standards, 112, 135
math problems, 144
matter, 84, 87, 91
Media Lab, 53–56
mind maps, 141–42, 164
mirroring, 116, 156, 181
misconceptions, 106, 142, 205, 221
  potential, 105, 140, 174, 204
models
  exponential, 115, 130–31
  machine learning, 99, 102, 183
  test learning, 84
molecules, 91–93
momentum, 84, 93–94
  total, 93–94
monitor students, 8
motion, 24, 64–65, 93
movies, 41–42
MPs (mathematical practices), 75, 111–16, 134, 144
multidisciplinary tools and concepts, 181
multiplication, 127–29, 135, 137, 139, 142
  polynomial, 141–43
mutations, 90, 98

Named entity recognition (NER), 147
National Council for the Social Studies. See NCSS
National Council of Teachers of Mathematics (NCTM), 112
National Research Council. See NRC
natural language, 40, 114, 147, 151, 179–80, 197–99, 204
natural language processing. See NLP
natural selection, 89–90, 98

NCSS (National Council for the Social Studies), 180–81, 198
NCTM (National Council of Teachers of Mathematics), 112
NER (Named entity recognition), 147
Netflix, 40–41
Netflix recommender system, 41–43
Next Generation Science Standards. See NGSS
NGSS (Next Generation Science Standards), 81–82, 99, 101
NLP (natural language processing), 21, 69, 129, 143, 147, 165, 183, 193–94
norms, societal, 43, 171
NRC (National Research Council), 82, 112
numerical data, 104, 107

online learning resource allocation, 133
online lessons, 5–6
online resources, 66, 75, 192, 203
operations, 111, 120, 126–27, 135, 137, 171
organisms, 98, 100–102, 105
origin, 182–83, 185–86, 190, 192

parents, 6–7, 11
parties, 5, 193–94
pattern recognition, 125, 149–50
PBL (Problem-based learning), 119
pedagogical, 33, 179, 217–19
performance tasks, 99, 103–4, 138–40, 172, 202
personalized learning, 4, 225
personalize learning, 167, 225
perspectives, cultural, 62, 66, 76–77
PhET Interactive Simulations, 69, 90, 92
phonics card, 157–58
photographs, 74, 117, 184, 187
phrases, 71, 161, 170
platforms, 8, 14–15, 26, 67, 70, 72, 190, 193
plausible arguments, 127
political parties, 193–94
polynomials, 135, 137–43
populations, 89–90, 100–102, 105, 220
position, 57, 65, 153, 193
power dynamics, 148, 168, 170, 172–73
preassessments, 105–6, 140–41, 174–75, 204–5
precision, 12, 48, 74, 115, 128, 131
predictive algorithms, 64–65
preparing students, 15, 226
privacy, 3, 5, 9, 17, 35–37, 43, 45, 49, 52, 168, 222

probabilities, 89, 117, 119, 123
  conditional, 113, 118–19
probability trees, 113, 118–19
problem-based learning, 119
Problem-based learning (PBL), 119
problem-solving processes, 37, 98
problem types, 138–39
professional development, 14–15, 60, 68, 226
professional development programs, 21, 61
professional learning, 62–63, 76, 226
project-based tasks, 214
properties, 91, 114, 120, 125–27, 129, 137–38
proponents, 56–57
proportional reasoning, 75, 131–33
psychomotor, 215, 217–19, 223
psychomotor outcomes, 215–17, 220, 223

quadratic, 115, 129–31
quantities, 91, 116, 118, 131, 147
quizzes, 103–5, 133, 138–40, 172, 202

rabbits, 89–90
real-world problems, 14, 31, 33–36, 51–52, 73, 135, 179, 216, 219
reasoning
  commonsense, 95–97, 147, 151, 165
  human-like, 96–97
reasoning methods, 134
reasoning problems, 65, 101, 135, 137–38
recommender systems, 26, 41–43
regions, 3–4, 188, 200, 205–6
regularity, 114, 123–24
representation
  graphical, 96–97, 104
  literary, 168
rescue targets, 53, 55
resource availability, 100–102, 104
resources
  accessible learning, 20
  data visualization, 144
  limited, 60, 98
  teacher, 71
  teacher-provided, 203
resources for ethical guidance, 37
resources for ethical guidance and data security, 37
rewrite, 135, 137–38
routes, 133, 140, 142–43, 203–4
routing system, 141–44
rubric, 186, 214, 222

sacrifice, 154–55
scaffolding student learning, 47, 50
scenarios, 4–7, 9–10, 21, 36, 50, 67, 88, 93–94, 119, 172
schemas, 135, 137–39
school bus routes, 140–43
science lessons, 81–82
science standards, 81–82, 99
scientists, 81, 83–85, 88, 95, 97, 106–7
Scratch Foundation, 53–56
search-and-rescue mission, 52–53, 57
senses data, 186–87
sensors, 24–25, 44–45, 83, 86–87, 94, 149, 182–84, 186
sensory data, 149, 182–83
SEPs, 75, 81–85
sequence, 120–21, 125, 206
Shelley, Mary, 172–73, 175–76
shoe size data, 122–23
Silk Road, 182–83, 188–89
simulation, 90, 92, 94–97, 144
skilled, 65, 138, 171, 201
skills, technological, 39
small-group work, 106
Social Studies Dimensions, 182–83
societal challenges, 56–57, 151, 166
solar panels, 86–87
SoLD framework, 32–33, 38
Somme, 182–87
species, 97–98, 101, 105
spectrograms, 70–71
Spiderman, 41–42
sprites, 53–54
  rescue, 55–56
stakeholders, 41, 169–71
standardized tests, 7
Standards for Students Technology Practices, 75
statistics, 113, 116–17, 119, 123, 130, 144
STEM Practices, 73
story, 152–56, 192, 202–8
storyteller, 202, 204–5, 207
strands, 112, 147–51
strength, 29–31, 55, 171, 175
strong literacy skills in students, 148
student annotation process, 155
student-centered learning, 148
student engagement, 63, 72
  monitors, 9
student-led initiatives, 35, 38
student populations, 58, 133
student privacy, 6, 7

subtraction, 114, 135, 137, 139
superconcepts, 137
supervised machine learning, 46, 91

teacher-centered approach, traditional, 62, 70
teacher training, 11, 13–14
teaching resources, 76, 176, 187
teams, common vowel, 156–57
tessellations, 114, 124–26
themes, 8, 50, 154–55, 172–73, 175–76
timelines, 67, 155, 182–83, 188
tools
    machine learning, 100, 102
    multidisciplinary, 181
traditions, 190, 192, 200, 202–3
training datasets, 99, 101, 106–7, 125, 127–28
transformations, geometric, 124–26
transportation, 57, 139, 141–42, 183, 188

UbD (Understanding by Design), 64, 66, 99, 141, 175, 205
Understanding by Design. *See* UbD
United Airlines, 25
United States, 82, 112, 180, 182–83, 190–92, 203, 207
unit groups, 104, 140
user data, 43, 216

videos, 106–8, 133, 166, 192, 207
viewpoints, 43, 66, 164, 182–83, 186, 193
virtual labs, 91, 104–5, 108
virtual lessons, 8–9
visual representations, 74–75, 119, 141, 143, 166, 186
voice assistant, 27, 157–58
voters, 193–94

weather prediction, 118

CORWIN

**To help every educator
help every student**

We believe that every single student
deserves a great education

We believe that knowing our impact is both
a privilege and a responsibility

We believe that a fair, stable, and thriving
society is built on education

PROFESSIONAL
SINCE 1990
LEARNING

Preparing students for a future we can't imagine

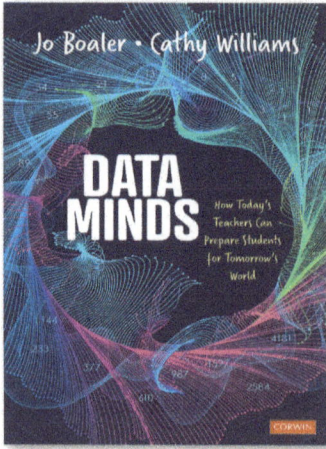

Jo Boaler, Cathy Williams

Introduce data science to your students across disciplines with real world stories and teacher testimonials to transform your classroom experience.
Grades K-8

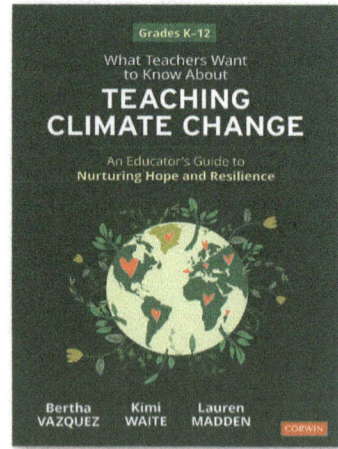

Bertha Vazquez, Kimi Waite, Lauren Madden

Use this inspiring road map to integrate climate change lessons into your existing curriculum and foster student agency across disciplines.
Grades K–12

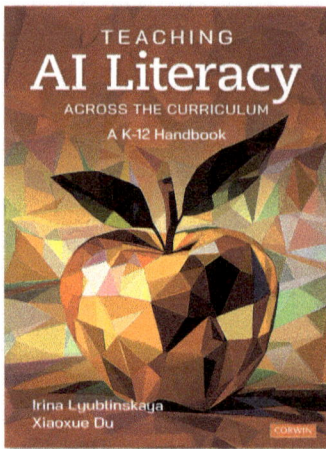

Irina Lyublinskaya, Xiaoxue Du

Integrate AI literacy into K–12 classrooms, blending theory, practical lesson plans, and ethical considerations to empower students as critical thinkers.
Grades K–12

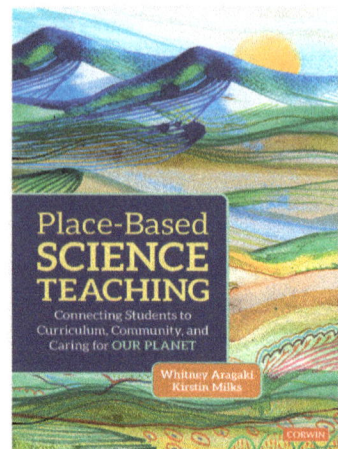

Whitney Aragaki, Kirstin Milks

Learn more about centering place (and the people who inhabit it) in science instruction across locations, from places rich in Native culture like Hawaii and Alaska to urban areas that have multiple histories and myriad cultural influences.
Grades K–12

Whether you're training students for an increasingly technological job market, striving for equitable access in STEM, or encouraging innovation and joy through scientific exploration, our books are here to support you every step of the way.

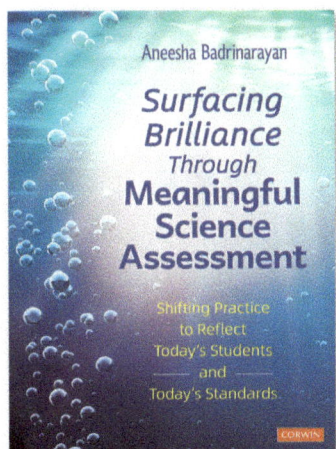

Aneesha Badrinarayan

Learn more about exploring science like scientists do and embracing an asset-based approach to formative and summative assessment.
Grades K–12

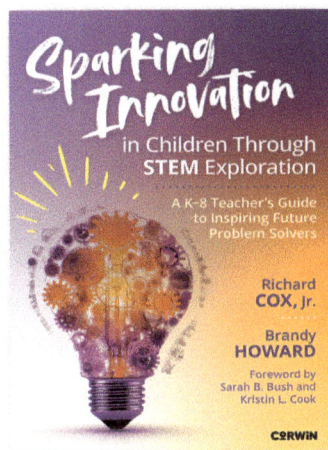

Richard Cox, Jr., Brandy Howard

This resource offers accessible guidance for teachers, instructional coaches, and administrators, detailing specific moves to facilitate imaginative learning.
Grades K–8

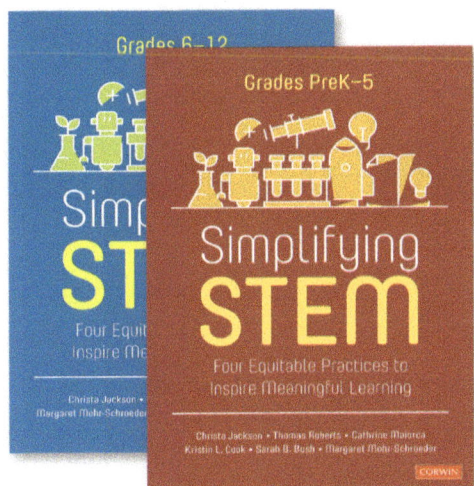

Christa Jackson, Kristin L. Cook, Sarah B. Bush, Margaret Mohr-Schroeder, Cathrine Maiorca, Thomas Roberts

Help educators create integrated STEM learning experiences that are inclusive for all students and allow them to experience STEM as scientists, innovators, mathematicians, creators, engineers, and technology experts!
Grades PreK–5 and Grades 6–12

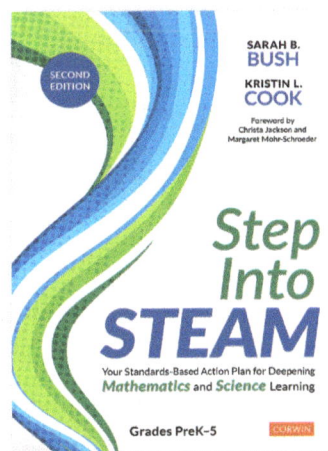

Sarah B. Bush, Kristin L. Cook

Going far beyond a collection of STEAM activities, this book shows educators—as well as school and district leaders—how to build a STEAM ecosystem that can measurably improve every learner's mathematics and science achievement.
Grades PreK–5